"A gift. A historian. A friend. Lalo Guerrero gave us a voice—para todos los Chicanos—that we never had before. He's a national treasure."—**Edward James Olmos**

"Through his music and prolific songwriting Lalo has been an inspiration to all Chicanos, expressing the joys and struggles of the Mexican American experience. He rocks."—**Louie Perez, Los Lobos**

"Fantastic story of an incredible life . . . Lalo, Musician, Poet." —**David Reyes,** coauthor of *Land of a Thousand Dances: Chicano Rock 'n' Roll from Southern California*

"Lalo is our mentor, maestro, and the granddaddy of Chicano humor. He's been an inspiration to us through his power of perseverance. May we be fortunate enough to grace the stage as long as he has." —**Culture Clash**

"Lalo Guerrero is the first great Chicano musical artist." —**Linda Ronstadt,** *Tucson Citizen*

"Over the years he pioneered new musical styles, invented bilingual communication through his lyrics and unique sense of humor, and became a wonderful role model for young and upcoming artists." —**Ricardo Montalbán**

"In 1980, the Smithsonian Institution named him 'a national folk treasure.' And we are honored to honor him today. . . . He still has his salsa."—**President Bill Clinton,** National Medal of the Arts ceremony

Lalo

Lalo
my life and music

Lalo Guerrero
Sherilyn Meece Mentes

THE UNIVERSITY OF ARIZONA PRESS   TUCSON

The University of Arizona Press

This book is printed on acid-free, archival-quality paper.
Manufactured in the United States of America

07 06 05 04 03 02   6 5 4 3 2 1

Pancho Lopez (The King of Olivera Street). Words by Tom Blackburn
and Lalo Guerrero; music by George Bruns. © 1955 Wonderland;
renewed 1983. Used by permission of Walt Disney Music Company.

Library of Congress Cataloging-in-Publication Data
Guerrero, Lalo
Lalo : my life and music / Lalo Guerrero, Sherilyn Meece Mentes.
p. cm.
Discography: p.
ISBN 0-8165-2213-8 (cloth : alk. paper)—
ISBN 0-8165-2214-6 (paper)
1. Guerrero, Lalo. 2. Mexican American musicians—Biography.
I. Mentes, Sherilyn. II. Title.
ML420.G88 A3 2002
782.42164′092—dc21   2001004256

British Library Cataloguing-in-Publication Data
A catalogue record for this book is available from the British Library.

Publication of this book is made possible in part by the proceeds of a permanent
endowment created with the assistance of a Challenge Grant from the National
Endowment for the Humanities, a federal agency.

This book is dedicated to my mother, Concepción Aguilar de Guerrero (Doña Conchita), who taught me how to play the guitar. She was my inspiration and whatever I have accomplished, I owe to her.

Special thanks to

Los Carlistas Quartet, with whom I began my career: Chole Salaz, Yuca Salaz, and Goyo Escalante.

Manuel S. Acuña, composer and arranger, who gave me my first opportunity to record and who was my friend and my partner in the music industry for many years.

Mario Sanchez and Jose Coria, with whom I formed the Trio Imperial and had many hit records in the forties.

All the great musicians who worked with me throughout my career. Space limitations do not allow me to name each one here, but you know who you are.

My first wife, Margaret Marmion Guerrero, who was my partner during the toughest of times.

Lidia Guerrero, my present wife, who for twenty-six years has been my right arm and my companion.

My two sons, of whom I am very proud. I like to think that both are chips off the old block. Dan is a well-known and highly respected television and theatrical producer, and Mark is a very talented singer-songwriter in his own right.

And, finally, Sherilyn Mentes, without whom this book would not have been written.

Contents

Photographs

Luis Valdez, Dan Guerrero, Linda Ronstadt, Lalo Guerrero, 1988
Dan Guerrero, Lalo Guerrero, Rita Moreno, Edward James Olmos,
    Cynthia Telles, and David Telles, Los Angeles, 1988
Lalo with Alma Award, 1998
Lalo in his zoot suit, 1999

Preface

In 1958, I wrote a song about a Martian who came to Earth to clear up certain misunderstandings about Mars. Now I have decided that it is time to set some things straight about Lalo Guerrero.

Over the years, a lot of words have been written about me—"about" me, but not "by" me. This is the story of my life as I remember it. Anyone who knows me will tell you that I have an excellent memory. I can even remember things that never happened. Seriously, I may have forgotten some names and dates, but I never forgot the songs.

All of my life, I just wanted to write music and play music. I loved it so much that I couldn't ever think of leaving it. My mind is always full of music. It's a joy—a delight—to come up with a rhyme that makes me laugh because I know if it makes me laugh it's good. Sometimes my music makes me cry, and I know it'll touch the hearts of other people because it brings back memories that we all share.

And I ain't through yet! Writing music and lyrics, entertaining—I still love it. When I'm going to have a show somewhere, I'm so excited I can't sleep at night because I'm looking forward to the next day.

I always was a dreamer and a lot of my dreams have come true. My life has never been planned; it just happened. It's a mixture of sadness and tragedy and a tremendous amount of happiness with a lot of humor and fun. I hope that people will find my story interesting and smile a little bit or shed a few tears with me.

Most of all I hope that it will give everyone who reads it a better understanding of what kind of people we Mexican Americans are—our customs, our values, what we do, and why we do it. And maybe it will create more appreciation for our culture so that all Americans—both Spanish and English speaking—can share the best of our two worlds.

—*Lalo Guerrero*

Three years ago while searching for music for a film that I was working on, I heard Lalo Guerrero's *Barrio Viejo*. I looked him up to see if I could get permission to use it.

In spite of twenty-five years difference in our ages and our very different backgrounds, we liked each other immediately. I was enthralled by Lalo's stories of his childhood in Tucson, of his triumphs as a young singer and band leader, and of his struggles to achieve recognition as a performer and composer during the years when discrimination against "Mexicans" was an accepted part of life in America and discrimination against "pochos" was rampant in Mexico. And I loved his dignity and his wonderful sense of the ridiculous.

I was also impressed—and often depressed—by my own ignorance of the Chicano culture. Over margaritas after a concert or backstage at a local fiesta, Lalo opened windows on a world that I had seen only dimly.

Spanish-speaking peoples have been a part of the Americas since the arrival of Columbus. Today people of Mexican heritage form the largest Spanish-speaking group in the United States. We are not just neighbors; we're living inside the same house. Salsa, both on the table and on the dance floor, is an integral part of American life. Ready or not, we are connected.

Bilingual and bicultural, articulate and creative, Lalo Guerrero invites us into his world and often gives us a different view of our own.

—*Sherilyn Meece Mentes*

Lalo

The Dream

It's a nightmare! Everybody's staring at me. I'm on a stage in front of a huge audience surrounded by famous people—actors, writers, musicians. The President is here. And the First Lady. They're coming right at me. They want to give me a medal. But I can't stand up! The old guy on the next chair keeps dozing off and falling over on me. Then the medal is around my neck.

The First Lady turns to leave. I can't let her get away; I gotta have a picture of this. I grab her by the waist. The President laughs and says into the microphone, "The old guy still has his salsa."

It's not a nightmare; it's real. It's one of my daydreams come true. I look down at the gold medallion and read, "The National Medal of Arts awarded to distinguished artists and scholars whose work reflects the strength and diversity of America's cultural heritage."

When I think back on that morning, I still shiver. That was such an incredible, marvelous, beautiful feeling. Up to that moment—I don't know exactly how to explain it—I thought of myself as a Mexican who happened to be born in the United States. When I looked at that medal, for the first time in my life, I felt like a real American.

While the President and First Lady were moving on to the next recipients, I was remembering a barefooted boy in a dusty barrio in Tucson and wondering how in the hell he got to the White House.

And I started to think that it was as if my whole life had been guided toward that moment. The people that I met and the choices that I made or that were forced on me by circumstances all sort of fell into place as if someone had been leading me by the hand.

Barrio Viejo

Viejo barrio, barrio viejo	Viejo barrio, old neighborhood,
Solo hay lugares parejos	There are only empty spaces

Donde un día hubo casas,
Donde vivió nuestra raza.
Solo quedan los escombros
De los hogares felices
De las alegres familias
De esa gente que yo quisé.
Por las tardes se sentaban

Afuera tomar el fresco.

Yo pasaba y saludaba,

Ya parece que oigo el eco

¿Como está Doña Juanita?
Buenas tardes, Isabel.
¡Hola! ¿Qué dices Chalita?
¿Como está Arturo y Manuel?
Viejo barrio, barrio viejo
Que en mi infancia te gozé
Y con todos mis amigos,
Iba descalzo y a pie.
De la Meyer hasta El Hoyo,
Desde El Hoyo hasta la acequia,

De la acequia hasta el río,
Ese era el mundo mío.
Dicen que éramos pobres
Pues yo nunca lo noté
Yo era feliz en mi mundo
De aquel barrio que adoré.

Viejo barrio, barrio viejo
Yo también ya envejeci,
Y cuando uno se hace viejo
Nadie se recuerda de ti.
Vamonos muriendo juntos

Where once there were houses
Where once our people lived.
Only ruins remain
Of the happy homes,
Of the joyous families,
Of these people that I loved.
In the evening, they would sit outside
To enjoy the coolness of the night.

I would pass by and greet them,

It seems that I can hear the echo.

"How are you, Dona Juanita?"
"Good evening, Isabel."
"What do you say, Chalita?
How are Arturo and Manuel?"
Viejo barrio, old neighborhood
That I enjoyed in my childhood.
And with all my friends
I traveled shoeless and afoot.
From Meyer Street to El Hoyo,
From El Hoyo to the irrigation ditch,
From the ditch to the river,
That was my world.
They say that we were poor,
But I never noticed that.
I was happy in my world
In that neighborhood that I loved.

Viejo barrio, old neighborhood,
I too have gotten old
And when you get old
No one remembers you.
Let us die together.

Que me entierran en tu suelo	Let them bury me in your soil
Y seramos dos difuntos	And we will lie together
Rodeados de mil recuerdos.	Surrounded by a thousand memories.

The Beginning

On a bitterly cold Christmas Eve in 1916, in the old barrio in Tucson, Arizona, "la señora Concepción de Guerrero dío a luz," as we say in Spanish, "brought to light" a healthy baby boy, and that was me. I was born at home and there was no doctor present. Mamá had had four children already, so I guess she thought she knew the routine. My aunts were all there—my mother's sisters.

But something went wrong. I'm not sure but it may have been my fault. It was so cold that night that icicles were hanging from the cactus needles and the coyotes were wearing serapes. It was so cold that after I stuck out one little toe, I changed my mind. I didn't want to come out.

They kept at me, and finally I had to give in. Just as I was being born, Mamá fainted. Her sisters tossed me down to the end of the bed while they revived her. After a while Mamá came to. When she was okay, somebody—I think it was the oldest sister, La Prieta—looked around and said, "¡El niño! ¿Dondé esta el niño?" (The baby! Where's the baby?)

El niño was at the foot of the bed, turning blue already. I could have frozen to death down there! Right then I realized how important it is to be the center of attention. I've been working at that ever since.

My aunts had a big discussion about my name. Every day in the Mexican calendar has a saint and the baby is supposed to be named for that saint, which is why you find a lot of Mexican boys named Maria.

So Tía Panchita looked at the calendar and said, "It's Santa Delfina's Day, so his name is Delfino."

Then Tía Joaquina said, "It's Christmas Eve, La Nochebuena; you have to name him Jesus."

But, thank God, Mamá was conscious by then and she said, "No way! His name is going to be like his father, Eduardo." So that was that.

Mamá

The angels sang in Bethlehem on the first Christmas Eve, but the first music that I remember was my mother's voice. She'd hold me close and croon, "A la roo roo baby, A la roo roo ya. Here comes that man with a tail and he will eat you up." Or "There's a hole up in the sky where old Calzones de Cuero (Leather Pants) looks down on you. (I still don't know who Leather Pants is, but he doesn't sound very nice.) And below the sky is a hole where a rat comes out. Kill it! Kill it! Kill it!"

Every lullaby I ever heard in Spanish is frightening. Mexicans scare their kids to sleep. The bebés conk out as fast as they can so they don't have to listen to that stuff.

Mamá had a beautiful soprano voice and she was always singing. If she was in the kitchen cooking, she was singing. If she was in the yard planting flowers, she was singing.

In the evenings, she would bring out her guitar and sing to all of us. She used to play some really difficult songs like *Ave Que Cruza por Lejanos Cielos* (Bird That Crosses to Faraway Skies). She had one special love song that she would sing to Papá: *Cuando Escuches Este Vals* (When You Listen to This Waltz).

Everybody loved her because she was all heart and she was always happy—always laughing, always smiling, always singing. When she'd walk down the street, everybody would call to her, "¡Doña Conchita! ¡Doña Conchita! ¿Como estas?"

Mexicans are usually short, but Mamá was two or three inches taller than Papá—maybe 5'10" or so. She had a good figure, black hair so long that it hung down to her tailbone, and big dark-brown eyes that dressed up her whole face.

She loved to dance, especially the Spanish dance *La Jota Aragonesa*. She'd wind up the Victrola and she'd dance through the house laughing, clicking her castanets, and kicking her heels way up.

Her braid would come loose and her long hair would wave like a flag as she whirled around and around. Then she'd stop, all out of breath, and she'd braid her hair and wrap it around the top of her head and pin it up again.

She was incredible in the way she found the energy to sing and dance with all of the work that she did—she washed clothes in a tub with a washboard and used a flatiron heated on top of a wood stove and cooked three meals a day for eleven people. Where she found the energy to do that and have all those babies—and still she could kick up her heels.

My dad said that Mamá had twenty-seven children, but I think that he was wrong because I can only remember the names of eighteen. She loved babies, and when she found out another one was on the way, she'd laugh and say, "Ay, tu papá—all he has to do is throw a sock at me and I'm pregnant again."

Only eleven of her babies lived past their first birthday. The others were stillborn or they died after a couple of months. There were two sets of twins and one of triplets. It seemed like almost every year there was another little white coffin in the living room.

She knew a lot of sorrow in her life, but if she ever cried, it must have been at night when we were all sleeping.

She gave me so much, but the greatest gift was when she taught me to play the guitar and to love it and to wrap my heart around it. I wish that I had asked her who taught her to play when she was a girl, but I never did. At the end of her life, when she couldn't recognize me anymore, I took her guitar to the nursing home, and she could still play it and sing the old songs.

She was such a wonderful woman. I'm sure everybody says that about his mother, but she was so special. I've never known anyone else like her.

Papá

The second most important person in my world was Papá, Eduardo Guerrero Ramirez. When he was young, Papá was a handsome dude. He had hair as shiny and black as shoe polish that he always combed straight back, and he wore a little moustache.

When he was eighteen or nineteen Papá was in the Mexican navy, and he used to make jokes about the ships. He said, "Our boats were so small that every time we gave some big shot a three-gun salute, the recoil would knock us out so far that it took three days to get back to port."

For several years, he worked in the shipyards in Guaymas, Sonora. In those years the ships still ran on steam, and he learned his trade so well that later he went to work for the Southern Pacific Railroad yards in Tucson.

At the time I was born he was the head boilermaker, and he made pretty good money for those days. Once, the shop foreman threatened to get him fired if he didn't join the union, but Papá was very Mexican, very proud, very stubborn. He just laid down his tools, folded his arms, and said, "Go ahead. Fire me!" He knew that they wouldn't, and they didn't.

He never became a citizen. Neither did Mamá. They were very proud of their heritage and their roots. They didn't want to live in Mexico, but they still wanted to be Mexicans. Mamá couldn't speak any English and Papá learned just enough to get by. They really didn't need it. Everyone in the barrio spoke Spanish and, in those years, more than three-fourths of the railroad workers in Tucson were Mexicans.

My parents had a good relationship but they were very different. Mamá liked to laugh and sing. At work Papá used to joke with his friends but at home he was always serious, always the boss—except he loved to tease Mamá.

My little brother, Ruben, told me about something that happened after I grew up and moved away. He said that one evening Papá came home real late. He was staggering and singing. I don't know what got into him that night, because he was not a drinking man. Mamá was furious! She grabbed him by the shirt and dragged him out to a washtub full of water in the yard and she dunked him. He came up sputtering but he started laughing, so she dunked him again and again. Then the tub tipped over. They both fell down and they just lay there in the mud together laughing.

With me Papá was really tough. He never teased me or joked with me.

In the morning he'd tell me, "Chop some firewood today."

He'd leave for work and I'd chop a little wood and then I'd run off to play. When I came home in the evening, he'd be waiting behind the door. He'd grab me and he'd say, "What did I tell you to do today?"

With my head down, in a little voice I'd say, "Chop wood."

"What did you do?"

"Well, it was awfully hot and the boys were all going to the irrigation ditch to swim. So I thought I'd go cool off for a little while before I chopped the wood. And the time just went by, and then it was too late."

Whack! He had a special whip for me made out of braided leather with a handle. And that son-of-a-gun hurt. He never used that whip on anybody else.

The last time he whipped me was one day when I was about sixteen. I went to a rodeo with my friends, and I found one of those long slender whips that they use on horses. It was just lying in the road so I picked it up and carried it home.

I'll always remember that night. For the first time my pal Yuca and I got paid for playing at a party. It was only a couple of dollars, but that was real money in those days. They had some maiz—some homemade corn whisky. The older boys kept at me to take a drink. I didn't really want to, but finally I gave in, held my breath, and had a shot. It was horrible stuff. It smelled bad and tasted worse. That one swallow made me dizzy!

I had told Papá that I would be home by eleven, but everyone kept applauding and asking for more songs. All that applause was

more intoxicating than the whisky. Never before in my life had I felt
so popular.

I got home about midnight and I sneaked in very quietly. We had
so many kids that we had to double up in bed, so I undressed and slid
in beside my brother without waking him up. Papá must have been
lying awake waiting for me, because just then he came into the room.
"Why are you getting back so late?"

"Well, they liked the music and they wanted us to stay longer.
They paid us an extra half dollar."

He leaned over me and said, "Blow in my eye."

I tried to act really sleepy. "What?"

He tapped his cheek, "Blow right here." I did, and my breath
almost knocked him over.

He said, "Stand up here on this bed." Then he whipped my naked
body with that same horse whip I had found in the road.

Papá hit me pretty hard sometimes, but I never hated him for
whipping me. Maybe I thought that I deserved it. Sometimes I've tried
to figure out why he was so hard on me. I wasn't that bad. I really
think it was because he loved me.

Maybe I just wasn't macho enough for him. When I was little, I
was Mamá's pet and I was a crybaby. Later I was very shy, and besides,
I started playing the piano and thinking about being an artist.

Or maybe it was because a lot of the older boys who played at
parties did booze it up. My oldest brother, Alberto, was already having
problems with alcohol, so Papá might have been afraid that I would
turn out the same way.

Later, Papá was very proud of my success. I know that, even
though he never told me so.

I loved the old man in spite of the beatings. Who knows what
might have happened? What I might have become? Maybe the whip-
pings served a purpose.

Sometimes I think that he wanted to talk about why he had
been so hard on me, but he didn't know how and then finally he
couldn't. He got Lou Gehrig's disease. He could get around okay but,
for the last year or so, he couldn't talk at all.

But he could still laugh. Once we went to the market together, and when we were about ready to leave I asked him, "Is this everything?"

He looked in the cart and then he tried to say something. I couldn't understand, and he got madder and madder. Then, finally, he grabbed his crotch and grunted "¡Huevos!" I picked up a carton of eggs, then—I couldn't help it! I started to laugh. And he started to laugh. It got funnier and funnier, and we both had to hang onto the cart to keep from falling down while all the other shoppers stared at us, trying to figure out what was going on with those crazy Mexicans.

At the end, we were all in his hospital room one night and, as we filed out, I said, "Nos vemos mañana, Papá." (See you tomorrow, Dad.) He looked at me in a strange way. He looked right into my eyes. I looked back, and his eyes followed my eyes all the way out the door. I think maybe he knew that we wouldn't see each again, and he wanted to tell me that he loved me and that he was sorry that he had been so hard on me. A few hours later he passed away.

Our Mexican Roots

I was born an American and I've lived my whole life in the United States, but the roots of my family tree reach way down into Mexico. Like most Mexicans, my background is mestizo (mixed). I don't know when my Indian ancestors walked to North America from Asia or even when my Spanish ancestors sailed over from Europe, but somehow some of them ended up in Baja California.

Papá was born in La Paz in 1885. When he was fifteen, the family moved to Guaymas, which was where my grandpa dumped my grandma a few years later.

Grandpa owned a pool hall in Burro Alley. It had a bar and some little rooms with ladies of the evening. When Papá and his three brothers were all teenagers they used to run errands for the ladies. He told me that some of them were very pretty and very nice.

In 1903 or 1904, my grandparents split up. I never knew why until just a few years ago. One night, after a concert in Los Angeles, a man came up to me and said, "I knew your grandfather in Guaymas."

I said, "He was a wonderful old guy."

"He was a son-of-a-gun. You know the reason that he left your grandmother? One day she was at home by herself and this fellow they called El Berrendo (the bull) came by. He said that he had some business with your grandfather, so she let him come inside to wait. It was a small house and the front door opened right into the bedroom, so he sat down on the bed and she went back to work in the kitchen. Your grandfather came in and yelled, 'What the hell are you doing on my bed? Get out of here!'

"He threw him out and then he got after your grandmother. The whole street could hear him. 'What was this hombre doing on our bed?'

"She tried to tell him, 'He was just waiting for you.' But your grandfather got so mad that he decided to pack up and take the three younger boys to Cananea, leaving her behind."

That bugged me. How could he be so cruel? Unless . . . maybe he caught Grandma in bed with the man! She wasn't a grandma then. Maybe he just had a lot of imagination, or maybe in those days he was real macho and it was a matter of honor.

Papá used to sing a very funny song someone made up about Grandpa's pool hall. The song is called *Adios Guaymas*. The lyrics describe some of the women and some of the customers. They all have funny nicknames. My grandpa is called Panzon (potbellied). And he was.

Mamá's family had a ranch in Santa Ana, in Sonora. Her maiden name was Murietta. Joaquin Murietta, the "Mexican Robin Hood," was born and raised on a farm not far from their home. He was either a bandit or a hero, depending on who you're talking to. I guess that you could say the same thing about the original Robin Hood.

One of Mamá's sisters was named Joaquina. I've wondered sometimes if Tía Joaquina was kind of brainwashed by her name. I know that she was a very independent woman. The story goes—I heard it a hundred times from Mamá—that when they all came to Arizona, Joaquina married a white dude. I don't know any of the details, but she killed him and did time in the prison at Yuma.

It was years before that, in Cananea, Sonora, that my parents met and fell in love. In 1906 they decided to get married.

About that time the workers at the copper mine there went on strike. The mine was owned by an American named Greene. Mr. Greene called in some gunslingers from Texas to come over and break the strike. They met some resistance from the local people, who also had guns.

The day of that gun battle was the very day that my mom and dad were saying their vows in front of the priest. Mamá told me that right in the middle of the ceremony, bullets came flying through the church windows and they had to dive under the pews. When the shooting stopped, they went back up to the altar and they got married and settled down to raise a family.

Later some of the mine workers still refused to go back to work, and the dictator, Porfirio Díaz, sent the Mexican army in to settle the affair. Several miners were killed. Some people say that these were the opening shots of the Mexican Revolution, which officially began in 1910 when Francisco Madero attacked the garrison at Piedras Negras, Coahuila.

Along the northern border people were being caught between the government forces and the revolutionary armies. One side was about as cruel as the other. There were a lot of Chinese in northern Mexico. They didn't have guns and they weren't fighting anybody, but Pancho Villa hated them just because they were different. Papá told us that he'd see their bodies hanging from the trees and the telegraph poles.

The fighting kept getting closer and closer to them so, in 1910, my dad brought my mom and the kids (by then there were four) over to Douglas, Arizona. In those days, you paid two centavos and you could cross the border in either direction.

My dad's oldest brother, Tío Crispín, was already married when the others left Guaymas, so he stayed behind with his wife and children. As the Revolution began to build up, the government needed more and more men to fight Zapata and Villa. They had a kind of legal kidnapping called la levita (the little tail). The name came from the little tails on the officers' coats.

The military was so powerful that the officers could just grab a young man off the street and put him in the army. In 1912, that happened to Crispín. A few weeks later he tried to run away, but they caught him and put him in a military prison in Torín, not far from Guaymas. My grandmother went to visit him on Sundays and to take him food. She told us that one week he was in the prison hospital and the next week his bed was empty. When she asked where he was, someone pointed to the cemetery.

Soon after my parents moved to Tucson, my grandpa came to live with them. To me, he looked like Santa Claus—big, fat, with a long white beard. He was a baker, so he'd cook all kinds of wonderful pastries. In the morning, he'd set me on his lap and feed me warm, wonderful Mexican sweet breads—pan de huevo, conchas, empanadas, coyotas. No wonder I loved him.

When I was very small, maybe four or five, he stepped on a rusty nail. The wound was very deep. It got infected and gangrene set in. The doctor wanted to amputate his leg, but my grandpa said, "I won't be a cripple; I'd rather die." And he did.

In those days, children were not sheltered from death like they are now, and I remember seeing him in the coffin. I knew that he was dead; I could understand that but I couldn't believe it. A few nights later, I woke up and I saw him . . . or I think I saw him. I was so happy that I screamed, "Mamá! Mamá! Tata's here. Tata's here. I saw him."

She came running in and she said, "No, you didn't. You didn't see him." But it was so real. I still wonder if I did see him. I loved him so much. Maybe he just came back to say adiós.

Raul and Alberto

When we were kids, we never celebrated the Day of the Dead because it was just too scary. Now sometimes I think life is like one of those old Mexican masks that remind us that death is always close by—that the skull is not far beneath the skin.

It was about the same time that my grandpa died that we lost Raul, my brother that was a year younger than me. The first song that I ever composed was for Raul.

We lived on Main Street then, in a house with a stone wall at the back. The level of the ground was the top of the wall on our side. On the other side way down below us were the railroad tracks, and about a half mile away was the depot.

When I was about four and Raul was three, Papá went to Mexico City to visit his brothers, and he was gone for a month. We missed him a lot, so Raul and I would sit on that wall with our legs hanging over the edge. A long way off across the desert, we'd see the smoke of a train and we'd say to each other, "I hope Papá is on that train." Then it would stop at the depot, and people would get off, but not our Papá.

As the train would leave the station, we'd feel really sad, abandoned. To help us feel less lonely, I made up a little song that I taught Raul. I can still remember the melody. We couldn't say "tren" so we'd sing, "Bye-bye tlen. Vete con Papá. Bye-bye tlen. Vete con Papá." (Bye-bye train. Go with Daddy.) We sang that every day until finally, one wonderful morning, we saw him get off the train and we went dashing inside to tell Mamá.

Raul was brighter and smarter than I was, and he was good at teasing. He could get my goat so easy. I'd run to Mamá crying, "Raul hit me" or "Raul took my ball."

She'd say, "Raul, you leave him alone now!"

And Raul would always say, "Mamá, look at Lalo. Chipili chillon (spoiled crybaby)."

Even though he was smaller and younger, he was such a little brat that he overpowered me. To calm me and comfort me, Mamá would hold me and sing one of her favorite songs, like *Estrellita* (The Little Star). "Come down from heaven, estrellita, and tell me if he loves me a little . . . si me quiere un poco . . . "

But then Raul would pop up and say, "Mamá, it doesn't say 'un poco.' It says 'un pollo.'"

"No, mi hijito, it's 'un poco,' not 'un pollo.'" (A little, not a chicken.)

But he was such a stubborn little kid that he would argue with her.

He died when he was four. I thought that I hated him, but we were constantly together, and once he was gone, I missed him so much. Sometimes I still miss him.

My little brother Raul was my first buddy, and my big brother Alberto was my first hero. He was twelve years older than me so I was more like his son than his brother. He always took care of me, and I loved him dearly.

Before he went bad, he was a kind soul and real funny. He never called me Lalo; he used to call me Chipili, which means "spoiled brat." Whenever he came into the house, he would yell, "Chipili, where are you?" I didn't mind. I liked being spoiled.

Alberto was short and light-complected with light brown hair. The rest of us were all tall and dark. I never thought anything about it. I was almost grown up before I found out that he was our half brother.

Before he married my mom, my dad had an affair and got a girl pregnant. She told him about the baby but he didn't do his duty and marry her. She was disgraced and her family disowned her—threw her out into the street.

After the baby was born, she came over to the house where my dad and his brothers lived with my grandpa. She put a note on the baby saying that his name was Alberto, and she laid him down on their step. Then she poured kerosene all over herself and set herself on fire.

So the four men found themselves with a tiny baby. The young men went off to work every day, and my grandpa stayed home to take care of the house and the little boy.

When the kid was almost two years old, my dad took my mom home to meet his father and his brothers. The little boy was there but she didn't know anything about him. The men had all agreed that they would say that he belonged to my Uncle Severo, and they taught him to call Severo "Papá."

After they were married, Mamá came to live in Grandpa's house. She was the only woman in a houseful of men and she was treated like a queen. I know that this is true because she told me so. My grandpa had always taken care of the cooking and the housework, and he loved her so much that he wouldn't let her do anything.

Mamá told me, "I had nothing to do all day so I got really close to little Alberto."

Sometimes women have a kind of sense, a kind of intuition, and she started to notice some things that were happening between the boy and her new husband.

One night at dinner she gave the child an orange and said, "Take it to your papá."

The kid went over to Severo and said, "Papá, isn't this a nice orange?"

And Mamá said, "This has gone far enough. Alberto, come here! Severo no es tu papá. ¡Este es tu papá!" (This is your father!)

When she told this story, she would laugh and imitate my dad. "He got all flustered. 'What do you mean? Are you crazy? What are you talking about, woman?'

"'Come on. You know that he's your son. He is drawn to you. He follows you around everywhere.'"

So my dad knew that the secret was out. Alberto grew up with us. He was our brother.

All through her life Mamá loved Alberto—maybe even more than the others, because she felt sorry for him. It shows what kind of woman my mother was that she could love this child of my father's even before she had one of her own. Or maybe he was a comfort to her because she was so young when her own baby, the first Eduardo, died.

When Alberto was a teenager he started boxing. He fought as a bantamweight, and that's only about 118 pounds. He became bantamweight champion of Arizona, then he went on to win fights in San Francisco, Chicago, and even Matzatlán, Sinaloa.

I used to live at the gym. I'd carry his bag for him and I'd watch him train and I'd watch him fight. He was a real showman, always nattily dressed. In his glory days in Matzatlán he liked to drive around town in a big black car with his German shepherd sitting beside him.

His mother had named him Alberto but his manager, Spider Kelly, said, "Alberto Guerrero. That's too long."

One of Spider's favorite fighters was Mike O'Dowd. Since my brother was so light-skinned, he decided to give him an Irish name, Mickey. And at that time there was a very popular governor of Sonora whose name was Obregón. So Spider Kelly said, "Mickey Obregon. That'll be your name from now on." That was the name that he fought under, but at home he was always Alberto.

Papá was so proud of him. And so disappointed when he started going downhill.

For several years Alberto made good money, but then he started to slide. He was never mean or bad, but he was irresponsible. He fell in with the wrong crowd, he got involved with a lot of women, and he was always coming home drunk.

Finally Alberto couldn't fight anymore. And he didn't want to work at anything else. Sometimes he would just lie around the house, and sometimes he wouldn't show up for days; then Mamá would say to me, "Go find your brother." Even then, she really loved him.

Alberto and my brother Frank were born in Mexico, and they never bothered to become American citizens. At that time there was no pressure from immigration. People came and went across the border as they pleased—unless you were "an undesirable."

One day Alberto got drunk and he beat up the woman he was living with. Legally a boxer's fists are considered to be a weapon, so when a boxer hits someone, the judge usually throws the book at him. As soon as they found out that Alberto was not a citizen, he was sentenced to be deported to Mexico—forever.

He moved to Matzatlán, and things were okay at first because people knew him from the time when he had fought there in his prime. He married a woman who was very good to him and he straightened out for a while, but it didn't last long. He couldn't adjust to living in

Mexico; he always felt like an exile. Like he was surrounded by strangers in a foreign land.

Once, it was in 1939, I was on my way down to Mexico City to see if I could get some publishers interested in my music. I hadn't seen Alberto in nearly three years so, when the train stopped in Mazatlán, I got off to visit him.

It was almost two in the morning when I knocked on his door. A woman called from inside, "¿Quien es?" (Who is it?)

I said, "I'm looking for Alberto Guerrero. My name is Lalo Guerrero."

I heard a man's voice from inside the house, "¿Eres tú, Chipili?" (Is that you, Chipili?) He still knew my voice, and I think that was one of the happiest moments he had had in a long time.

When I think about that meeting, it brings tears to my eyes. I spent three or four days with him. When I had to go, it almost broke my heart to leave him there. I never saw him alive again.

His wife told me later how he died. He was in the bar where he always drank, and he fell asleep with his head on the table. The bartender shook him and said, "Wake up. We're going to close." But Alberto was dead.

My big brother, my first hero, died all by himself in that crummy old bar in Matzatlán. It's a sad ending to his story, but this is the way it happened. I still love to remember the closeness that we had when we were very young, when he was on top of the world and I got to carry his bag.

The Old Barrio

When we talked about our part of town, we usually referred to it as "mi barrio" (my neighborhood). Sometimes people think that a barrio is something bad—like a prison. But when I was a child, the barrio was a sanctuary where everyone knew the rules and where everything was familiar.

Most of the houses were bulldozed away in the seventies and eighties. I wrote *Barrio Viejo* (Old Neighborhood) in memory of the world that I knew as a child. I performed it for the first time in 1990 at the Mariachi Conference in the Tucson Convention Center, which now stands on the site of my barrio.

Like refugees everywhere, the Mexicans who came to Tucson tried to recreate the best of their homeland. They didn't want the violence of the revolution, but they wanted to be around Mexican people and to shop in Mexican stores.

We lived on the southwest side of the city and los güeros (the whites) lived in the northeast, on the other side of the tracks. In those years, they seldom came into our territory and we seldom went into theirs, except the women who cleaned their houses and the men who took care of their gardens. When we were kids, we were so segregated that I never knew I was a minority until I went to junior high.

I guess that this is as good a time as any to talk about "us" and "them." Over the years, I have referred to my English-speaking friends as blancos, güeros, gringos, whites, Americans, and Anglos. They have called me Mexican, Mexican American, Hispanic, Latino, and Chicano. And those are just the nice names! It's hard to keep track of them all. About the time I get used to the politically correct designation, it becomes an insult. Throughout my story, I'll use whatever terms we were using at the time I'm talking about.

Now back to the barrio: When I was six, my parents moved to Meyer Street, and I spent the happiest years of my life in that house. It was the best house in the neighborhood. In front of our house, we had a green picket fence, a couple of big trees, and Mamá's flowers. We had a long front porch where we would sit in the evening and watch the people passing by on the street.

Inside, the floor was just bare wood, but Mamá scattered some rugs around and she put pretty curtains on all the windows. There was a piano in the living room, and a Victrola. When we had the money, Mamá would go over to one of the stores that sold records in Spanish. She'd look at every one of them before she would choose one or two to bring home.

A big fireplace took up one wall of the dining room. That was what kept us warm on winter nights. Tucson is supposed to be a sunny winter resort, but it can get pretty damn cold, I tell you. Years later I got into real trouble with the Chamber of Commerce when I let out that secret on a national radio broadcast.

Our house had windows all around it. The windows were always open in the summertime and there were no screens. We probably had flies, but I didn't notice them.

All the kids in the neighborhood used to come there to play. On Saturdays, my buddies and I would go downtown to the Lyric Theater to see cowboy movies. When we got home, we'd replay the whole show; we'd be Tom Mix or Ken Maynard or Tim McCoy. We didn't have guns so we'd point our fingers and go "Bang! Bang! I got you!" We'd run into the house and fly through the windows from the bedroom out to the yard and back through another window into the living room. In and out! In and out!

Mamá must have had the patience of a saint. Or maybe she had decided that she'd rather have me playing around the house than going off somewhere and getting into trouble. Now and then we'd go too far and she would say, "Boys, stop making that noise! Lalo, it's enough already!"

Once Papá got home, all the fun would stop.

A screened porch ran across the back of the house and it seemed like there was always some stranger eating out there. These were the years of the Depression and the Dust Bowl. The men riding the rails to

California would get off in Tucson and start looking for a handout. A lot of the hobos were Anglos, but they would always come to our side of town. They knew they could get a free meal easier than they could in the rich white neighborhood, because the Mexicans were good-hearted people who would share whatever they had.

The railroad tracks were not far from our house, and the hobos must have had a mark on our place. Mamá was such a kind soul; she couldn't turn anybody away. "Pobrecito" (poor boy), she'd say as she warmed up the frijoles (beans). "He looks so hungry."

Out in the back yard, Mamá raised chickens and I kept my homing pigeons.

We usually didn't eat the pigeons, but whenever Mamá was going to have a baby, her sister would cook pigeons for her. I guess they didn't hurt her. She lived to be 86.

Right behind the house there was a ramada. Papá had put up posts and a frame, and grapevines went up and over it. In the summertime it was so hot that we couldn't sleep inside, so we'd take our beds out there at night. It was cool and it was beautiful. Between the leaves I could see the stars. The sweet purple grapes hung down, and I could reach up and pick off a bunch and eat them whenever I felt like it.

When I was six or seven years old, I would lie there and look up at the stars and think until I fell asleep. Maybe because of the movies, or maybe because of Alberto, it was already in my heart that I wanted to be in show business. I wanted to be somebody. Every night I'd make up a dream and every night it was different.

I'd close my eyes and I'd picture myself on a stage. At that time Rudy Vallee was my idol, so maybe I would be a crooner. I'd stand there in the spotlight in a suit with a bow tie and my megaphone and I'd sing, "My time is your time. . . . " Then I'd take a bow and the crowd would give me a standing ovation.

Some nights I'd be a boxer like Alberto. At home on fight nights, we'd all sit around the table watching the radio. Nobody even thought about TV then, but when I listened to the announcer, I could see the fight inside my head. This was in the glory days of Jess Willard, Max Schmeling, and Jack Dempsey. Many of our neighbors didn't have a radio. So the moment the fight was over, the boys were out selling newspapers. They'd run down the street yelling and people would grab the papers. And they didn't just want to know who won; they wanted to know all the details. Was it one-sided all the way? Was it a knock-out? Was it a really great fight?

In my daydream, I'd be in Madison Square Garden in New York fighting for the title. I'd be out there punching, and maybe I'd be hurt and bleeding, but in the end, I would knock the other guy out. I'd walk around the ring with my arms up and the people would be on their feet screaming! When I listened to the radio, that was me up there! That was me!

I was very skinny as a teenager, but I did fight one fight. It was a curtain raiser for the real matches. I lost. The other boy wasn't very big, but he was a lot faster than me.

Under that ramada in the old barrio, I was always a winner. I'd dream about the praise and the applause and the spotlights. Even now, when I listen to the applause after a concert, sometimes I think back to those daydreams under the stars.

In the morning when I'd wake up, the house always smelled of wood smoke from the stove. I'd hear Mamá singing while she patted out tortillas. She bought corn tortillas from a Yaqui Indian woman, but she made her own flour tortillas Sonoran style. She'd take a little ball of dough and slap it back and forth until it was as big as dinner plate. Fried eggs and spicy Mexican sausage, chorizo, would be sizzling in the frying pan. We had breakfast burritos a long time before Taco Bell.

After breakfast, I'd get outside as fast as I could. If I was lucky, I'd make it before Papá found some job for me to do.

Meyer Street was the main thoroughfare where everything happened. As soon as I stepped out through the front door, I was in the middle of the action.

On one corner of Simpson and Meyer was the house where I was born. On another corner of that intersection was Martinez' Bakery, so the morning air was filled with the sweet fragrance of Mexican pastries and breads.

Across the street was a store called Las Cuatro Esquinas (The Four Corners), where Señora Irun sold herbs and folk medicines of different kinds.

On the fourth corner was a grocery store run by El Chino Gordo (the fat Chinaman). He was the biggest man in the barrio; he must have weighed more than three hundred pounds.

Some people go on and on about how hard it is to grow up bilingual, but for me it was a great joy. In the barrio, we could choose the best of two cultures, so there was always something happening.

We celebrated the Fourth of July and we celebrated Mexican Independence Day on September 16. Papá played the French horn in the Southern Pacific Railroad Band. On both holidays, he'd march in the parade down Congress Street. Then we'd go to the Elysian Grove for a barbecue.

We kids loved El Día de San Juan in June. That was the day when St. John baptized Jesus in the Jordan river. Everybody would get up before daybreak. While it was still dark, we would trudge down to the big irrigation ditch two or three miles away. You had to get up that early to claim your space. By sunrise, hundreds of people would be lined up along the ditch. As soon as the air started to get a little warmer, we'd all take a dip in the water and have a picnic. All the popular bands in Tucson would come down, one after another, and each one would play for an hour or so.

It was the tradition to dress very casually. When anybody showed up in a suit and a tie, the boys would rush him and throw him into the ditch, clothes and all. Jacinto Orozco, the popular radio announcer for the Spanish music programs, always showed up in a white suit. Sooner or later someone would yell, "Let's get Mr. Orozco!" And in he would go—suit and all.

One year when I was playing with the Carlistas quartet, we went down to perform like the other bands. We were wearing our new fancy black charro outfits with black sombreros and silver trim. As soon as we got out of the car, some of the guys started after us. And you should have seen how fast we got back into that car! Our wonderful suits would have been ruined.

Our family celebrations were a hodgepodge of Mexican and American traditions. My favorite holiday was Christmas. It was doubly special because Christmas Eve was my birthday.

Mamá and the girls would make tamales—sweet ones with raisins and brown sugar, and others with meat and chiles. I never had a birthday cake, but we always had buñuelos. Mamá would fry big round flour tortillas until they were crispy, then she'd break them up in a bowl and pour a very light syrup on top of them.

In Mexico, los Tres Reyes (the Three Kings) come and bring the gifts on the sixth of January, but that was old-fashioned. We were Americans and we adopted Santa Claus. I don't think Mamá and Papá exchanged any gifts, but we children always got toys—little cars, skates, dolls for the girls.

The Christmas that I remember most vividly was the saddest one for me. I had my doubts but, in my heart, I still believed in Santa Claus, and I loved finding my presents under the tree on Christmas morning. That year I got exactly what I wanted, a BB gun and a football, but Papá just handed them to me and said, "Merry Christmas." I tried not to show it, but I was heartbroken that Santa was over. I was twelve years old and I guess Papá figured that it was time for me to grow up.

I loved Santa so much that years later I gave him a Mexican cousin, Pancho Claus. I wrote the song one December when I was listening to *The Night Before Christmas* and I started to wonder about what would happen if this lily-white, uptight, Dutch saint came into a Latino home in East L.A. He'd arrive expecting to find the children all snug in their beds and, instead, the whole family would be singing, dancing, boozing, and "getting their lowriders ready for cruising." Jolly old Saint Nicholas would probably hightail it out of there; on the other hand, Pancho Claus, with his big sombrero and eight cute little donkeys, would feel right at home.

Even apart from the holidays, there was always a lot of activity in our neighborhood. All the vendors in Tucson used to travel up and down Meyer Street.

The most important one in the summer was El Hielero, the ice man. As he drove along in his little blue Ford truck, he would lean out the window and yell, "¡Hielo! ¡Hielo!"

When the ladies heard him, they'd yell back, "Bring me fifteen cents' worth" or "Bring me a quarter's worth." His son was my best friend, and sometimes I'd help with the deliveries just so I could ride in the truck. Nobody I knew had a car.

We never put ice in our drinks. It went into the icebox to keep the food from spoiling. My mother's sister La Prieta worked in a white man's house, so we knew that in the kitchens over across the tracks they had real refrigerators.

Papago Indians from the reservation south of town would come down the street with their rickety wagons filled with wood. It was mostly mesquite, which smells real good when it burns, or a very hard wood, palo fierro, that they call ironwood in English. The logs were four or five feet long, and I had to chop them up so they would fit into our stove. Over on the other side of town they cooked with gas. If we'd had gas, I would have had a much easier childhood.

The snow cone vendors came out in the summer. In some parts of Mexico they call them raspadas, but most of our families were from Sonora so we called them cimarronas. They are just crushed ice covered with red, yellow, or green syrup, but I loved those things. On summer afternoons when the desert sun was beating down and you could fry an egg on the hood of the iceman's truck, it was like heaven to sit with my friends on our shady porch freezing my tongue on a strawberry cimarrona and talking about all the things that we were going to do someday. The truth is that none of us really thought that "someday" would ever come. It was so far away then, and now, here it is!

There were two menudo vendors who came around. Menudo is a very spicy stew made out of some parts of a cow that I'd rather not think about. It's flavored with dried red pods of chile tepín. That's the hottest chile in the world—about ten times hotter than the runner-up, the jalapeño.

Don Angel was always clean and neat. He dressed in pure white and wore a white cap. On his cart he had two huge aluminum pots filled with the steaming hot stew. He'd come down the street yelling, "¡Menudo! ¡Menudo fresco!" (Fresh menudo—just made.)

Menudo is good for hangovers so, on Sundays especially, people would stagger out with pans and bowls and say, "Give me twenty-five cents' worth," or, "I'll take fifty cents' worth."

Don Angel's menudo was great—it was clean and light-colored. The broth was golden and the corn was white.

But if you slept late and missed Don Angel, you had to get

menudo from Don Pedro. He never wore a cap and his hair was long and straggly. He was always covered with grease from head to foot. When he'd get grease on his hands from the menudo, he'd wipe them on his filthy apron. His menudo was dark muddy brown and it tasted terrible but, if you were desperate enough, you'd hold your nose and swallow it.

There was another old hombre who sold eggs. We'd all laugh and make jokes when he came by. He'd yell "Huevos frescos." That's "fresh eggs," but in Spanish huevos has a double meaning, so he was yelling "fresh testicles."

The lady next door to us had been done wrong by a man. She lost her mind over this and she hated all men. Every time she'd see the egg vendor go by, she'd make dirty signs with her hands, and she'd yell, "Huevos, huevos, y más huevos."

Then there was the old man called El Venadito (The Little Deer). I don't know why they called him that. Maybe he had been fast and graceful when he was young. He carried a little table full of pastries and he'd yell "Frutas de horno" (fruits of the oven). He was usually out of his skull with marijuana. He was not too steady, and when he'd drop a concha or an empanada down to the road, he'd pick it up, dust it off, and put it back onto the tray.

Besides the regular vendors, a lot of door-to-door salesmen came through the barrio, and they caused problems in our house. Mamá and Papá usually got along real well together. About the only reason that he would get upset with her was that all the salesmen in Tucson knew what a soft touch she was. They could sell Mamá everything. Papá would give her orders not to buy so much stuff, but she had a very good heart. She just couldn't turn them away.

Mr. Romero sold patent medicines for a cough or a sore throat or whatever. He'd say, "Doña Conchita, just try this. It'll work a miracle."

At first, she'd say no.

He'd keep at her and finally she'd say, "Okay. Give me one little bottle." Most of his medicines tasted good, but I can't remember if any of them worked.

Another salesman was San Dimas. He was an Arab, and he spoke Spanish with a funny accent. He went from house to house selling clothes and curtains and similar things. "Doña Conchita," he'd say,

"You don't have to buy. Just look at what a beautiful blanket I have here. And it's very cheap."

"No, no. I don't have any money."

"Just give me fifty cents a week."

"No, I can't do it." But he'd keep on, and he'd talk her into it.

Papá would come home and he'd roar, "What's this? I told you not to buy anything from those vendedores!" He would get upset because they had to feed and clothe nine kids on his salary. Mamá would promise not to do it again. And she wouldn't . . . for a while.

We weren't poor, but Papá never had any extra cash, so when we kids wanted spending money we'd sell anything that we could get our hands on.

During Prohibition, the bootleggers provided us with a source of easy income. They manufactured the moonshine in a basement somewhere, and then they sold it in pint bottles. Respectable people took their bottles home or to a club. The bums' version of a club was a vacant lot or an alley. When a bottle was empty, they'd just throw it aside. For us, those bottles were like found money because we could sell them back to the bootleggers for a nickel apiece.

In the late summer, someone would say, "Vamos a los sahuaros," and we'd run up the mountain to collect cactus fruit. Saguaros are so tall that we had to take a long pole with a hook on it to get the sweet red fruit down. We'd sell those three for a nickel.

Tía Panchita worked for a rich rancher who had a big orchard, and he let us pick there. Then I'd have to carry the fruit down the street going from door to door. "Would you like to buy some pomegranates?" Or figs or peaches or whatever was in season.

When there was no fruit, I sold the local Mexican newspaper. One door after another. "Would you like to buy *El Tucsonense*? It's only a nickel."

"No, gracias." And on to the next one and the next one, block after block. A lot of rejections, but now and then somebody would buy one. Looking back, I guess all those rejections prepared me for my future career in the recording industry.

I always was a proud little boy, and there was one thing that hurt my pride even more than selling door to door.

During the Depression years, Southern Pacific cut all the workers down to three days a week. And they got paid every two weeks. So every month, with only twelve days' work, Papá had to have enough money for the rent and for feeding eleven of us.

Usually, by the end of the second week we'd be out of money and out of food, with two or three days to go before he got his check.

So Papá would say, "Lalo, go over to Manuel Felix and ask him to lend me five dollars. I'll pay him back on Saturday."

I'd say, "Okay, Papá." I knew that we had to have the money so I never said no, but how I hated it. Manuel Felix was our landlord, and he was arrogant because he was pretty well set compared to the rest of us.

So I'd go over like—like with hat in hand. I didn't wear a hat, but that's how I felt.

It was demeaning. Humiliating.

His wife would come to the door and demand, "¿Que quieres?" (What do you want?)

"Please. I want to see Señor Felix."

"Espérate" (wait here), she'd snap. Then she'd go inside the house and he'd come out.

I'd feel about two inches high. I'd look down at the ground and I'd say real meek, because I was so embarrassed, "Dice mi papá que le mande cinco dólares." (My papá says won't you please lend him five dollars.)

He'd just look at me kind of disgusted like, then he'd say, "Momento." And he'd go get the money. He'd shove it at me: "Toma" (take it). I'd take the five dollars home to Papá, and we'd be okay for another couple of weeks. Then it would happen all over again.

The lack of money wasn't the only problem we faced. I don't know how anyone survived childhood in those days. I had just about every disease a kid could have: scarlet fever, measles, whooping cough. The biggest epidemics came in the years after the First World War.

The most deadly was influenza; they called it the Spanish Flu. We were all sick—even my father. I don't know how my mother didn't lose her mind. My sister Lolita was eleven. She died just before Christmas, and Maria Cristina died a week later. She was twelve.

When smallpox showed up in Tucson, I was five years old. Mamá and Papá wouldn't let the doctor vaccinate us. They were very conservative, old-fashioned Mexicans and they were suspicious of the Americans. They didn't want anyone to hurt their children.

So Frank got the smallpox first, then Alice and me, and finally Mamá. For weeks our house was quarantined. My father stayed away from us because he had to go to work. He used to sneak over the back fence into the house at two or three in the morning to bring us food and money.

For days I was in bed with sores all over my body. The itch just drove me crazy. I scratched and scratched until the blood and pus would run out and leave gaping holes. When my mother saw this she told me not to scratch, but I couldn't help myself. Finally she tied my hands to the side of my bed.

I couldn't stand it; I cried and screamed for hours. Then one night, even though my hands were tied, I struggled until I got my face against the rough plaster of the bedroom wall. I rubbed it and rubbed it until all the skin was torn off the side of my face. In the morning when my mother came into the room, she started to cry, "Oh, mi hijito! My son! Why did you do that?"

The scars were terrible. When I finally got well enough to get out of bed, the first time that I walked by the mirror, I saw this—this monster! I let out a scream that I can still hear. "Mamá, Mamá! It's horrible! What happened to me?"

It was a really scary moment, but she put her arms around me and said, "Don't worry, son. Don't cry. It'll be fine. It'll go away."

"Are you sure? Will it really go away?"

She hugged me closer and she said, "Yes, yes. It'll take a little time, but it'll be all right, son. It'll be all right." And I felt her tears falling on my head.

I don't know where my mother got the strength to live through all those horrible times; I don't remember her going to church. She did have a little shrine at home with the Virgin of Guadalupe, and she'd light candles and pray there.

It was a custom that when you wanted a miracle, you made "una manda," a promise to a saint to do something very difficult if he or she would help you.

Sometimes Mamá would call on Saint Xavier. In exchange for his help, she'd promise that she would walk all the way out to Mission San Xavier del Bac south of town. That's the one that they call "The White Dove of the Desert."

Papá was at work all day, so she'd take all the kids and a couple of baskets of food. We'd leave very early in the morning and we'd get back at dusk. I don't know how far it is, maybe seven or eight miles; now I drive over sometimes and it's still a long way out there. When I was so sick with the smallpox, Mamá had made a manda to El Santo Niño de Atocha. He's the one in the form of the Christ Child about ten years old wearing a robe with a braided belt. She promised him, "If you'll help my little son get well, he'll be so grateful that he will wear your robe and sandals for a year."

So for a year, all the time, I had to run around dressed like a little priest, and that didn't help much with all the tough kids in our neighborhood.

I Go Out into the World

My older sister, Alice, and I were so pockmarked that Papá decided to keep us away from the public school because the kids there were so cruel. The students in the Catholic school behaved much better, and they were taught to respect the nuns and each other.

When they sent me off to kindergarten, I didn't speak a word of English and bilingual education hadn't been invented yet. All the kids were from the barrio so we used Spanish on the playground, but in the classroom the nuns always spoke to us in English. Everything was new and confusing, and not being able to communicate was so frustrating.

The first day was very hot and I was dying of thirst. In Spanish, I whispered to the boy next to me, "How can I get a drink?"

He was a little more savvy than I was and he said, "Hold up your hand and say 'water.'"

I held up my hand. The teacher looked my way and I whispered, "Water?"

I can still remember the thrill, the incredible sense of wonder, of power, when she nodded her head.

It was hard, it was frustrating, but I took for granted that I had to learn English. And little by little, I did. We all did.

My parents encouraged us a lot. They knew that the language was important if we were going to make it in this country. And there was no danger of forgetting our Spanish because we were surrounded by people who didn't speak any English.

Most of us used two or three versions of our names depending on where we were and who we were talking to. In my family, we had Francisco-Pancho-Frank, Alicia-Alice, Eduardo-Lalo-Eddie, Concepcion-Conchita-Connie, Eugenio-Gene, Teresa-Terry, and Ramona-Mona.

For example, "Pancho" is the pet name for Francisco, like "Lalo" is for Eduardo. When I went looking for my big brother, sometimes I'd say "¿Dónde está Pancho?" and sometimes "Where's Frank?" It sounds really confusing, but we switched back and forth without ever thinking about it.

Even before I learned English, I loved kindergarten—drawing, singing, playing games. The nuns were really strict but they were fair.

Then the next year Papá didn't have enough money to pay the tuition any more. It was only ten dollars a month, but in those days you could get a pound of frijoles for a dime and a dozen tortillas for a nickel.

When he told me that I would have to start first grade in the public school, I thought that I would die. I knew what was going to happen. I saw those boys on the street all the time and they were mean!

Mexicans use a lot of nicknames and some of them are really cruel. My face was badly scarred from the smallpox, so the boys called me Cacarizo (pockmarked). Then for short they'd call me Cacaro. That was the kindest name they gave me.

In Mexico, there's a rough stone they use to make metates for grinding corn and chiles. It has a lot of little holes in it. So sometimes they called me Cara de Metate (Metate Face).

The one that was really terrible, that used to hurt the most: You know how out in the pasture when there's a fresh pile of manure on the ground and it rains while it's still soft, the water makes little holes in it? They used to call me Cara de Mierda Llovisnada (Face Like Rained-On Shit)—that's what they called me. And they'd all laugh and laugh when they'd say it! You can see why I wasn't thrilled about meeting those same guys in school every day. But what could I do? I was only six years old. I couldn't fight the whole school. It was rough, I tell you. They were merciless, but after a while they got their fill of it and left me alone.

Now the city of Tucson is going to make my old grammar school into low-cost housing for the elderly. They plan to keep the façade so it'll look just like it did when I went there. And guess what they're going to call the place: Lalo Guerrero's Barrio Viejo.

Who could have imagined that someday they'd name the school after poor little Cacaro? Even my daydreams weren't that far out.

School was so terrible that, for a while, I took refuge in the church. We were all brought up Catholic. I got baptized as a baby and later I went to catechism. The priest told me to study hard so that I could go to confession and take communion. By the time I finished those classes, I was so into religion that I felt like it was my duty to go to confession every Saturday.

I'd walk up to the little booth and kneel. A voice would say, "Tell me, young man, have you sinned?"

"Yes, Father, I have sinned." Now think about it. I was only eight years old. I was a quiet, lonely kid. I was so pockmarked and ugly that I didn't have many friends to lead me astray, so I didn't many chances to sin. But I had to confess, so, if I hadn't done anything bad all week, I'd make up stories.

I'd say, "Well, I disobeyed my father. He told me to do my chores and I went off to play. And I was disobedient to my mother and I lied to her."

"Say ten 'Our Fathers' and twenty 'Holy Marys.'" Then I'd go sit in the pew and pray. I'd feel very clean and good and, the next morning, I'd go to mass and receive the host.

I did this for weeks, maybe for months. Then one Saturday, while I was confessing my made-up sins, I thought, "I'll probably go to Hell. I'm lying to the priest and telling him that I have sinned." It got so complicated that I just stopped going to confession.

The Beginning of My Career in Music

Apart from my family, I think that the biggest influence in my life when I was a child was the movies. After I outgrew the Westerns, I started going to musicals starring Ruby Keeler, Gene Kelly, Dick Powell, Ginger Rogers, and Fred Astaire.

If I saw a movie with a song that I liked, I'd keep going back until I learned it. They'd only sing it once, so I'd have to see a film five or six times until I got all the lyrics and the melody exactly right. When I was nine or ten, I taught myself to play our piano. I didn't care about an audience; I just enjoyed it. The first song that I remember playing was *St. Louis Blues*.

It was in grammar school that I got started on my career as a performer. When I was in fifth grade, my music teacher, Miss Davis, gave me my first solo. Our class was going to put on an assembly program for the whole school. I was always very shy because I was embarrassed by the ugly scars on my face, but I think that she realized how much I wanted to be up on that stage with the other kids.

That was the year I saw *The Jazz Singer* about a dozen times. One day when nobody else was around, I showed her how I had learned to tap dance from watching the movies. I don't remember whether I asked her, or she asked me, if I could do an Al Jolson imitation for the assembly.

She got me a little black suit with a black hat, a bow tie, and white gloves. Then she made up my face. When I looked in the mirror, I hardly knew myself. The scars didn't show at all. I couldn't wait to get on stage.

Try to picture this little Mexican kid down on one knee in blackface singing "I got a mammy in Alabamy." I was a smash! When I heard the applause, I was hooked. Miss Davis had to drag me offstage that day, and I have been addicted ever since.

It was also Miss Davis who opened up the world of classical music for me. The following year, when I was in the sixth grade, all the schools in Tucson took part in a music appreciation contest.

The music wasn't like any that I had ever heard before—Debussy, Bach, Schubert, Mozart, Beethoven, all those guys. She had these great big records—or maybe they just seemed big to me because I was small. She'd play a record and we had to learn the title of each work, the composer, his place and date of birth, and what instruments were playing the solo parts. She'd tell us, "This is the cello," or "This is the oboe."

She was a great teacher and pretty soon I began to understand the music. I was so excited that I wanted to tell people all about it, but nobody was interested. Although my mother listened to me, I don't know how much she understood. I tried to play some things for her on our piano, but it was too difficult. It was frustrating because I had all of that great music in my head but I couldn't communicate it.

At the end of three months, Miss Davis picked out three of us to represent the class in the contest: Delfina Reyes, Aurelia Ramirez, and me.

Every school in town, all the grammar schools, the junior highs, and the high school, was represented in the high school auditorium that day. They played the records over the speakers and we had to write all that information about every song. It took hours.

When they compiled the results, the judges announced, "The winners are from Drachman Grammar School: Edward Guerrero, Aurelia Ramirez, and Delfina Reyes."

We couldn't believe it—three little chicanitos from the wrong side of the tracks beat out all the kids from all over Tucson! We were so proud.

I was only twelve, but that contest had a great impact on me. To this day, I enjoy listening to classical music, all of those wonderful melodies. They would fill up my head when I would lie awake at night. That was when I really began to think that music was the road that I should take in my life.

I think that my childhood ended when I went to high school. Up until then most of the students in my classes were from Mexican families. A lot of those families didn't place much value on education, so many of my friends decided to quit school and get jobs. But my parents took it for granted that we would all go to high school, so we did.

The high school was way over on the other side of town. I knew English by then but I was inhibited and shy. The teachers always treated all of us fairly, but some of the students didn't. I only remember a couple of real bigots, but I just didn't feel comfortable with all those white kids. I didn't even fit in with the Mexicans because most of them were from families that were better off than mine, and they looked down on me.

At first, I would go off by myself at lunchtime. Every morning, Mamá would pack me a brown bag and, at noon, I'd take it across to a little park close to the school. Then one day a couple of boys came over and asked if they could eat with me. Their names were Arthur Ruff and Bobby Ross. They both had Mexican mothers and Anglo fathers, so they spoke Spanish but they were used to being with Anglos and they knew their ways. We became friends and I learned a lot from them.

I did okay in high school but I wasn't a terrific student. There were no music classes unless you wanted to pay for them, and I didn't have any money. The only subject that I really liked was mechanical drawing. I still like to sketch and doodle when I'm thinking.

Bobby and Arthur used to tell me, "Don't be embarrassed; don't be afraid to try something different." They gave me so much confidence that I decided to go out for athletics.

First I tried out for football. I was 6'1" and weighed 135 pounds. The coach told me, "You're crazy. They'll kill you."

I said, "I can play end, Coach."

"Yeah. But when you catch the ball, those monsters are going to flatten you. I don't want your blood on my hands."

I tried boxing . . . once. I told you about that match.

I didn't give up. I had long legs and I could outrun a jack rabbit, so I joined the track team. I could have been a star, except my vanity did me in.

The first big meet for that year was between Phoenix, Nogales, and Tucson high schools. The coach put me down to run the hundred-yard dash and one leg of the relay race.

When I raced with the boys I knew, I'd run in my regular shoes. But for a big track meet, I thought that they'd look tacky. I wanted tennis shoes like the other guys on the team.

The department store downtown was owned by Sadie Turk. My mom used to buy clothes for all of us there because Sadie would give her credit.

We didn't have any money but I really wanted those shoes, so I talked Mamá into going with me to the store.

Sadie looked at my feet and said that she didn't have any tennis shoes big enough to fit me. I was determined, though, and I finally found a pair that I could get on if I bent my toes under. They looked great.

I ran the hundred-yard dash with these shoes and I came in fifth out of five. I was in such pain that I could barely limp back to the bench. The worst part was telling the team that I couldn't run my part of the relay. We lost.

I took off my new shoes and threw them as hard as I could. And that was the end of my athletic career in high school.

I wasn't a hero, but Bobby and Arthur stuck with me anyhow. I don't think that I could have stayed in school without those friends and a few others who came along later, like Ralph Johnson and his sister, Mary. I've forgotten many things over the years, but I can remember the names of all the people who have ever been kind to me.

The most important thing that I learned in high school was if you spoke English well and showed a little confidence in the way that you carried yourself, people usually let you alone. If you looked timid or afraid, somebody was always ready to pounce on you.

Music and More Music

When it came to music, I was like a funnel. I'd take everything in. I didn't care where it came from or whether it was in English or in Spanish. I liked Burl Ives' ballads and Bob Wills and His Texas Playboys. I learned American songs from the movies and Mexican songs from Mamá's records and both from the radio.

It's hard to believe now, but, at that time, you didn't hear much Spanish on the radio. Early in the morning when the air was clear, our Philco could bring in Pedro J. González and Los Madrugadores (The Early Risers) from Los Angeles, and we could get the station from Piedras Negras.

The music that was played on those stations was mostly ranchera (Mexican country-western style). Often a vocalist was backed up by one or two guitars. There were some groups who used the bajo sexto, a kind of bass guitar, and the accordion, which was brought in by the German immigrants along the Texas border. That style of music is called norteño (northern) or Tex-Mex.

There were beautiful waltzes like *Sobre las Olas* and *Ojos Tapatios*. And there were popular ballads called corridos that tell a story about a person or an event. Some of them were about kidnappings and murders; others were about horse races on the Mexican ranches. The races were usually between just two horses and they sounded very exciting—as if they were broadcasting the actual race.

One evening when I was about fourteen, I was listening to my mother play her guitar and I asked, "Mamá, will you teach me?"

She said, "I can teach you if you'll promise to really pay attention and practice."

I said, "I promise, Mamá."

So she taught me the classic Mexican songs that she loved, like *Morir Soñando* and *Adelita*.

At the same time I was inspired by a young man, Reedy Mothe, who was on one of the local stations every morning. He played the guitar and sang American pop songs. That was the start of my dream to record in English, because I knew that was where the money lay.

In high school, I got together with a couple of friends, Rudy Arenas and Manny Matas, and we formed a trio. "Eddie, Manny, and Rudy"—three voices and my guitar. We went down to KGAR and we got our own program for an hour every Monday. We sang in English and our repertoire was made up of the most popular songs of the day, like *My Blue Heaven, Lazybones,* and *Darkness on the Delta.*

Everybody listened to our show, and we became big shots in the neighborhood. When we walked down the street, the little kids would nudge each other and say, "There go Eddie, Manny, and Rudy. They're on the radio."

People in the barrio started to ask us to play at backyard fiestas. They would decorate the place with paper streamers, balloons, and lanterns, bring in some beer, and have a party. The younger people wanted American music and the older ones wanted Mexican. It didn't matter to us; we could play both kinds.

The back yards were just dirt. After an hour or two of dancing, it would get pretty dusty, so they'd pour on some water to keep the dust down. Then they'd churn that up with their feet, and they'd be dancing in mud. We boys used to laugh about that; what's worse— dust or mud?

It was fun but, after a while, Manny started to play trumpet with the school band. He was always busy and that was the end of our trio.

Three or four blocks from our house there was a nightclub called The Beehive. The owner, Louie Gherna, was Greek, but all the customers and musicians were black.

The Beehive was always packed and every night was Saturday night there. Blocks away you could hear the trumpet and the sax and the electric guitar.

My friends and I were drawn to that music. We weren't old enough to go inside, but The Beehive had four windows that were usually open for ventilation. For hours, we'd stand outside looking in.

The music was jazz and blues, and the dancers were fabulous. They were all so graceful; it was just a joy to watch them.

When I was nineteen or twenty, I became friends with a guitarist there, Teddy Essick. I was a tall, skinny kid and he was a big, heavyset guy about forty. Sometimes he'd show me little licks on the guitar. What a musician! I still shiver when I think about his solos on the blues numbers.

I was captivated by that music. Night after night, I'd be there watching the dancers and listening to the band. At closing time, the customers would come out all happy and laughing.

Those black musicians definitely had an influence on me. I'm very grateful that their music got into my blood, because it is so wonderful. All the blues and swing music that I wrote years later started in The Beehive.

There weren't many blacks in Tucson in those years, and most of them lived in a community right near our barrio. When I was a teenager, the Ku Klux Klan showed up in town. One night, they burned a cross over near the African Baptist church.

Then they started after the Mexicans. First they painted three big Ks on the sidewalk in front of Santa Cruz Catholic Church on South Sixth Avenue. That same night, they placed a bomb in the church. It went off at three in the morning, and the whole barrio was shaken by the explosion. I guess at that point the authorities must have stepped in, because that's the last we heard about the Klan.

Tucson wasn't as bad as some places in the South. The blacks were allowed to sit beside us at the movies. But we didn't go to the same schools and we couldn't eat in the same restaurants.

When I was eighteen or nineteen, I played at the El Charro Cafe at night. A lot of black people would show up there because they loved Mexican food. And they wouldn't serve them—in a Mexican restaurant! They had to stand in line outside. You would have thought that we were in Memphis or Atlanta, but this was Tucson, Arizona!

The line would get to be a half block long. They'd go in one at a time and the boss would say, "What do you want?"

"I want three tacos."

"Stand over there until I call you."

It used to make me mad when I'd see them out there waiting. I felt bad because I knew a lot of them.

I'd hear, "Hey, Lalo, how you doing?"

And I'd say, "Hey, Eddie." Or Joe or whoever.

I'd smile at them but sometimes I thought, "If that was me, I'd say, 'Take your Mexican food and shove it.'"

Once the war started, and the country really needed them, all that stuff stopped. We all became equals.

One afternoon while I was out feeding my pigeons, I heard music coming from the back yard next door. I peeked over the fence and saw a dark-skinned, curly-haired boy sitting there all by himself playing and singing. He was just a kid, two or three years younger than me, maybe thirteen or fourteen, and he was very good. I wanted to sing with him, yet I didn't dare ask because I was afraid that he would reject me. I didn't even say "Hi." I just climbed up on the top of the fence to watch him play. He glanced up at me but he kept on singing.

Then he stumbled and forgot a lyric, and I was bold enough to speak up and tell him the words. Then he looked at me and said, "You know the song?"

"Yeah. I know the song."

"So why don't you come on over?" So I jumped down on his side of the fence.

He said, "Can you harmonize with me? Do you know *Las Gaviotas* (The Seagulls)?"

I said, "Yeah. I know it." He had a baritone voice and I was a tenor, so we sounded great together.

He said, "You're good, man. Do you play the guitar?"

I said, "I don't play as good as you do. I do mostly harmony."

"That's all right," he said. "I can play melody."

So I ran home, got my guitar, and pushed it over the fence to him. Then I jumped over and we started playing, and that was the beginning of our long friendship.

He told me that his name was Joe Salaz. Everybody called him Yuca, which means a black man in the Caribbean. He wasn't African, but he was very dark.

That's how Yuca and I became a duo. He already had been playing at parties around the neighborhood, so the next time someone asked him to perform, he brought me along.

People liked the sound of our two voices harmonizing and, pretty soon, every time there was a party, someone would say, "Go get Lalo and Yuca and bring them over!"

And there were a lot of parties. Mexicans can always find something to celebrate. Where they get the money for those parties, I don't know. They just love to dance and sing, and they can usually find a reason to do it and a way to do it.

At first they paid us a quarter an hour apiece; then we got so popular that we raised our price to fifty cents an hour. If you define a professional as someone who gets paid for his work, then that was the beginning of my sixty-year career as a professional musician.

At that time trios were hot in Mexico. Some of the young groups today have crazy names, but even then we had El Trio Calaveras (The Skulls) and Trio Los Murcielagos (The Bats).

Yuca's older brother, Chole, was an excellent guitarist—even better than Yuca. "Why don't you come along and play with us?" we asked him. "The three of us would sound great."

But he'd say, "Nah—I don't want to play with you little kids." He was twenty, so he felt like a real man.

After a while Chole noticed that we were making quite a bit of money at those parties. Then we got our own radio program on KGAR every Tuesday morning for half an hour. Even though most of the programming was in English, we sang Mexican songs in Spanish. Finally he decided to join us, and we formed El Trio Salaz y Guerrero. We got so popular that we started singing on station KVOA also.

Then by a twist of fate, Greg Escalante came into our lives. Sixty-five years later Greg and I ended up together on a mural in downtown Tucson. He was very nice, very soft-spoken, and I'm glad that he's the one on that wall with me since we are going to be up there together for a long, long time.

At that time Greg was twenty-four. He and his partner, Bull, were on the air every Saturday and Sunday morning. Greg and Bull had some kind of falling out and Bull quit. Greg was really in a spot. He came to me and said, "Would you accompany me next weekend?"

I said, "I can't do it. I play with Chole and Yuca."

He said, "So what? It's just for a couple of programs until I find another partner."

I didn't want to be disloyal to my friends, so I talked to them. "Greg wants me to help him out next Saturday and Sunday."

Chole said, "You can't do that. You go tell him that we're a team and if he wants you, he's got to take all of us."

So I said to Greg, "Chole says 'no way' unless you can work them in and we can have a quartet."

He wasn't happy about it but he said, "I guess I have no choice."

We rehearsed a little so that we'd be in sync. With four guitars and four voices, we sounded real good right from the beginning.

After people heard us on the radio, they wanted our quartet for weddings, anniversaries, and quinceañeras—the traditional coming-out parties for girls on their fifteenth birthday.

One of the people who used to hire us now and then was Gilbert Ronstadt. I knew him from high school. Although we weren't in the same class, we became friends because he was interested in music. His family was Mexican American, but they owned a big hardware store and they lived over on the other side of town.

Gilbert had a great personality and lots of spending money. And he was very good-looking—a real lady-killer. Every now and then, he'd come get our quartet to serenade his girlfriends. If we were playing at a party or a bar, we didn't finish until one or two in the morning.

Several times he took us to the girls' dormitory over at the University of Arizona. We'd be out there singing at 3:00 A.M. All the girls would throw open their windows and wave, "Hey, Gilbert! How are you, Gilbert?" The security guards would come yelling—"Get out of here! Stop that noise! We don't allow music at this time of the morning." We got chased off the campus a half dozen times or more. Then he got married and settled down, but he'd still call us up for parties and birthdays.

His daughter, Linda, loved it when we came over to their house. No matter how late it was, as soon as she heard us, she came running downstairs. When she was so little that she was still wearing a diaper, she'd sit cross-legged on the floor to listen. She wouldn't take her eyes off my face and she wouldn't move. Her favorite song was La Burrita, about a little girl donkey. She couldn't sing the words yet, but she already had a great sense of rhythm. She learned to do the "clip clop" of the hoofbeats with her tongue when I sang.

She was still small when I moved away from Tucson, so it was a surprise years later when I heard her singing American pop music on the air. Who was to think that the little girl with the big eyes would grow up to be such a beautiful woman and such a wonderful entertainer in English and in Spanish?

To this day, I think the world of her as an artist and a person. In 1996 Linda and I performed *La Burrita* together in front of 5,000 people at the Tucson International Mariachi Conference. She still knows how to do the "clip clop."

Gilbert had died a while before that performance, so in his honor Linda and I sang *El Sonorense* (The Man from Sonora). He loved that song because he was born in Sonora.

To get back to the thirties, in addition to the private parties, our quartet started playing in the Mexican restaurants and bars. Sometimes we didn't get paid anything, but we would go strolling from table to table playing for tips. We played strictly Mexican music. My real passion was still American popular music; I just couldn't make any money with it.

My First Love

To complicate matters even more, about this time is when I fell in love.

In 1999, they put up a big mural at the entrance to the old subway under the tracks in downtown Tucson, and it has a picture of me when I was eighteen. The artist didn't know it, but that wall is like a memorial to the first girl that I ever kissed more than 60 years before.

Emma was beautiful. She had green eyes and light brown hair. She was very gentle—very soft-spoken, very quiet. She was like una gota de agua, like a drop of water—so pure and beautiful. I was madly in love with her. I was seventeen and she was fifteen.

One reason that I loved her so much was because she was the first girl that ever paid any attention to me. I was tall and skinny and I still had the pock marks all over my face. And I was very shy. About as attractive as a walking skeleton and less interesting than a long drink of water. Most girls wouldn't give me a tumble, but Emma liked the way I was and the things I talked about. She made me feel like somebody.

I used to see her around the neighborhood and I'd say "Hi." And she'd say "Hi," and that was it. Then I found out that she worked cleaning houses over across town on the north side where the well-to-do Anglos lived.

Every morning at 6:30, when it was barely daylight, she walked through the subway to the other side of the tracks. It was a long tunnel and very dark, so I thought that it might be dangerous if she ever got caught in there by some stranger.

One day, I worked up my nerve to say, "I know that you have to go through the underpass every morning; would you mind if I walked with you?"

She said, "Thank you. That would be nice."

So the next morning I waited for her out in front of my house. Then we walked down Congress Street into the underpass. When we could see the light at the other end, she said goodbye and I said, "See you tomorrow?"

"Yeah. See you tomorrow."

I watched her walking until she disappeared into the light of day, and then I ran home.

After that, every morning at six, I'd drag myself out of bed just to meet her. Those walks meant a lot to me. We'd stroll along slowly and talk about school and music and other things. It went on like that for a couple of weeks until one day, one very, very important day, when I said "Good-bye," she looked at me and I looked at her. And it happened. I kissed her very softly right on the lips. I'll never forget that thrill!

I took off like a rocket! That morning I ran home without touching the ground.

After that, every day when we could see the light at the other end, we'd stop there where it was still dark and I'd get my kiss—a little peck and a hug. And I'd just melt.

I don't know if she loved me or if she kissed me because she was grateful to me or maybe she felt sorry for me because I was such a terrible sight.

Emma's mother discouraged her from seeing me. To begin with, she didn't like Emma having any boyfriends. And she didn't like me in particular. Quite a few musicians around town were always drunk, so she probably thought that I was going to grow up to be some kind of ne'er-do-well. She wanted a son-in-law who had a real job like a mechanic or a clerk in a store or something more substantial than a guitar player.

We never had a real date because we couldn't see each other in the neighborhood. I'd just walk with her in the morning, and we'd have a kiss or two and she'd go off to work.

And in the evening, I'd meet her and walk her back home. And that was our relationship.

Then my world came crashing down. Papá decided to take the family to Mexico City. The tears flowed between Emma and me because, supposedly, I was never coming back.

Mexico City

My parents had left Mexico during the Revolution along with a million other Mexicans who came pouring across the border into Texas, California, and Arizona. Then the Depression hit and, in 1930—31, to open up some jobs, the American government offered Mexicans living here $200 or so if they would return home. Thousands of people accepted the offer; they were called Los Repatriados (The Repatriates).

So many of our neighbors were leaving that I guess my father finally got itchy feet. At that time the economy of Mexico was as good as that of the United States, so maybe he thought that there would be more work, or maybe he just wanted to go back to his homeland and be near his brothers.

It was 1934, my senior year in high school, when he decided to move. I don't think it ever entered his head that I could stay with my big brothers, finish school, and then go to Mexico. Or maybe he thought that if we were going to live there forever, I didn't need a diploma from Tucson.

There were six kids at home and none of us wanted to go, but he was our father so we had to do what he said. Only the two oldest boys stayed behind; Frank was married and Alberto was already a boxer. Our house on Meyer Street was rented, so we gave notice to Señor Felix; Papá sold all the furniture, including the piano, and we packed up.

We took the train south because Southern Pacific gave Papá free passes for the entire family. It took three days and two nights to get from Nogales to Mexico City, sitting up the whole way.

My father's family lived in a vecindad, in a big building with three apartments. The front entrance had a tall, wide door for moving large objects in and out and a small door that the residents usually used.

Uncle Severo got my father a job at the Aguila Oil Company, where he worked. I don't know how much Papá made, but I do remember being hungry sometimes. There were eight of us and there just wasn't enough food to go around.

In the vecindad, we were a regular tribe—maybe 25 or 30 people in all. One apartment was occupied by my uncle Severo, my father's oldest brother; the next one by our family; and the third one by Uncle Romulo's widow, Tía María, and her three sons.

I think that those three cousins were the brightest part of our family; one of the boys became a general, another a doctor, and the third a college president. Maybe they were inspired by their names: Romulo, Marco Antonio, and César Augusto.

Tío Romulo was killed just a few months before we arrived. He had a very important position with the government, but it really didn't pay to have too much power in Mexican politics in the 1930s. I don't know whether he made enemies because of his job or somebody just wanted to step into his shoes, but one day as he was walking home from work, he was shot and killed right on the street in front of his house.

My dad was the only one of the four brothers to die a natural death. We never really learned the details of how and why Crispín died so suddenly in that military hospital. Uncle Severo, the oldest brother, was an engineer, and he just wouldn't retire. When he was 86 years old, he was supervising the construction of a bridge near Mexico City. He insisted on going up all the way to the top of the crane to make sure that everything was going right, and he slipped and fell.

In 1934 Mexico City was already a huge, beautiful metropolis with wide boulevards, parks, and statues everywhere. They called it "The Paris of the Western Hemisphere." That's not so far-fetched as you might think. It still has a European atmosphere. Even today, I think that some parts of the city compare very favorably with Paris.

It was like the other side of the earth from Tucson. We'd had almost no musical connections with that part of the world. We didn't get any of their radio broadcasts and very few of their recordings. Almost as soon as I got off the train, a whole new world of music opened up for me with tremendous orchestras, beautiful melodies, and rhythms like huapangos, sones, bambucos—music that I didn't know existed.

The Mexican music that we knew up north was simpler, and maybe it was happier, but it was not half as beautiful as this music from the heart of Mexico. There were giants like the composers Luis Arcaráz, Gonzalo Curiel, Consuelo Velásquez (who wrote *Bésame Mucho*), María Grever (one of the few women composers to make a mark in Latin music), and Agustín Lara, who became my idol. And there were great singers like Pedro Vargas, Toña LaNegra, Jorge Negrete, and Pedro Infante.

I never saw an entertainer in person because we couldn't afford concerts or clubs, but the air around me was filled with music. The radio was on from morning to night, and my cousins and their friends were always getting together to play and sing. My cousin Danny was only fourteen, but he could play the guitar like you wouldn't believe. During the next three months I learned a lot about music from Danny, and I learned so many songs that I bought a tablet and wrote them down. I wanted to be sure that I wouldn't forget anything. I was never satisfied. The more I heard, the more I wanted to hear.

Canción Mexicana

Hoy que lleno de emociones
me encuentro con mi jarana.
Voy a rendir homenaje
A la canción mexicana.
Voy a rendir homenaje
a la canción más galana
la canción más primorosa
que es la canción mexicana.

Pa' hacer pesos de a montones
no hay como el americano.

Pa' conquistar corazones
no hay mejor que un mexicano.

Y como es lo que consigue
si no es que contando canciones
como es el *Cielito Lindo*
que alegran los corazones.
No hay otra cosa más linda
que en las mañanitas frías

Mexican Song

Today filled with emotions
I'm here with my guitar.
I'm going to pay homage
To the music of Mexico.
I'm going to pay tribute
To the most gallant music,
To the most beautiful music,
And that is the music of Mexico.
To make pesos aplenty
There's no one like an American.

To conquer hearts,
There's no one better than a Mexican.

And how does he do it
If not by singing songs
Like *Cielito Lindo*
That makes all hearts happy.
There's nothing more beautiful
On a crisp, cool morning

cantarle a mi rancherita	Than to sing to my little country girl
Mañanitas Tapatias.	*Mañanitas Tapatias.*
Que causa más alegría	That which brings a lot of happiness
y emociona el cuerpo mío	And emotion to my heart
que los sones abajeños	Is the music of a mariachi
de un mariachi tapatio.	From the lowlands of Jalisco.
Es la canción mexicana	It is the music of Mexico
la que se merece honor	That deserves to be honored
y es la más primorosa	And that is the most beautiful
porque alimenta el amor.	Because it nurtures love.
Hay canciones extranjeras	There are foreign songs
que alborotan la pasión	That arouse passion
pero ninguna se compara	But none can compare
con esta linda canción:	To this beautiful song:
"Si Adelita quisiera ser mi novia	"If Adelita would be my sweetheart,
y si Adelita fuera mi mujer,	And if Adelita were to be my wife,
le compraría un vestido de seda	I would buy her a dress of silk
para llevarla a bailar al cuartel."	and take her dancing at the camp."

When I was seventeen, before I ever set foot in Mexico, I wrote *Canción Mexicana* (Mexican Song). It's a corrido (ballad) that includes a medley of well-known tunes from different parts of the country and praises the beauty and joy of Mexican music. It was kind of a gift to the people of my old barrio to remind them that, even if we were poor, we had something to be proud of. It's the most enduring song that I have ever written; it's still being played and recorded today. I have written hundreds of songs since then, but of all of them, *Canción Mexicana* is number one in my heart.

At the same time that I was being immersed in all of the great music in Mexico City, I also learned another, an earthier, kind of music from three old men who used to go from house to house begging for coins. When we heard them coming down the street, we'd all run outside. One of the viejitos (old men) would start singing a little song, and the second one would pick it up. They'd take turns and they'd make up the verses right on the spot. Everything rhymed, and some of them were really clever.

I enjoy playing with words so, from that time on, I started making up funny verses. I still love it when I come up with one that cracks me up, because I know if I laugh, other people will laugh. I've been writing lyrics and verses so many years that sometimes when I'm not thinking, I talk in rhymes. It's kind of scary.

In the middle of all that music, my mother stopped singing. She was pregnant, so maybe she just didn't feel well. I know that she missed our house and she missed Alberto and Frank. She would cry, and she'd tell Papá, "I want my boys. I want to go back. I want to go home."

I was homesick all the time. The Mexicans were nice to us, but we missed our friends, and my big sister, Alice, and I had left sweethearts behind. Danny and I used to go up on the roof in the evening with our guitars. I'd look out over the big city and I'd sing songs that would remind me of Emma. I wanted to go home so bad.

We were really grateful when Papá decided to return to Tucson because of some complications with Mamá's pregnancy. I didn't want my mother to get sick, yet, deep inside, I couldn't help thinking, "At least we'll get to go home."

So we came back. Everything turned out okay. Mamá was the first woman in Arizona to have a Caesarean section. The baby was my little sister, Mona.

While we were away, my class graduated without me. I didn't get my high school diploma because I refused to go back to school with a bunch of strangers who were younger than me.

It always bothered me that I never finished high school. In 1954, when I had become the "famous" Lalo Guerrero, I went back to Tucson High to perform at an assembly program. It was a strange feeling to walk down those halls where I had felt so out of place as a teenager.

At the end of the show, the principal announced, "And now we have a surprise for you, Mr. Guerrero. We know that you had to leave the country before you graduated, so here's your high school diploma."

It was so unexpected! I remember it like it was yesterday. The students gave me a standing ovation and I was so choked up that I couldn't even say thank you.

Although our sojourn in Mexico City was a hardship in some respects, those three months were very important to my career. My music would never be the same.

Back to Tucson and on to Los Angeles

When we returned home, first I looked up Emma and then Yuca. Yuca, Chole, and Greg had played as a trio while I was gone. Right away I started teaching them the new music that I had learned in Mexico City—and that's how I lost Emma.

Late one night about a week after we got back, I went over with Yuca to serenade her. I stood real close to her window and sang a beautiful love song very, very softly.

Chalita, the lady across the street from Emma's house, yelled, "Lalito! Yuca! Come over here and sing us a song."

We went over and she said, "Sing us something funny. Sing that song from Mexico about the 'huesos de mi suegra' (the bones of my mother-in-law). So I started to sing: "From the bones of my mother-in-law, I'm going to build a ladder so that I can climb down into her grave and spit on her skull." And then I went on to another one: "When my mother-in-law dies, I hope they bury her face down so if she tries to get out, she'll just dig herself in deeper."

Believe it or not, these are happy songs, happy melodies, and they're really funny in Spanish because everything rhymes. Mothers-in-law get a real bad rap in Mexico, and there are a lot of mother-in-law songs. They're not supposed to be disgusting or mean, but Mexican humor is a little weird sometimes.

It was three in the morning. The parties were all over; everybody had gone home. The whole barrio was as quiet as a graveyard. You could have heard a feather drop. My voice rang out as clear as a bell. Chalita was happy and I went home to my bed.

The next morning my mother came in and shook me awake. "Lalo, Lalo, what did you do last night?"

"I didn't do anything, Mamá."

"Yes, you did. You went and insulted Mrs. Fenochio."

"I did? I did not! I went over to serenade Emma."

"Yeah? You sang some silly songs about a mother-in-law."

I'm a little slow sometimes, but I caught on.

"Wait a minute," I said. "That wasn't for Mrs. Fenochio. Chalita asked us to sing that funny mother-in-law song. We were across the street."

"The whole neighborhood heard it, and everybody thinks that you were singing to her. So you get up and go right over there. You knock on her door and apologize. You tell her that it was not meant for her, that you were singing it for Chalita. Go right now."

I went to her house and knocked on the door. Mrs. Fenochio opened it and I said "Doña Maria—" And slam! She shut that door in my face. I knew right then there was no point in trying to explain.

So she forbade Emma to see me anymore. I tried to meet her and talk to her like before, but when her mother found out, she beat her. One day Emma showed me the bruises on her arm, and I never tried to talk to her again.

I was heartbroken. My brother Frank had moved to Los Angeles, so I decided to go out there to work with him.

I could have ridden in the train. I had a free pass because Papá worked for the railroad, but I enjoyed being with my friends. Besides, I was adventurous, so a couple of my buddies and I decided to hop a freight.

We went down to the tracks to wait for a freight train headed west. After a while, a train came flying by. We were ready to go and we didn't want to wait for a slower one. I grabbed the ladder on a boxcar. Before I could get my feet on the rungs, it shot me out like a flag. I had to hang on for dear life until I could climb aboard. Then I couldn't get into the boxcar, so I had to ride in between the cars until the train stopped an hour or so later.

My friends came running up to see if I was okay. Then we all piled into an empty boxcar and settled down for the ride. By the next day, we had made it as far as the Coachella Valley, about a hundred miles from Los Angeles.

The train stopped just before it got into Indio. The yard bulls came around and pulled all the bums off, including us. They were tough-looking dudes and they carried clubs like baseball bats for braking the train. And for breaking heads, too, I guess.

The biggest one said, "You guys are going right back where you came from. First of all, empty your pockets. If you got any money, go buy a ticket."

We didn't have any money but some of the others did, so they had to go over to the station.

He told the rest of us, "Line up here on the other side of the tracks. When the next train comes headed for Tucson, you'd better be on it."

We were standing there waiting for the train going back to Tucson, and pretty soon here comes one headed in the same direction as the one we'd been on!

We looked at each other. "That train is going to L.A."

"What about the one they told us to catch back?"

"The hell with that. Let's jump this one." And we did.

My older brother Frank was already in Los Angeles, so I moved in with him. He was staying with the Snyders—friends of our parents from the time they came from Mexico. They had three children and a home in East L.A.

Frank had a bed; the kids had beds, everybody had a bed . . . except me. Marina Snyder fixed me a place to sleep in a closet. I was six feet tall. If it got cold and I wanted to close the door of the closet, I had to fold my legs up like a pretzel. It's kind of an understatement to say that it wasn't very comfortable.

Frank had a job painting cars, and my cousin Chris Gonzales and I went to work for him. We'd wash the cars and sandpaper them to smooth out the cracks. After he painted them, we'd smooth out the paint. When we finished, the car would look just like new.

Frank got paid $300—$400 every Friday. He was very generous and, if he had money, he was an easy touch for a loan. As soon as he got paid, we'd go out to the bar and he'd say, "Set 'em up for everyone."

By Monday, the money would be gone. He'd have to borrow a few dollars from his boss so that we could eat until the next Friday. At times all we had was "air sandwiches"—two slices of bread with nothing between.

We finally moved up in the world. Not very far up, but I did get out of the closet and into a bed. The only place that we could afford was over on Skid Row on Fifth Street near Main. We had two rooms— one for Frank and me, and one for anybody else who'd drop by looking for a free bunk.

Everybody who'd come in from Tucson knew where Frank Guerrero lived. Frank was his mother's child—all heart; he'd never turn anybody down. It was still Depression times, so sometimes we had four or five extra people.

Frank and I had beds, but the others would just get a pillow and a blanket and they'd sleep on the floor. Sometimes it looked like the morgue with wall-to-wall cadavers. It was a lot of fun for a while, but then I got tired of it all and I went home to Tucson.

Los Carlistas

Back in Tucson, I started to play with Yuca and the boys again. I brought out my notebook from Mexico City and pretty soon we had a whole new repertoire made up of music that had never before been heard in Tucson. We were more popular than ever. About then our quartet got a name.

A local fellow, Frank Castelan, organized a social club for young people. He was an admirer of Prince Carlos, the pretender to the Spanish throne in the nineteenth century, so he decided to name the club for Carlos' followers—Los Carlistas. All our friends belonged, so we joined, too.

Right away whenever there was any kind of event, they'd say, "Be sure to bring your guitars, fellows. . . . "

Then, at a meeting one night, somebody stood up and said, "I move that this great quartet be called Los Carlistas." They voted for it, and everybody cheered.

It was supposed to be an honor and we were too embarrassed to turn it down, but I didn't think it was a good name. Most people had never heard of Prince Carlos, so they were always asking us about the name and we'd have to go into the whole story.

Besides the parties in the barrio, we started to play every Sunday in concerts in the band shell at Armory Park. First the WPA band would play, and then we were featured as special entertainment. Hundreds of people attended those concerts every week.

Pretty soon we were discovered by the other side of town—the white folks. We played in some fancy places—the Arizona Inn, the El Conquistador Hotel, the Pioneer Hotel. It was fun. They were all very friendly, they loved the music, and they paid us really well.

One of those parties was almost the death of me. A dude ranch hired us to play for a moonlight ride. People think that everybody in Arizona is a cowboy, but not me. All I know about horses is that one end bites and the other end kicks. Every year at rodeo time, when we boys rented horses to ride around town, I would always pick the slowest and dumbest one I could find.

The party was on a beautiful summer night like only Tucson can have, with a big, full moon so bright it was almost like daylight out on the desert. We four were singing softly, riding along behind a whole line of people, and all the horses were just walking along quietly.

Then all of a sudden my horse took off at full gallop! I dropped my guitar and I hung on for dear life. He dodged around saguaros and jumped over boulders and left all the other horses behind. I kept yelling "Whoa!" and pulling on the reins as hard as I could.

I saw a barbed wire fence in front of me, and the horse went straight for it! I dropped the reins, closed my eyes, and hung onto the horn. Just as he got to the fence, he made a 90-degree turn to the left and he headed for the corral like a bat out of Hades.

As soon as he got through the gate, he stopped dead. I opened my eyes and I was still alive! The horse put his head down to munch some hay in a trough, and I got off as fast as I could.

The others came riding up. Chole yelled at me, "Why did you go racing off like that?" Like I'd had a choice.

My guitar was a bunch of kindling wood and so would I have been if I had fallen off. I was grateful that I still had my life. I did lose my dignity that night, but that was nothing new.

At that time one of our biggest fans was Frank Robles, a former congressman. He kept telling us that we needed to expand our horizons. "You boys have to get out of here and go to Los Angeles. I'll be your agent."

He was a politician and a real good talker. Finally he convinced us, and we all went to Los Angeles.

My brother Frank was living in a couple of rooms in a small hotel on Figueroa Street, so we moved in with him. Leo Carrillo, the actor, used to say that his English was "not too good-looking," and you could have said the same thing about Greg and Joe. The first morning that we sat down at the counter for breakfast, the waitress asked, "What're you going to have?"

Joe said, "Gimme a cuffa coppee."

And Greg said, "I wanna hamburger with everybody in it."

They weren't kidding; their English was atrocious. Chole and I almost fell off our stools laughing at them.

Right away Frank Robles got us a job on a very popular radio program that aired every morning from 6:00 to 8:00. Spanish-language programs were always on early in the morning because the air time was cheaper and people could listen while they were getting ready to go to work.

We broadcast from the stage of the California Theater on Main Street. The theater was usually full of people on their way out to breakfast and drunks on their way home after being out all night. The master of ceremonies was Jose Arnaiz. We felt that we were in great company because we were performing with artists we had heard on records in Tucson, like Las Hermanas Padilla, Chicho y Chencho, and a very fine tenor, Carlos Bracamonte. We'd each do our turn and at the end of the show, we'd all come out together for a big finale.

Meanwhile Frank Robles met Francisco Miguel, a Hollywood agent, and he got us a job at Omar's Dome. We didn't have any costumes to wear and no money to buy anything, so Mr. Robles bought yards and yards of white muslin that my friend Marina Snyder used to make us shirts and pants with drawstrings at the waist. Our ponchos were just bright-colored curtains with holes to put our heads through, and our straw hats came from Woolworth's.

We couldn't afford real huaraches (sandals), so Frank got some old tires that somebody had thrown out into a vacant lot. He measured our feet and cut slabs of rubber for the soles, and we tied them on with leather thongs. No socks, just bare feet.

When we walked out for the floor show some people laughed, but then they started applauding like crazy even before we started to play. They thought that we were real cholos (peasants) from Mexico.

As a matter of fact, if you want to see what we looked like, watch for a replay of *Boots and Saddles*; Mr. Miguel got us a job in that film with Gene Autry, and we used the same costumes.

Before they started shooting the movie, we finished our engagement at Omar's Dome and we started playing at the Cotton Club in Culver City. Culver City is not far from Republic Studios in Hollywood, but we lived way over in East L.A. So instead of driving all the way home, we'd finish at the club at 3:00 in the morning, get to the

Republic lot about 4:00, sleep in the car, and show up at the studio at 7:00.

Maybe it wasn't very glamourous, but it was a thrill to be there in Hollywood working with Gene Autry, who was a big star. I loved cowboy movies, so I had seen all of his. He was very friendly to everyone on the set and he was especially nice to me. He kept trying to calm me down because I was so nervous.

Our big scene is one where Gene is having dinner with Judith Allen in a beautiful Mexican restaurant. We are playing our guitars with Aaron Gonzalez' orchestra when Gene starts to sing to her. We stroll off the stage down to the table where they are sitting and we join in on the chorus. Then we stand by the table and sing a Mexican song called *Ayer, Hoy y Mañana* (Yesterday, Today, and Tomorrow).

When that movie played in Tucson, the marquee read, "Los Carlistas with Gene Autry." And there we were, up on the screen of the Lyric Theater, playing and singing with one of the biggest stars in Hollywood. The hometown crowd was really proud.

I never actually spoke to Gene Autry again until almost 40 years later. At that time, he owned the Gene Autry Hotel in Palm Springs. One night, I stopped by the lounge for a drink and he came in. I stood up and said, "Mr. Autry, you know what? You and I did a movie together. I sang with you in *Boots and Saddles* over at Republic Studios."

He said, "Yeah? That was a long time ago. Of course, I remember the movie but I'm afraid that I can't say that I remember you personally." Then he invited me to sit down and we talked a little bit about the old days when we were both in Los Angeles.

After that, every now and then I'd drop in at the bar and he would be around. He was still a real nice guy just like I remembered. He called me "Lalo" but, to me, he was always "Mr. Autry," just like when I was a teenager.

To get back to Los Angeles in 1938, very early one morning, my brother Frank shook me awake and he was crying. Without a word, he handed me a telegram: "Alice was killed in an automobile accident. Come home immediately." We told the boys. They had all liked Alice and they wanted to go with us, so we packed up Frank's car and went home.

My big sister Alice was twenty-four. She had finished her courses at the beauty school on Friday and on Monday she was going to get her diploma. She already had a job all lined up. Mamá was so proud of her.

Sunday night one of Alice's friends came by and said that she and her boyfriend were going to a dance about thirty miles outside of Tucson. The boyfriend had a friend who needed a date, so she persuaded Alice to go with them. Alice told Mamá that she'd be home early and she went off.

About midnight, someone pounded on the front door. When my mother opened it, a young man, a stranger, was standing there. He said, "Are you Mrs. Guerrero?"

"Yes."

"We have your daughter at the mortuary. She just got killed on the Nogales Highway."

Maybe he was new at the job, maybe he had never had to tell anybody that before, because he didn't say another word. He just turned around and walked away. My mother screamed once and fell to the floor.

It was a gray, drizzly morning when with my brothers, Frank and Alberto, and the other Carlistas I carried Alice from our house to St. Augustine's Church. I don't remember it very well . . . just that we walked down the middle of Stone Avenue with my sister's coffin on our shoulders.

My little brother Ruben says that morning after we left the cemetery he saw our father all alone leaning against the side of a building, with tears pouring down his face. It was the only time in his life that he ever saw Papá cry.

As for me, it was such a shock—so unbelievable, so hard to accept—that I hadn't been able to weep for my sister. I wanted to cry but the tears wouldn't come . . . not even while the wake was on and she lay in her coffin in the living room. But that morning, as we started back to the house, all of a sudden the grief came over me. I ran down the street away from everyone and threw myself onto a pile of dirt beside the road, screaming and crying like a baby. Alice had worked so hard and we had been so happy for her. It wasn't fair. It just wasn't fair!

A few days later we returned to Los Angeles and went to work at a place on Spring Street around the corner from Olvera Street. The sign outside said Club La Bamba but most people called it "the Bamba Club." Chuy Perez was playing there with his orchestra, and our quartet used to stroll among the tables during intermissions when they would take a break. For the floor show, we'd open by singing a couple of songs and then we backed Bobby Ramos. At that time he was working as a waiter, but later he had his own band and a TV show called *Latin Cruise*.

The piano player was a very talented and funny guy named Pete Alcaraz. Who was to think that not many years later I would have my own club and he would be working for me!

I worked at the Bamba Club several times from the late thirties onward. Before the war, 95 percent of the customers were Anglo. At first, almost all that we played were the Mexican standards that they were familiar with.

The music gradually changed. Música Tropical became popular. The danzón from Veracruz has been around forever; now we added the conga from the Caribbean, and the customers would form long lines and dance around the room and among the tables.

The movies brought in the samba from Brazil and the tango from Argentina. And now and then we'd throw in some nice slow ones, some boleros. The other dances and rhythms changed over the years, but the bolero was always there.

Something new developed there off the bandstand, too, but explaining it is pretty complicated. It had to do with an act on the floor show called the Dancing Cansinos, Eduardo and Margarita, a father-daughter team. They did ballroom dancing—semiclassical waltzes, tangos, Spanish dances. She had a beautiful body, and she wore very elegant gowns.

At that time Ensenada was popular with the Hollywood crowd because gambling was legal there. For a couple of seasons the Cansinos danced there in the Riviera Casino, which was owned by Jack Dempsey. I knew Frank, the bartender at the Riviera, because he worked at the Bamba Club sometimes, and he was a real fan of the Cansinos.

The most popular drink in Mexico was straight tequila with a squeeze of lime and a lick of salt. It's pretty strong. I was at the bar one night when Frank came up with a prettier, gentler concoction of tequila with sweetened lime juice in a glass frosted with salt, and he said to Miss Cansino, "I'm going to call this drink the Margarita in your honor."

Later Margarita went into the movies and changed her name to Rita Hayworth, but the name of the drink has remained the same to this day.

Havana was another great resort city of that era, and Cuba gave us another popular drink, the Cuba Libre, which is rum, Coca Cola, and lime. From Cuba we also got the rumba. The first rumba that I ever heard was "¡Ay! Mamá Inez, ¡Ay! Mamá Inez,—todos los negros tomamos café." (All us blacks drink coffee.) "I started to scrub a black man to see if the black would come off, but the more I scrubbed the blacker he got." The lyrics are probably considered racist now, but that was then.

At that time, I still wasn't sure that I could make a living with music. I knew that I had the talent to write melodies and lyrics, but I was not doing well financially. Of course it was the Depression, and nobody was doing very well. Somehow I didn't take that into account.

Like a lot of aspiring young musicians, I had a "day job." Mine was in a factory where we'd take old tires and turn them inside out. Then I had to cut the lining inside the tire with a very sharp knife and pull it away from the rubber. I don't know whether they used the rubber or the lining, I just did my job. It was hard work and I used to cut my arms and my hands, and then I had to play the guitar at night.

My First Records

At that time, quite by chance, by the most incredible coincidence, I met Manuel S. Acuña.

I was walking down Main Street wearing my fancy cowboy boots and a white hat that I had gotten for the annual rodeo in Tucson. I was tall and lanky, so I stuck up like a sore finger. It happened that Manuel was walking the opposite way. When we met, he said, out of the blue, "¡Hola! ¿De dónde vienes?" (Hey, where are you from?)

If I had been white, he might have walked on by thinking, "He's a Texan; they dress like that all the time," but he could see that I was a Mexican.

I said, "I'm from Tucson."

"Oh," he said. "With the boots and hat, I thought that you might be from Sonora like me. What are you doing in town?"

When I think back, this was one of the most important moments in my entire career. And we were just standing there on the sidewalk talking with people passing all around us.

I said, "I'm a musician. I play guitar."

"What kind of music?" he asked.

I said, "Mostly Mexican music, but I can sing in English. And I write songs also."

"I'm the A&R man for Vocalion records right down the street here. Why don't you drop off a couple of songs someday and I'll take a look at them. Maybe we can use them." A&R means Artists and Repertoire; he's the one who picks the songs that will be recorded by certain artists.

I said, "Great. I'd like that very much."

A few days later, I went by. Manuel wasn't there so I left three songs with his partner, Felipe Valdez Leal.

He couldn't call me because I didn't have a telephone, but the following week I went back to his office. Manuel was in so I said to him, "What'd you think of my songs?"

"I liked a couple of them and I think they're right for the Padilla Sisters."

I could hardly believe my ears, because the Padilla Sisters were real stars. Their records were very popular all over the Southwest. He gave me a contract for those two songs, *Estamos Iguales* (We're Even) and *El Norteño* (The Man from the North). As I was leaving, he added, "Bring me some more music when you can."

He asked me if I'd like to audition as a vocalist. Maybe I just didn't have enough confidence, but it didn't seem right for me to record without the boys, so I told him that I was working with a quartet. He said, "Bring them in," and the next week we went in for an audition. He liked the group and he gave us the opportunity to record four songs that I had written. One was a funny song called *El Aguador,* about the boy who carries water in a bucket for the workers out in the fields. On the flip side was *Así Son Ellas* (That's the Way Women Are). The other two were *Cuestión de una Mujer* (Question of a Woman) and *¿De Que Murió el Quemado?* (What Did the Burned Man Die Of?). We got paid $50 apiece and nobody mentioned royalties in those days.

The songs were good and we sounded good. We played four guitars and vocalized in harmony. The records were well received, although they were not great hits. Manuel liked the group and we cut about a dozen records together during the next few months.

We could have done more but we were homesick. Even though the music scene in Los Angeles was exciting, we all missed the friendly atmosphere of Tucson. Years later, in *Barrio Viejo,* I wrote about the closeness between people that was a part of our lives in that place where "everybody knew each other."

So we went home.

The New York World's Fair

Los Carlistas was the most popular musical group in Tucson. We had played some good clubs in Los Angeles, we had cut some records, and we had been in a movie. We didn't have a name everywhere, but we were such big shots in town that the Chamber of Commerce decided to send us to New York City to represent our hometown in the Arizona Building at the World's Fair. They wanted to promote Tucson as a winter resort for the snowbirds up north. The exhibit included cactus, Hopi pottery, and Navajo blankets. Our group would remind them of the warm desert climate and of Mexico only an hour away.

The Chamber paid all of our expenses. One of the local car dealers, Monte Mansfield, put up a brand new 1939 Ford, and the secretary of the Chamber of Commerce, Roy Wollam, volunteered to drive us across the United States.

Now it's true that the winters in Tucson are usually very pleasant, but it does get cold. Sometimes if a faucet outside is dripping, the next morning you'll find a thin sheet of ice on the puddle or an icicle hanging down. That winter it had snowed one night. It was only about an inch and it melted in a few hours, but all the local people were thrilled to see it; the whole city was pure white and beautiful.

The Chamber of Commerce was not so thrilled. We were scheduled to appear on one of the most popular radio programs in America, *The Major Bowes Amateur Hour*. Before we left Tucson, the Chamber members suggested things for us to talk about on the air.

Actually they did more than "suggest," they brainwashed us: "Whatever you do, don't mention the word 'snow.' Don't mention snow.

It didn't ever snow in Tucson. You don't know anything about snow. Forget the word 'snow.'"

On the road sometimes Mr. Wollam coached us on what to say when we got on the radio, and he told us over and over, "Now don't forget. Nothing about snow."

"Oh yeah. Sure, sure."

What a trip! I was nineteen, Yuca was two years younger than me, Chole was twenty-two, and Greg was twenty-four. None of us had ever been north of Phoenix nor east of Tucson. All across the country we got to see places that we'd read about in our history books.

In Valley Forge, we found a rock with a GW with a circle around it and we said, "Wow! George Washington himself tagged this!"

We went through Gettysburg and many of the other Civil War battlefields. We stopped in Washington D.C., and, finally, we arrived to New York City.

Just imagine four little cactus flowers from the desert in that city which, even in 1939, was awesome. With our mouths gaping open, we bent as far back as we could to see the tops of the sky-scrapers.

The Chamber of Commerce had made reservations for us at the best hotel in town, the Astor. Mr. Wollam checked us in and we were going up to our rooms when the elevator came down. The doors opened and who's standing there? Someone that we all knew from the movies! I stared and went "J-J-J-Jimmy Durante."

He smiled, "Hi, fellows," and walked out.

To celebrate our first night in New York City, Mr. Wollam took us to a fancy Chinese restaurant. We were tired and thirsty, but there weren't any glasses on the table. The water was in some little bowls at each place. We looked at them and at each other, but we didn't want to say anything to show how ignorant we were. Finally Chole picked his up and took a drink. The waiter snickered and Mr. Wollam looked sort of embarrassed. That's how I learned about finger bowls.

We stayed in New York about a month. We were real tourists. We rode the subways, ate at the Automat, and saw the Statue of Liberty.

We must have been wearing little signs on our heads saying "Hayseed" because people kept trying to separate us from our money.

And a lot of them succeeded.

The first time that Yuca and I went to a movie, we were sitting there waiting for the film to start when a boy came down the aisle with a trayful of candy bars. We looked at him and he threw us a couple.

"Free candy at the movies," we thought. "This is a great city."

Just then the cartoon came on, so we ate our candy and enjoyed it very much. When we got up to leave, the boy waylaid us. "That'll be twenty-five cents each."

Twenty-five cents! For a nickel chocolate bar! We knew that we owed him so we paid up, but it was humiliating.

Another time a kind of rough-looking fellow came up and said that he had something that we might be interested in. They were those little books where you flip the pages real fast and it's like a movie. He had three or four, but the one that I remember best was Dagwood and Blondie doing all kinds of things that you never saw in the Sunday comics.

The books were a dollar apiece, but they were so funny and so cute—and so dirty—that we each bought one. He disappeared pretty fast and we started flipping our books. The pages were blank!

Everybody was out to get us. We didn't know any girls in New York and didn't know how to meet any, but Yuca and I found this ballroom where you could pay a dime to dance with a girl. My partner was pretty and kind of flirty, and after a couple of dances I decided to see how far I could get. I asked her, "Do you ever go out with guys you meet here?"

"Sometimes, but they have to buy me out."

"What's that mean?"

"If you buy my whole roll of tickets, I can leave." It was only three or four dollars, so I consulted with Yuca. He had been dancing with a girl that he liked, so we decided that it would be a good deal. The girls were real nice and, of course, we had our hopes up for the evening.

They said that they had to check out with the cashier and go upstairs to change clothes, so we should wait for them at the front door. We waited and waited, but they didn't show up. Finally we decided that maybe we were at the wrong door, so Yuca stayed at the front and I went around to the back door. After standing there in the alley for about half an hour, I caught on. Did we feel dumb!

When we weren't busy being bamboozled, we spent hours exploring the Fair. The symbol of the 1939 World's Fair was a big white ball, the Perisphere, and beside it was the Trylon, a tall obelisk like the Washington Monument.

The theme of the fair was "The World of Tomorrow." In one building I saw television for the first time. The screen was only about six or eight inches wide, the images were all blurry, and the voice was a crackle. But the picture was coming out of thin air! "The City of the Future" took up a whole room in another building. It had model skyscrapers with glass walls and miniature freeways filled with little cars with tiny headlights racing through underpasses and overpasses. Chole said, "We'll never live to see that day." As a matter of fact, we didn't have to wait long; the first freeway in Los Angeles, the Pasadena freeway, was built just ten years later.

Every morning we'd go out to the Arizona Building and play for three or four hours. Whenever it was time for us to perform, a big crowd would gather. There weren't many Latinos around New York in the 1930s, not even Cubans or Puerto Ricans. A lot of New Yorkers had never seen a Mexican in their lives. And we didn't have the crazy white cholo costumes any more; we wore fancy black charro outfits with silver trim, bright-colored serapes, and big sombreros.

The building next to us belonged to the country of Belgium. We were curious to see what was inside it, so one afternoon we walked over there. We had just finished playing so we were still in our costumes. We looked around a while and, as we were leaving, we heard a tourist say, "Oh! Look at the Belgians!"

It was so funny. As soon as we got out of her sight, we laughed so hard we were holding on to each other to keep from falling down.

The crowning point of the trip was our appearance on *The Major Bowes Amateur Hour*. When we stood up on Radio City Music Hall stage and belted out "¡Guadalajara! ¡Guadalajara!" the whole country could hear us. The studio audience loved it. The music was new and different and strange. Most of them didn't understand the words, but they could feel the rhythm.

I would have been even more thrilled if I had known that I was following in the footsteps of a boy who would be both a hero and a friend 50 years later; Frank Sinatra got his start in show business on *The Amateur Hour* in 1935.

After we sang, Major Bowes said, "What can you tell me about your part of the country? What is Tucson like?"

Chole went first, and he said, "Well, we have a lot of ranches. And people like to ride horseback in the desert."

Then Yuca got into a little history about Father Kino and the old Spanish mission, San Xavier del Bac, right outside town, and the colorful Indian dances every Easter. Greg described the flora and the fauna—the saguaro cactus and the wildflowers in the spring. Things that we had been told to talk about.

Then it was my turn. I don't know what got into me; I was so nervous. The other guys had come out with all this stuff and they didn't leave me very much. "Well we have a rodeo every year—Día de los Vaqueros. It's in February and everybody in town dresses up in cowboy outfits."

"Anything else you can tell us?"

I got more nervous. I just wanted off the hook. That's when I did it. I said, "This last winter we did get a little bit of sssssnow." I could hardly say it. As much as I wanted to hold it back, I couldn't. After all Mr. Wollam's drilling, it was the only thing that came into my head.

"Oh, you get snow in Tucson?"

"It was just a little bit—not even an inch. Just a few flakes." Then I said real fast, "It doesn't get cold at all." But I knew it was too late; I'd already blown it.

Of course, everybody in Tucson heard what I said. There was a story in the Arizona Daily Star: "Wollam Stymies a Canard. Roy Wollam decides his psychology is nothing to brag about." For weeks after we got home, I was razzed by everyone who knew me. Sometimes I'm just too damn honest.

Concepción and Eduardo Guerrero Sr.,
Lalo's parents, 1910

Lalo Guerrero at age 5 in Tucson, Arizona

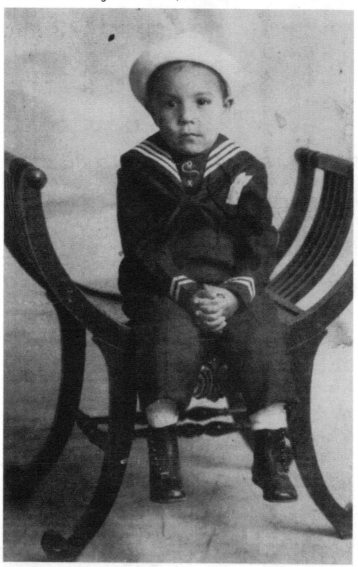

First Holy Communion,
sister Alice and Lalo,
1925

Lalo and Lupe Fernandez,
Café Caliente, Los Angeles,
1939

Los Carlistas Quartet: (standing left to right) Chole Salaz, Lalo, Greg "Goyo" Escalante; (seated) Joe "Yuca" Salaz, Tucson, Arizona, 1938

Lalo performing at Café Caliente, Los Angeles, 1939

(right) San Diego Naval Hospital,
San Diego, 1943

Lalo Guerrero and Margaret Marmion, wedding portrait, Tucson, Arizona, 1939

Lalo and Lolita performing at the Mexicali Club, San Diego, 1943

(right) Wetmore's Ballroom, party to celebrate solo artist Imperial record contract and success of *Pecadora:* (seated, left to right) Concepción Guerrero, Lalo, wife Margaret Marmion Guerrero; (standing, left to right) sisters Teresa, Connie, Mona, brother Ruben, and unidentified friend, Tucson, Arizona, 1948

Lalo and band at
Club La Bamba, Los
Angeles, 1946

Trio Imperial, guest
appearance at the
Mayflower Club: (left
to right) Jose Coria,
Lalo Guerrero, Mario
Sanchez, Los
Angeles, 1946

Lalo and band, Oxnard Ballroom, Oxnard, California, 1951

(middle photo above) Lalo as Pancho Lopez, *The Al Jarvis Show,* Los Angeles, 1955 (© CBS Photo Archive)

(right photo above) Lalo on beach with sons, Ensenada, California, 1953

(right) Lalo and his band on the road: (standing, left to right) Bill Castagnino, unidentified person, Bill Trujillo, Frank Quijada; (kneeling) Al Leon, Lalo Guerrero, 1958

La Capital Night Club, Lalo y Sus Cincos Lobos: (left to right) Pete Alcaraz, Lalo,
Frank Quijada, Nacho Barranco, Tino Isgrow, and David Lopez, Los Angeles, 1956

Lalo and his wife Lidia, Las Vegas, 1974

Lalo as Santa Claus, Los Angeles, 1972

Lalo and Las Ardillitas on the
Talina Fernandez Show, ECO-TV,
Mexico City, D.F., 1991

(above) Lalo and Amigos Tribute Concert: (top row, left to right) Carmen Moreno, Jose Hernandez, Cheech Marin, Lupita Castro, Marcos Loya, Dan Guerrero, Mark Guerrero, Juan Ortiz, Cesar Chavez, Lalo Guerrero, Edward James Olmos, Rosana De Soto; (bottom row, left to right) Willie Loya, Diane Rodriguez, unidentified person, Daniel Valdez, Paul Rodriguez, Little Joe Hernandez (with hat); (bottom right corner, left to right) Richard Montoya, Herbert Siguenza, McCallum Theatre, Palm Desert, California, 1992

President and Mrs. Clinton presenting Lalo with the
Medal of Arts, Washington, D.C., 1997

(left) Dedication of the star on the Palm Springs Walk of
Fame: (front row) three members of Culture Clash (Herbert
Siguenza, Richard Montoya, and Ric Salinas), Lalo
Guerrero, Cheech Marin; (second row) unidentified person,
Dan Guerrero, Mark Guerrero; (above Lalo) Lidia Guerrero,
Palm Springs, California, 1992

Lalo addresses 2,000 Tucsonans gathered to dedicate artist Stephen Farley's Broadway Underpass mural, 1999; © Stephen Farley

Luis Valdez, Dan Guerrero, Linda Ronstadt, Lalo Guerrero, 1988

Dan Guerrero, Lalo Guerrero, Rita Moreno, Edward James Olmos, Cynthia Telles, and David Telles, Los Angeles, 1988

Lalo with Alma Award, Los Angeles, 1998

Lalo in his zoot suit, 1999

I Get Married

It was about this time that I started giving serious thought to getting married.

For a while, my brother Frank had a job that made him one of the most popular guys in Tucson. He worked nights for a company that delivered beer to bars. When someone called, he'd take a keg over; the rest of the time he was just sitting there all alone. Naturally some of his friends started to drop in to keep him company. Frank was always generous, so he would tap a keg and they'd have all the beer they could drink.

One night I stopped by to see him and there was a young man sitting there staring straight ahead, drunker than a skunk, and that was Ralph Marmion. When I started to strum my guitar, Ralph woke up. He loved guitar music. From that moment, we became friends.

One night I said to him, "I'd like to have you for a brother-in-law. Do you have any sisters?"

He said, "Two—sixteen and eighteen. Which one do you want to meet?"

I was only nineteen. I didn't know much about girls, so I thought the older one might be more than I could handle. I said, "The sixteen-year-old."

"That's Margaret," he said. "Come over for dinner tomorrow night."

I found out later that his mother worked as a maid in the Santa Rita Hotel. His father was dead. There were four sons and two daughters, so I sort of think that Ralph was eager to marry off the girls as quickly as possible.

As luck would have it, Margaret was late getting home the next day. We were already sitting at the table when she came in. Ralph said, "Margaret, I have a friend that I want you to meet. This is Lalo Guerrero, a fine singer and guitar player."

I stood up and said, "Pleased to meet you."

"Thank you. I'm pleased to meet you, too." Then she said, "Mom, I gotta go over to Marie's house." And she left.

I was so disappointed. I guess that she wasn't impressed with me, but I liked her as soon as I saw her. She was very pretty. I think that part of her attraction was that she didn't look Mexican. Her mother was from Durango, so Margaret grew up with the customs and culture of Mexico but she looked a lot like her Scotch-Irish father. Having suffered so much from discrimination, I wanted to spare my children. I thought that their lives would be easier if they were lighter-complected than me.

I didn't get a chance to talk to her until Ralph asked Yuca and me to play at his wedding. Margaret was always pretty, but that day she was gorgeous. She was wearing a new dress, her hair was different, her makeup was perfect. For the wedding, I sang some very romantic songs and I sang them directly to her.

We sat next to each other at dinner and I asked her to go steady with me. She sort of hemmed and hawed and wouldn't say yes or no, so finally I said, "I want you to be my girlfriend, but this is the last time that I am going to ask you."

She thought about it for a few minutes, then said, "Yes." I thought that she would because of the way she watched me when I was singing. I didn't look like much, but I had my guitar and my love songs and she was still a schoolgirl.

As our custom was, I asked her mother's permission to come over and see her. She said okay, and it was official.

Not long ago I came across a song that I wrote for Margaret. It's on a page with a sketch of a charro I had drawn. The lyrics are in Spanish and I wish I remembered the melody, but I couldn't write music and we didn't have tape recorders then. "Eres: ¿Que tanto vales para mi? How much do you mean to me? Ask me. What you are to me—let me tell you. You are the soul of my soul, the life of my life, my guardian angel, and the sun that makes me happy. You are the light in my darkness; you are the love of my loves. You are the blood of my veins; you are my maiden of marble. You are the lyre with which I write my music. You calm my soul. You are the queen of my blue heaven."

By this time, 1939, I had written quite a few songs that I thought were pretty good, and I decided to see if I could get them recorded in Mexico City. The records produced there went out all over Latin America.

I took the train south and started knocking on the doors of the music publishers. I had confidence in my music and my voice. I thought, naively, that they would let me record my own songs. That's when I found out how much the Mexicans discriminated against "pochos," or Mexican Americans.

I had interviews with eight or ten different publishers. They liked my music, but the moment they found out that I was an American their attitude would change completely. They'd say, "Come back next week and we'll see what we can do."

I'd go back and the boss wouldn't be there. "Señor so-and-so had to go to Guadalajara." Next week I'd come back and they'd say, "Oh, he had to go to Rio de Janeiro." They just kept putting me off until I finally caught on.

They were interested in my music; they just didn't like me. I was young, my voice was clear and pure, but they wouldn't give me an audition. They wouldn't even give me the chance to sing my own songs.

Talk about injustice. In the United States I was discriminated against for being a Mexican, and in Mexico I was discriminated against for being an American!

Finally Promotora Hispano Americana de Música (PHAM), which is associated with Southern Music Company in the United States, gave me a contract for four songs. When the publishing company signs on the songs, they don't pay you anything and they don't promise they're going to release them. The songs go into the archives and they may never see daylight again. The publishers say if they find the right singer, and the singer likes the song, they'll record it. If it is recorded, the writer gets paid royalties from the record company, a fee from the publishing company for the use of the music, and performance rights so that he gets a royalty every time it's played anywhere.

I went home feeling disappointed that I didn't have the chance to record my music, but at least those four songs were with PHAM in Mexico City where the big stars could find them. I had high hopes. A month went by, then two months, then a year, and nothing happened. I wrote a couple of letters and got no answer. After a while I quit hoping.

Meanwhile Los Carlistas were playing at Cosme's Restaurant in Tucson. Although Greg was the oldest of us, he was very quiet and mild. Chole was always bossy and he appointed himself our leader. As time went by he got more and more domineering, and it all came to a head one Sunday afternoon.

We didn't go on until 6:00, so I took Margaret to the matinee dance at the Blue Moon Ballroom. We had a lot to talk about and the hours kind of slipped away. When I suddenly realized what time it was, I took her hand and we rushed over to Cosme's.

As soon as we walked in, Chole came over roaring, "Who do you think you are? Coming in late like this!"

He started telling me off and swearing right in front of Margaret. I said, "Calm down. It's only 6:15. And don't use that kind of language in front of my girl. If you keep cussing like that, I'm leaving."

"Well, leave. Who the hell needs you, anyway?"

I had known for quite a while that he wanted to get rid of me. I think that he was jealous that I was overshadowing him. I was the writer, and people were always saying how much they liked my material. Besides, with me out of the way, they could split the fees three ways instead four

So I left and that broke up the quartet. I was ready to work alone but, before this incident, I didn't have the heart to leave the guys. We had all started together so young and had shared so many wonderful experiences.

Actually Chole did me a great big favor. I told Margaret, "I'm going to Los Angeles, but I'll be home when I've got a job and some money. We'll get married in the fall and I'll take you back to California with me."

So I got on a train heading west. Not a freight train—I was getting too old for that. I went to L.A. and looked up Lupe Fernandez. I had met him when Los Carlistas were playing at the Bamba Club. Lupe and I went to work as a duo in the Cafe Caliente on Olvera Street. We strolled among the tables during intermissions and made pretty good tips, but not enough to save anything.

I had a friend, Lamberto Leyva, who was playing with El Trio Guadalajara. We were both ready to get married and we decided that it was time to go back and officially get the families' okay. We made the trip in Lamberto's 1929 model A Ford. He dropped me off in Tucson on his way to his girlfriend's home in Nogales.

It sounds like the Dark Ages, but at that time it was the tradition for the man's father to go with him to ask for the girl's hand in marriage. My dad didn't want me to get married. He liked Margaret; he just didn't approve of me getting married.

He still had four kids at home. Maybe he thought that I was getting old enough to start earning some real money so that I could help him out a little. I begged him, "I want to get married. I'm in love with this girl." And I finally coaxed him into going with me.

Even then he tried to sabotage us. Margaret's mother opened the door and we went in and sat down. Right away Papá said, "Well, it looks like these kids want to get married. What do you think?"

Mrs. Marmion realized that he wasn't too keen about the idea, but the people from Durango have a lot of pride, so she said very softly, "Mr. Guerrero, maybe you think that my daughter is not good enough for your son, but your son is good enough for me. I like him and I give them my blessing." My dad was embarrassed but he had to accept it.

The next day, Lamberto came by to pick me up. I asked him, "How'd it go?"

"Okay. How about you?"

"There was a little problem but I got the permission."

So we started back to California. Lamberto's grandmother lived in Los Angeles and I guess she was kind of homesick for Mexico, because she had asked him to bring back four of those big parrots made out of plaster. They were two feet tall and painted bright green and red. They almost filled up the back seat of the model A.

For years it seemed that every time I'd pass through the Coachella Valley between Tucson and Los Angeles, something bad would happen. This time we ran out of gas, we ran out of money, and we were stuck in Indio!

We just looked at each other, then at that back seat full of parrots. All of a sudden it was just like I was a little kid again, because we had to go from door to door. "Would you like to buy a parrot?"

I was glad that our future in-laws couldn't see us.

From the parrots, we got enough money to limp back to L.A. I went back to my gig with Lupe at the Cafe Caliente and about six months went by.

While I was in Tucson, I had promised Margaret that we would get married in October.

In the Catholic church for several weeks before the wedding the priest always announced it. He'd say "Esta rodando." (You are rolling— up the aisle, I guess.) "El sabado, 15 Octubre, se casará la señorita· Margarita Marmion con el señor Eduardo Guerrero." So the whole community knew about our marriage plans . . . and I didn't have enough money yet. I couldn't afford a wedding! I didn't know what to do.

I had forgotten all about those records that the Carlistas had recorded the previous year. Then one day Mr Acuña came by the Cafe Caliente and said, "Hey, Lalo, I've been looking for you. Your royalties came."

I said, "What royalties?"

"For those songs you wrote."

We had been paid for the recording, but I had not gotten anything for writing the songs.

He didn't say how much, and I was hoping that it would be at least a hundred dollars so that I could send it to Margaret. I went over to pick up my check and I almost fell over. It was for $500! With that we could have a real wedding. That was enough to pay for Margaret's dress, the flowers, the fancy cake, and the reception. I even had a hundred dollars to give to my mom.

My partner, Lupe Fernandez, drove me back to Tucson for the wedding, and I bought my bride a beautiful white dress with lots of lace. For myself (this sounds like a rerun of my track career), I got some shiny black patent leather shoes. After I wore them a little while, I knew that they were too tight, so I put them into the shop to have them stretched. I was supposed to pick them up on Friday afternoon before the wedding next day.

That was my last night as a free man, so my buddies took me out to party and I forgot all about picking up my new shoes. So I had to wear my old shoes to the church. They had two "half-dollars" on the soles, but Mamá polished them and they didn't look bad as long as I was standing up.

Then the priest said, "Kneel."

I whispered, "Do I have to, Father?"

And he said, "Yes. Kneel." When I knelt down in front of the altar, everyone in the church could see the holes in my shoes. Nobody said anything, but I heard a few giggles.

Except for my shoes, the ceremony was very dignified and beautiful. Afterwards we went back to our house for the reception. This was not your typical Anglo reception in the Country Club with champagne and hors d'oeuvres. We were drinking tequila and cerveza, and the house was packed with friends and relatives all laughing and talking.

Papá had this cousin, Vicente, who had a really weird sense of humor—especially after a few drinks. I was sitting on the couch with my pretty young wife when cousin Vicente staggered over to us and yelled out, "Weddings are for the birds. All women are whores!"

My mom grabbed her broom and started hitting him over the head and yelling, "Get out of my house, you nasty pig!" Pow, pow, pow over the head right in front of all the guests in their Sunday best clothes. "Get out and don't ever come back."

Vicente covered his face with his arms and backed out the door, laughing all the time.

Our Gypsy Years

That same night, Lupe took Margaret and me back to
Los Angeles and we moved into Mrs. Williams' Apartments on Stanford
Avenue.

The next night when we went in to work, Mr. Vega, the boss,
bawled Lupe out for something or other. Lupe was very short and the
boss was more than six feet tall, but Lupe got mad. He hauled back
his fist, reached up, and floored Mr. Vega. Then he was out the door,
and Mr. Vega took off after him with a big butcher knife. Lupe got
away, and when Mr. Vega came back he said to me, "You can work
here, but I don't want to ever see that son-of-a-bitch again."

I appreciated his offer but I wasn't ready to perform solo. I felt
that I needed Lupe. So that was how I got fired the day after I got
married.

Lupe and I found another job, but he was really a bad influence
on me. There were always girls around, so he'd try to talk me into
going out with some of them after work. I liked to get home as soon
as I could because I had my new wife waiting for me. Lupe was a lot
older than me and he'd say, "What kind of man are you? You let your
old lady tell you what to do?" I was young and stupid and people
could talk me into anything, so sometimes I went with him.

I don't know how much Margaret knew about our shenanigans,
but I know that she didn't like being alone in the apartment at night
in a strange city, and she didn't like Lupe at all.

Finally, I got tired of Lupe getting me into trouble all the time,
so I took Margaret back to Tucson. We moved into a little house in the
old barrio. By this time, Margaret was pregnant. A few months later,
Dan was born in a little birthing center nearby called The Stork's Nest.
He was a beautiful baby—fair-haired and fair-skinned like Margaret's
family. In fact, my dad suggested that maybe Margaret had been

fooling around, because he didn't believe that beautiful child could be mine. I think that he was joking.

The Depression was still on. There just wasn't much money to be made in Tucson, so after a while we went back to L.A. Our apartment was so tiny that we didn't have room for a crib for Dan, so we'd open a dresser drawer and put in a pillow and his little blankets and he'd sleep right next to us.

Dan looked like a little angel, but from Day One he was a pain in the neck. He liked the best of everything. And he still does.

As hard as those times were, the kid wouldn't drink milk at 15 cents a bottle. He had to have a special prescription milk powder from the drug store.

The powder cost $3.00 a can. You have to remember that a loaf of bread was only a dime. But our baby had to have three-dollar milk. I said to Margaret, "Send this kid back."

We kept him, though. Dan is Mr. Big Shot now, but I remember him sleeping in that dresser drawer.

It was very hard to make a living with music, but I didn't know anything else. And I guess that I was kind of like my brother Alberto, who had to be a boxer or nothing at all. Maybe another woman would have insisted that I go out and get a real job, but, through all those hard years, Margaret understood that my music was my life.

I looked up Lupe Fernandez again. He and Mike Ceseña were working as a duo. Mike was from Tijuana and he was a wonderfully talented young man, a good guitar player with a great voice.

We formed a trio and we worked in several clubs. Music didn't pay much, but we got enough tips so that we could live. Then we got an offer to work in a club in Phoenix called El Chico.

Mike was only 18 but he had gotten married about a year before. The day that we left for Phoenix, his wife had a baby. Mike never got a chance to hold his baby. He looked at him through the window in the hospital, and he never saw him again.

We got to Phoenix and we started working right away. At night we'd play at El Chico, and every morning at 7:00 we'd go on the air on KOY. The announcer there was an old friend of mine from Tucson. At least I thought that he was a friend.

I'd had to leave Margaret and Dan with my brother Frank and his wife. Frank was a nice, easygoing fellow, but his wife made Margaret's life miserable. Everything that she or the baby did was wrong. When I got my first check, I sent it to Margaret to pay for our share of the rent and the groceries. She had a little money left over, so she packed up Dan and got on the first train to Phoenix.

I was broke because I had sent her my check. Carlos, my boss at the radio station, knew Margaret from when she was a little girl, so I went to him and I said, "Look. My wife is here with our baby and I don't have enough money to rent a room for them. Could you advance me a little? When you give me my check Saturday, I'll pay you back."

"I don't do business that way," he told me.

I couldn't believe my ears. "What do you mean? All I need is ten dollars and it's just for a couple of days."

"No. I feel sorry for Margie but I don't do business that way. You go find your money somewhere else." And he shut the door right in my face.

I didn't know what we were going to do. Somehow I found a small adobe shack that we could use for two or three nights. It didn't even have a floor—just dirt. When I looked around that little room I felt terrible, but Margaret said, "I don't care if we have to sleep under a bridge as long as we're together and we have milk for the baby."

I found out that I had one real friend in Phoenix: an ex-boxer, a friend of Alberto's. His name was Pipa Fuentes and he owned a restaurant called La Poblanita.

I was embarrassed, but I had to go to him and ask if he could just let us have some milk for Dan. He said, "Oh, sure. All three of you can come and eat whenever you want three times a day."

I said, "I'm getting paid on Saturday at the club and at the station. I'll bring you the money then."

He said, "Don't worry. It's on me."

Pipa fed us for almost a week. When I went to pay him, he wouldn't take any money. He said, "No, no, no. Your brother was a good friend of mine. Forget it." That almost made up for the other jerk.

We had been in Phoenix maybe a month or two and we were doing fine, when we had this terrible, terrible accident.

It was so hot that almost every morning after the radio show we guys would go to the swimming pool and cool off. But this one day, I said to them, "You go on. I'm really tired, really sleepy. I just don't feel up to it."

They went on to the pool but it was closed for cleaning.

There was a local guy, a friend of Lupe's, with them, and he said, "Let's go swimming in the irrigation ditch."

So they walked over to the ditch. Lupe dived in and so did his friend. Mike just sat on the edge with his feet in the water.

Lupe yelled, "Come on in, man! Come on in!"

"In just a little while."

"Come on in, you chicken. You been telling us what a great swimmer you are. Come on in and show us."

You see, Mike had told us, "When I was in Tijuana, we used to go swimming all the time in the dam." He meant in the reservoir behind the dam where the water was calm. This irrigation ditch ran pretty fast, and he was afraid.

But Lupe kept egging him on. Finally he said, "Aw, we're getting out of here. You're never going to come in. You're too chicken." He started climbing out.

"Oh, no, no, Lupe. I'm coming in right now."

I wasn't there, but Lupe's friend told me what happened. Mike could swim a little but not against a current like in that ditch. All of a sudden he started to drown. Lupe grabbed him to pull him out, but Mike panicked. He tried to climb on top of Lupe and he pushed him down. Then the current grabbed them both. And the third man was standing up on the edge of the bank watching.

He was crying when he told me later, "I don't know what happened to me. I couldn't believe it. I couldn't move. I just froze."

Lupe was scratched up and bleeding from trying to hold on to Mike. Finally he couldn't breathe anymore so he had to turn loose of Mike and save himself. The current took Mike away.

They found Mike's body about four or five miles downstream, torn to pieces by the rocks on the bottom of the canal. He was just eighteen years old, and he left a teenaged wife and a newborn baby back in Los Angeles.

As soon as we had buried Mike, I said to Lupe, "I quit, man. I'm not going to work with you anymore." Then I told Margaret, "Get the baby. We're going home."

In Tucson, I got a job performing by myself at El Charro Cafe. I'd stroll through the restaurant with my guitar singing a mixture of American pop and Mexican music, whatever people wanted to hear. I got paid just five dollars a week to play nine hours a night six nights. Margaret, Dan, and I lived on my tips. In those days a quarter was a pretty good tip. I did okay, but I sure wasn't getting rich.

In 1941 Tucson was pretty much segregated, but the white folks from the other side of town were sometimes lured over to our side because they loved Mexican food.

I was always glad to see students from the university come in. A lot of them were from well-to-do families and they were usually pretty generous.

One of my funniest memories about tips was one night when two Mexican fellows were sitting at one of the tables. They had had a few drinks before I came by. At that time there was a popular song called *Zenaida*. It went: "The girl that I love lives four hundred kilometers from here . . . "

One guy says: "Do you know that song about the four hundred kilometers?"

"Yes. I know it."

"How much?"

He was pretty drunk so I decided to push my luck. I said, "A dollar."

He put his hand into his pocket, pulled out a fifty-cent piece, kind of frowned at it, and said, "Just play me two hundred kilometers."

I almost choked. I couldn't laugh because the guy was serious about wanting to hear the song and I wanted the fifty cents.

A lot of Westerns were filmed in Tucson because of the desert and the saguaros and mountains. For one of them, for a change, I was hired not for my music but for my looks. The star was a very young and very handsome William Holden. Opposite him was the beautiful Jean Arthur. The film was called *Arizona,* and it won a couple of Oscars in 1941.

The first morning, when I went out to the set in the desert, they slapped a black wig on my head and made me up to look even more like an Indian than I actually did. We were just ready to go to work when someone asked for my Social Security card, which I had left at home. The director was not happy, but he sent me back in a big limo. We had to stop for gas about a block from my house just as Margaret came down the street with Dan in her arms.

I guess the makeup was pretty good because when I called to her, "Margaret, Margaret," she started running away.

I yelled again, "It's me!"

She stopped and said, "Lalo? My God, what have they done to you?"

I said, "Well, that's Hollywood!"

When the movie opened in Tucson, there was a big hullabaloo. I went with a bunch of friends to see it and I kept whispering, "I'll be coming on the screen pretty soon. Pretty soon."

Finally my big scene came on. I was sitting on a horse watching over a herd of cattle.

It was a very long shot and one of my buddies said, "Where are you?"

"See that horse over there on the hill?"

"Yeah, yeah."

"That's me."

"That's you? That horse is you?"

"No. The guy on the horse." I thought that I would never hear the last of that.

Every morning I'd sleep until ten because I worked from six in the evening until 3:00 A.M. at El Charro. Our apartment was really tiny, so Margaret would get up very quietly and she'd take Dan to a little restaurant on the corner called La Concha. They'd have breakfast there while I slept.

One morning she came rushing back into the house. She shook me, yelling "Wake up! Wake up, Honey!"

I sat straight up. "What's going on? What's the matter?"

"We're at war! The Japanese just bombed Pearl Harbor!"

I was still half asleep. "What?"

"The Japanese attacked Pearl Harbor. They sank a whole bunch of ships and we're at war!"

I got up and I turned on the radio. We hugged each other and our baby while we listened together and, like young couples all across America that morning, we were very frightened.

World War II

Like a lot of other Americans, I got very angry.

So many young men died; it especially hit us in Tucson because more than a thousand went down with the USS Arizona, and that was our ship. I just sat there with Margaret and I didn't know what to think or what to do. ·

I loved my country and I wanted to do my duty, but I was crazy about the baby and so in love with my wife—I just couldn't imagine leaving them.

I registered for the draft, but I decided to get a war job to see if I could hold off the army for awhile. We moved to San Diego because Margaret had a sister living there, and I went to work building airplanes.

One evening, after we had been in San Diego for several months, I was listening to the Tijuana station on the radio and the disc jockey said, "And now here is Lucha Reyes with her latest hit, *Canción Mexicana*." Then I heard the most popular woman vocalist in Mexico singing my song!

I couldn't help myself; I started jumping up and down and screaming, "Listen, Margaret! Lucha Reyes recorded my song." And then we were both jumping up and down and screaming. Dan was too little to jump up and down, but he probably joined in the screaming.

Right away I got a friend to drive me across the border to a big music store in Tijuana. I found the record and looked at the cover. It said "Singer Lucha Reyes" and—my heart just sank—"Writer Lucha Reyes."

The next day I got an emergency leave from work and I headed down to Mexico City on the train.

I was angry. It took four days to get there, and all the way the train wheels were singing, "They want to steal my song. They want to steal my song."

I went straight to PHAM and I stomped into the office mad as hell. "My song, *Canción Mexicana,* has been recorded by Lucha Reyes and it has her name as the writer. You have a contract with me for that song."

"Lucha Reyes recorded that? I haven't heard it."

I said, "I have a copy right here" and I slammed it down on the desk.

"I'll be dammed." He went through the files and there was my signed contract with the words and music. "Let's get over to RCA Victor right away."

The president at RCA was Mr. Barragán. The fellow from the publishing company said, "We have a problem here. This gentlemen has had this song registered with us for months and Lucha Reyes put her name on it."

Mr. Barragán said, "Well, she said a young man by the name of Luis Moreno gave it to her." I just about went through the ceiling. I didn't find out the whole story until later.

The Mason Theater in Los Angeles booked a lot of shows from Mexico City. The program was always headed by a big star and the rest of the performers were local entertainers. One week the headliner was Lucha Reyes. One of my former partners, Luis Moreno, was playing there with a trio. *Canción Mexicana* was a part of their repertoire and they played it every night. When Lucha heard it, she asked, "Who wrote that song?"

Luis was a joker, so he piped up and said, "It's mine. I wrote it."

"I like it very much." she said, "I'd like to it take back to Mexico and record it."

"You can have it. I want to give it to you because I admire you so much."

He wrote out the music and lyrics for her. He probably never thought that she would record it.

At first I was really angry with Luis because he gave away my song, but then I thought what the hell . . . at least it got off the shelf. The publishing company just stores the music until somebody asks for a certain kind of song. The chances of that happening are like winning the lottery, a million to one. I left four songs with PHAM in 1939 and the others were never released. If Luis hadn't played that joke, my song might never have been recorded by such a big-name artist.

I never met Lucha Reyes in person and I don't know if she ever knew about all this. It was one of her last recordings. Not long afterward she committed suicide.

Canción Mexicana has been recorded by some big stars, including Lola Beltran, the "Queen of Ranchera Music." It's still a part of the repertoire of mariachis everywhere.

Back in San Diego, I'd work at the factory during the week. On weekends I played at the Mexicali Club. Our band was very good, and the club was always packed with marines and sailors from the port. We were doing mostly Mexican songs with English lyrics, and I would also do some songs with one chorus in Spanish and one in English. When I sang in English, the band would play American style; when I'd go into the Spanish half, they would switch to a Latin rhythm.

Many people in the music industry had gone to war and there was a shortage of new music to record in this country. The publishing houses looked to Latin America, especially to Mexico and the Caribbean. They brought back the prettiest melodies and wrote English lyrics to them. Some of them got new titles: *Cuando Vuelvo a tu Lado* (*What a Difference a Day Makes*), *Te Quiero Dijiste* (*Magic Is the Moonlight*), and *Duerme* (*Time Was . . .*). *Amapola* and *María Elena* kept the same names for the English versions.

One of the most popular songs, *Aquellos Ojos Verdes* (Green Eyes), was written by a Cuban, Nilo Menéndez. I knew him from when I was playing at El Zarape and he was the pianist in the band. One night Pete Alcaraz, who later became my piano player, got a little bit of a shock when he asked Nilo how he was inspired to write such beautiful lyrics. Nilo kind of sighed and said, "I just fell in love with the most gorgeous green eyes . . . on the most beautiful black man."

I have some newspaper clippings about the show at the Mexicali Club: "Bunny Weldon presents *The Little Devils* with Lolita the Latin Beauty." And, "The colorful place was packed. Eduardo Guerrero, the tenor troubadour, was held onstage by wild applause from the audience which just wouldn't let him stop."

One photo caption says, "Eddie Guerrero, Romantic Troubadour"—that's me, surrounded by girls. I was the only man in the show and I had never been in a show with girls before. Onstage they didn't wear much, and backstage they would run around in the raw. With all that skin showing, I didn't know where to look. They would come by and pinch my cheeks and laugh when I blushed. I was glad that Margaret never came to see the show.

Regarding my first name: My birth certificate says Eduardo, my family called me Lalo, my teachers called me Edward, and my school buddies called me Eddie. Later, whenever I was performing or recording in Spanish, I went back to Lalo because it has that cute, warm, fuzzy feeling.

In 1947, I got the chance to cut one 78 rpm in English, and I used the name Don Edwards. Ever since I was a boy, I wanted to sing real American songs like my heroes Rudy Vallee and Dick Powell; I wanted to cross over into the English language market.

I had a beautiful, clear voice, and, if I may say so, I did a good job on that record, but I was years ahead of my time. In the forties, nobody could even conceive of a Mexican American with the face of a cactus singing *Tiptoe through the Tulips,* or whatever. The sales were only so-so, and I went back to Spanish.

During the war years, I worked for Ryan Aeronautics and Consolidated Aircraft Corporation. Both companies had groups of entertainers who volunteered to put on shows to sell war bonds and raise money for projects like buying playing cards for the troops overseas.

We had one show on a British aircraft carrier that came into port. The men couldn't get off, so we went on board. It was a hot day and I was dying of thirst. As soon as we finished the show, I went up to the bar and said, "Give me a beer."

The bartender handed me a mug. I took a big gulp. Aaacch! It tasted terrible.

What a shock! I said to the bartender. "This beer's hot."

He said, "That's the way we British drink it."

I said, "I'm glad that the Americans won the Revolution."

One night a group of people from the USO came into the club and they liked what I did and what I sang. So, for two or three years, I worked with them. I'd be given permission to take time off from the aircraft factory for a few days to entertain around Southern California. We had an orchestra, vocalists, dancers, and comedians. And we entertained at the marine bases, naval bases, military hospitals, places like that.

There were no celebrities like Bob Hope in our USO troop, but the performers were professionals and very talented. There was an 18-piece orchestra and some very pretty dancers. We didn't get any pay, but we had the fun and satisfaction of doing the shows.

The most satisfying of all was performing in the military hospitals. The men would really get into it and I could see that while they were having fun with us they'd forget about their wounds and their illnesses. There was so much happiness on their faces; that made those shows very special to me.

Sometimes we performed at the officers' club in the beautiful old hotel on Coronado Island. The room was like a movie set with all the men wearing gold braid on their shoulders and "fried eggs" on their caps. It was a treat just to be there, but that wasn't the only perk. In those days everything was rationed. Even with the stamps, you couldn't get much meat or sugar, but after we finished playing at the Club, they would always load us up with beef, pork, chicken, and all kinds of cakes and pastries to take home. Margaret and I would feast for a week after I played there.

One of the positive effects of the war was that all kinds of people were thrown in together in the service and in the factories, so overall there was less discrimination, but we still felt it now and then.

Sometimes I really didn't know whether to get mad or not. For example, our next-door neighbors were Anglos. They had a little boy named Billy who was the same age as Dan, and they were good friends. One day Dan came in crying. "Mama! Mama! Billy says I'm a Mexican! And I told him, 'I am not a Mexican. I'm Dan.' but he keeps saying I'm a Mexican."

I went over there and I said to the father, "Your son called my son a Mexican and I want you to know that I am an American. I was born in Tucson—so were my wife and my son. I am of Mexican descent and I hope that Billy never heard you use that word in a derogatory way."

He said, "No, no. He may have heard us mention that you're a Mexican family and he just picked up the word. You know how kids are."

I said, "Dan doesn't even know what a Mexican is, but Billy made it sound like something bad."

"I'll talk to Billy," he said. After that the little boys went back to playing just like before.

The worst incidents of anti-Mexican American feelings were the zoot suit riots in Los Angeles. We had been in San Diego almost a year when those broke out.

A zoot suit has a long jacket with wide lapels and very wide shoulders. The pants are high waisted and real loose except at the ankle. In the forties, zoot suits were worn by cool young Mexican Americans who called themselves "pachucos." They kept their hair long with a duck tail and they usually had a tando—a wide-brimmed hat with a feather. The pachucos were just the opposite of the servicemen with their neat uniforms and crew cuts.

In the summer of 1942, the Sleepy Lagoon case in Los Angeles made the national news. Nine members of the 38th Street gang were convicted of the murder of Jose Diaz. All of a sudden all Mexican American youths became identified as draft-dodging pachuco hoodlums.

The following year, hundreds of marines and sailors went on a weeklong rampage through downtown Los Angeles and they proceeded to beat up every zoot-suiter they could find. Whenever they caught one, they would rip off his clothing and cut his hair. Nobody got killed, but quite a few young Latinos got beaten up.

I didn't even own a zoot suit; when I wasn't performing, I usually wore ordinary khaki pants, but I looked Mexican and that was enough to get me in trouble. Not long after the riots in L.A, I was walking down Broadway in San Diego with a friend and his father when three marines came up behind us and tripped the father. My friend turned around and said, "What's the matter with you? Can't you see his gray hair?"

The marines didn't bother the old man any more, but they yelled and came after us. Me and my buddy ran like hell. They were ready to beat the frijoles out of us. Some more marines joined in—maybe a dozen of them.

Just down the street, I saw a movie theater with a lot of people standing around in the lobby. I ran inside without slowing down to buy a ticket. I cowered in a corner in the dark and I was so nervous that I couldn't even watch the film. The marines didn't find me, but they got ahold of my buddy and beat him up pretty good.

After a few weeks, the government moved in to restrain the servicemen. We were at war and that kind of news was really demoralizing to all of the Mexican Americans who were fighting for our country.

The years went by and I kept getting deferments every six months because I was married with a child and because of my work at the factory and with the USO. Someone at the draft board may have figured that I was doing more good than if they gave me a gun. I think that they were right, because I'd probably have shot myself in the foot first thing.

My big brother Frank got drafted when he was 33 years old. They shipped him to the South Pacific right away. When he got to Papua, New Guinea, some officer looked at his papers and said, "You were born in Mexico and you're not an American citizen. Why didn't you say so? You wouldn't have been drafted."

"I guess nobody asked me."

The officer said, "Well since you're already here. . . . " and they made him a citizen right on the spot. He served four years in the Pacific, most of the time in New Guinea, and he was in the invasion of Leyte Gulf in the Philippines. When General MacArther said, "I shall return," Frank was right there with him.

I got my draft notice in the summer of 1945. I took the family to Tucson so Margaret could stay with my parents, and I went to Phoenix for my physical. It was almost a joke because by then they were drafting everybody. Then I went back to Tucson to wait.

Very early on the morning of August 6, a couple of days before I was supposed to leave for boot camp, all the church bells in the city began to ring and there were mobs of people in the street. I asked Papá, "¿Que pasa?"

He said, "The war's over." He had just heard on the radio that we had dropped the atomic bombs and Japan had surrendered.

The Pachuco Years

After the war, Margaret and I returned to Los Angeles. I went back to work at the Bamba Club but this time as a solo vocalist. A lot of the Hollywood crowd used to show up there: George Brent, Ida Lupino, Ann Sheridan, Ricardo Montalban, John Garfield, Anthony Quinn. . . .

One night in 1946, Manuel Acuña came by and told me that he was now working with Lew Chudd at Imperial Records. He said that they needed a trio, so I got together with two of my friends, Mario Sanchez and Joe Coria, and we formed El Trio Imperial.

In the next couple of years, with the trio or with a mariachi, I recorded more than sixty songs. We didn't get royalties but they'd pay us $50 a side each, so I'd get $200 a session because we did two 78 rpm records, four numbers, at a time. For me, the money was like a bonus. My real reason for recording was to make a name for myself so that I could make some big money as a performer.

At Imperial, we were recording mostly Mexican ranchera-style romantic music along with a few humorous songs. This was about all that was available in Spanish at that time. Manuel Acuña and I decided to branch out into some more modern, more popular music with a dance band.

I met a lot of performers at the clubs where I played, and so I picked out the ones I thought were the best musicians and the most compatible with me and with each other. I chose them well because that group—Pete Alcaraz, Frank Quijada, David Lopez, Carlos Guerrero, and Alphonso Rojo—stayed with me for twenty years. We worked together in the clubs, recorded together, and went on the road together.

I called my band Lalo y Sus Cinco Lobos (Lalo and His Five Wolves). At that time a "wolf" was one of those guys that was always on the prowl, and my boys fit that image.

The group was originally formed just for recording, but after we cut a few records, we got a gig at Club El Acapulco on Los Angeles Street. That was my first job as a bandleader. We were there for almost a year, and then we moved on to other clubs around town.

The Latin music scene in Los Angeles after the war was very diverse and very exciting. Although American musicians were not welcome south of the border, groups from Mexico like Mariachi Vargas de Tecalitlan and Luis Arcaráz and his orchestra were very popular in Los Angeles. From New York City, we got the high-energy Caribbean sounds of Música Tropical, the pachanga, the cha cha cha, and the mambo. The bands of Pérez Prado, Tito Puente, Machito, and Noro Morales played at The Trocadero, Coconut Grove, Ciro's. . . . There were so many Latin clubs in those years: El Sombrero, El Babalu, La Bamba, La Casa Olvera, El Bolero. They were filled almost every night.

The Música Tropical thing didn't stop but, during the forties, the pachucos started to have an effect on the music in Los Angeles.

My first encounter with pachucos goes back to 1933 or so when young men from West Texas would hop on a freight train to go to California. They spoke a kind of slang called caló. They called El Paso "El Chuco" and California "Califas." If they were headed west, they would say they were going pa' Califas. If they were headed home, they were going pa' El Chuco, so people started calling all of them "pachucos."

Later, when the fad reached Mexico City, people called them "Tarzanes" for Tarzan the Ape Man, because they wore their hair long. They dressed in baggy clothes that they called drapes or un tacuche— a zoot suit. We didn't know it then, but the fashion had started with the black musicians in Harlem; I still don't know how it got to El Paso. We thought they looked real sharp, but our parents didn't agree.

One time four or five of these boys got off in Tucson and they got a job at a bakery. Two of them played guitar and sang very well, so Yuca and I started hanging out with them. We'd go over at night while they were baking bread. We sang for them while they worked, then they'd sing for us while they were taking a break. They knew a lot of songs from the border area around Juarez and El Paso—songs we'd never heard before.

I started learning some caló. It's a mixture of Spanish and

English and weird words that are neither. For example: una sura was a quarter, 25 cents; un toleco was a 50-cent piece; and a dollar was una bola, a ball. A tortilla was una sória. Sometimes to tease my mother, I'd say, "Hey, jefecita! Deme una sória." (Give me a tortilla.)

She'd get upset."Don't come in here talking like that! In this house, you speak English or Spanish."

The next time the pachucos had an impact on my life was almost ten years later, at the time of the zoot suit riots in Los Angeles. Even in San Diego we could feel the vibrations of the violence, like being on the edge of an earthquake.

Respectable people, both Anglos and Latinos, looked on the pachucos as gangs because they always ran in bunches. Sometimes there would be some friction between groups over turf or girls and they would fight, but always among themselves. It wasn't like the gang warfare today; they didn't harm any other people. When two guys would get into a fight they used a little knife, like a penknife. They didn't kill each other; the first one to draw blood was the winner. It was more like some kind of ritual than a fight.

Most of them worked as bus boys, waiters, whatever. The girls wore short skirts and stockings that came to just below the knee. Kind of flirty, kind of sexy, a little bit provocative. The boys were very neat, very clean, and they loved to dress up. They'd save for months for a tailor-made zoot suit that would cost two hundred dollars or more. They were the epitome of "cool" before the word "cool" was ever used for anything except the weather.

Usually nobody else would go to the clubs where the pachucos went. When we played at El Hoyo on Main Street, just about every man on the dance floor would be wearing a zoot suit. The clubs that catered to them hired groups like mine that could play swing and boogie-woogie because they liked to jitterbug. The pachucos admired me because I talked their lingo and I wrote their kind of music.

About two in the morning, after we got off work, some of the musicians from the clubs nearby used to go eat at a restaurant on Main Street called La Golondrina. The owner, Mariquita, was like a mother to us. The bars were all legally closed by then, but if we asked for a cup of tea, she would hand over a cupful of booze. Someone would bring out a guitar, another guy would bring out a set of bongo drums, and some fellows would start singing. We had jam sessions that lasted until three or four in the morning.

A lot of pachucos used to hang out there, too, and I enjoyed listening to them talk. One morning, I heard one of the pachucos say to Mariquita, "¡Esa carnala! Traigame unas de lamina con unos de cemento."

She said, "What?"

So one of his friends translated for him, "Unas tortillas de harina y unos refritos con queso." (Some flour tortillas and refried beans with cheese.) Lamina is corrugated tin like you use on a roof. When flour tortillas are fried they bubble up like that. And I guess they thought that the melted cheese on the beans looked like cement.

The nearest thing I know to caló is the cockney slang in London. The pachucos often used words that rhymed with or began like or sort of sounded like the Spanish or English word that they meant to say. Like all slang, it was constantly changing, it was understood only by the "in" crowd, and it irritated the outsiders.

I wrote *Nuestra Idioma* (Our Language), making fun of the way that the pachucos were destroying the Spanish language. My boss at Imperial Records, Lew Chudd, got a real kick out of that song. So I wrote *La Pachuquilla,* about the girlfriend of one of the pachucos, and that was a big hit. After that I wrote El Pachuco about the boyfriend. Then I wrote *El Pachuco y El Tarzan* about a guy from Mexico City who tried to come between them. I did a whole series, almost like una telenovela (a Mexican soap opera), all with this weird language that they spoke.

I love playing with words and, just for fun, I would skip from English to Spanish to caló in the same song and sometimes even in the same sentence. In all I recorded more than a dozen pachuco songs with El Trio Imperial.

These songs were just for listening and laughing, but the pachucos loved to dance, so it seemed natural to write boogie-woogie and swing with caló lyrics. That's when I wrote *Vamos a Bailar* (Let's Dance), *Los Chucos Suaves* (Cool Cats), *Chicas Patas Boogie* (Pachucos' or Chicanos' Boogie), and *Marijuana Boogie.* I recorded all of these with my Cinco Lobos.

The music was rock and roll, swing, and blues, but the lyrics were in Spanish and caló with a lot of English, because most of the pachucos were born in this country so they spoke English. The songs were a big hit with them—they liked being noticed and sung about, and they bought a lot of records because I spoke their language.

Vamos a Bailar is a good example of this music. It's a medley—American swing combined with Latin rhythms.

Vamos a Bailar

Cuando salgo yo a bailar,
Yo me pongo muy catrin,

Las huisitas gritan,
"Daddy, vente,
Vamos a bailar el swing."
Cuando voy al vacilon,
Y me meto yo a un salon,
Las chavalas todas gritan,
"¡Papí!
Vamos a bailar danzon."
Tocan mambo sabroson,

Se alborota el corazon,
Y con una pachucona
Vamos a bailar el mambo.
De los bailes que menté,

el bolero y el beguiné,

De todos los bailes juntos,
¡Me gusta bailar el swing!

Let's Dance

When I go out to dance,
And I'm dressed up like a king,

All the young chicks yell,
"Daddy, come on.
Let's swing."
When I go out on the town,
And I go into a ballroom
All the girls scream,
"Papí!
Let's dance danzon."
They play the mambo so sweet,

It excites my heart,
And a sexy lady says,
"Let's dance the mambo."
Of the dances that I mentioned

As well as the bolero and the beguine,

Of all these dances
I still prefer the swing!

Another example is *Chicas Patas Boogie,* a swing song with a rumba bridge. It names a lot of the places where pachucos would show up when my band played for dances.

Chicas Patas Boogie (excerpt)

Swing chicas patas, ese es mi borlo.
Swing Chicanos, this is my dance.

Lo bailo en Tula, con una chula,
I dance it in Tulare with a cute girl,

Lo bailo en San Jo con una guisita a todo tren.
I dance it at full steam with a chick in San Jose.

Lo bailan los carnales allá en San Fra.
All the brothers dance it over in San Francisco.

. . . Se pone a todo dar Cuando bailan boogie.
They really turn it on When they dance the boogie.

For *Tin Marin De Do Pingue* (a rock and roll version of a children's game) and *Muy Sabroso Blues* (Delicious Blues, music so good that you can taste it), Manuel located a group of black musicians over in South Los Angeles. He gave them the music to practice for a few days. One of them had a studio in his garage, so I came in one night and we recorded both sides in that one session. It was a great experience; they were incredible musicians.

All of these songs were about what I could see going on around me. For example, I wrote *Marijuana Boogie* because they smoked a lot of pot—they called it grifa or yerba.

Sometimes when one of them would come up to say good-by, he'd shake my hand and leave a joint in my palm. When I was a kid, the only guys in the barrio who smoked that stuff were the filthy old bums we called marijuanos. I didn't use it but, just to fit the pachucos' image of me as one of them, I let them think that I did.

In the late forties, the pachucos just disappeared along with their music.

Thirty years later, in 1979, Luis Valdez wrote the play *Zoot Suit,* which was based on the incident in 1942 at Sleepy Lagoon. He was looking for music from that era. He consulted Philip Sonnichsen, an ethnomusicologist at UCLA. I didn't know anything about this at the time, but Phil had collected and taped a lot of my records for his files. He dug them up and sent several selections to Luis.

Luis used four of my songs—*Los Chucos Suaves, Chicas Patas Boogie, Marijuana Boogie,* and *Vamos a Bailar*—in the play, and much of the dialogue was based on the caló in my lyrics. *Zoot Suit* premiered in Los Angeles at the Mark Taper Forum and went all the way to the Winter Garden Theatre on Broadway in New York. Later it was made into a movie that was released by Universal Studios, and now it's out on videotape.

In reality, the pachuco mystique never really went away; the shadow of the zoot suiters hung over us. The music faded, the styles changed, but they never disappeared completely. In the late 1990s, bands like Brian Setzer's started to play swing in the style of the forties.

One day I got a call from a young man named Ben Esparza. He and my son Mark were in Garfield High School at the same time. He had been a fan of Mark's band, Mark and the Escorts, and he knew my name and my music.

Ben said, "Why not bring back your swing music? I'd like to put out a CD from my company, Break Records. We'll call it *Vamos a Bailar—Otra Vez* (Let's Dance—Again)." He got together a sixteen-piece band of first-class musicians and me, the oldest living pachuco, doing the vocals. For me, it's marvelous to know that a whole new generation is dancing to the music that I wrote more than fifty years ago.

As a perk, in 1999, I finally got a zoot suit and a tando. I get to wear them for TV interviews and concerts.

On the Road with My Band

Back to the forties . . . my next big break came in 1948. Imperial had a soloist from Mexico City who was selling records like crazy, but it went to his head and he started drinking. Sometimes he wouldn't even show up for a session. He got fired, and Manuel suggested to Lew Chudd that they try me.

My first record as a soloist with an orchestra was *Pecadora* (The Sinner) by Agustín Lara. It was a hit.

When I visited Tucson the first time after *Pecadora* was released, I was given a hero's welcome with a big dance at Wetmore's Ballroom. In those days it was very difficult to get on records as a soloist and there had never been a local boy, black, white or brown, who had done it. My mom was there, my brothers and sisters, and my friends. I sang for them, and it was a wonderful, wonderful experience to come home a success.

Manuel Acuña and I worked together for about thirty years with different companies. We even organized a music publishing company, NACO. It's the name of a town in Sonora near where he was born. Manuel did some beautiful arrangements for the orchestra and he was a wonderful composer. Over the years, he picked out a lot of the songs that he thought were well suited for me and that I should record. Sometimes we disagreed, but most of the time he was right.

After the success of *Pecadora,* my records really took off and they started to sell all through the Southwest wherever there were Mexicans or Mexican Americans. And there were a lot of them around in the late forties.

During the war, we needed workers because so many U.S. citizens went off to fight or to work in factories. During those years, tens of thousands of Mexicans crossed the border. Some of them came legally as temporary migrant workers; others were undocumented, but the authorities kind of looked the other way because our country needed workers. They were called "braceros" (arms); in Mexico, that name is used for a day laborer, someone who lends his arms to do a job. Anglos use the word "hand" the same way—like a farmhand. Most braceros worked in the fields, but a lot of them worked on the railroads; they usually did real hard jobs like building and maintaining the tracks. The trains were very important in those years because they carried everything across the country: coal, iron ore, tanks, and soldiers.

Even though they were here legally, and we needed them, a lot of the braceros were mistreated by the people who employed them. I wrote several songs about their suffering here in a strange land with a language they couldn't understand.

The braceros were around at the same time as the pachucos. Later I wove some of my funny songs into a story of a bracero and pachuco who fall in love with the same girl. The bracero is from a farm in Mexico and the pachuco is an American city boy, so there are all kinds of misunderstandings because of language.

One night my Cinco Lobos and I were playing at a place over on the west side of town when I got a phone call at about 10:30. I walked out leaving David Lopez in charge. It's the only time in my career that I ever left in the middle of a set, but I had to get to the hospital; Margaret was in the process of having a baby. I drove as fast as I could, but I had barely settled down in the waiting room when a nurse came out carrying our second son, Mark.

With two children to look out for, I really needed some extra cash. All across the Midwest and the Southwest, people knew my name and bought my records. My music was out there and I knew that they would pay to see me in person. I kept thinking, "I've got to get on the road," but I didn't know how to do it.

Then, in another one of those lucky connections in my life, I met Paco.

It was 1949. I was booked as a soloist at the Cinema Curto in Mexicali, across the border from Calexico. On the bill was Francisco "Paco" Sanchez, an incredibly talented comedian.

After the show that night, he said, "You want to make some real money, Lalo? I can make you a lot of money, but you gotta trust me."

I got suspicious. "Trust you? What is it you want to do?"

"I was on the road as a circus clown with Barnum and Bailey a long time. Mexicans love circuses, so I know where to find them. And they're starving for entertainment. I can book a month's tour in just a couple of weeks. If you can get a mariachi group, it'll be just you, the mariachi, my straight man and me doing my clown act. That would be the whole show."

From watching him work that one night I already knew that he was a very bright man, so I said, "Keep talking."

"But," he said, "I don't have any money and I will need transportation. My old car is not very reliable. So you'll have to trust me with your car and enough money for my expenses. When I come back, we'll go on the road."

I went home and talked it over with Margaret. We had a little bit of a doubt but we agreed that it was worth a chance, so I gave Paco some cash for expenses and sent him off. For three weeks, I rode the trolley to work wondering if I'd ever see my car again. Meanwhile Paco was busy booking the whole tour: Arizona, New Mexico, Kansas, Nebraska, Colorado. He ate and slept in the car, and he kept going day and night. That's the kind of hustler he was. As soon as he got back, I signed up the Mariachi México del Norte. I had recorded with them several times and we worked well together. A few weeks later, we went on the road in Paco's old Packard and my Pontiac—Paco's straight man, John Rocha; Paco's 14-year-old nephew, Juanito; the six musicians; Paco; and me, plus all the instruments.

We started east hitting the towns where Paco had booked us, and it was just like he predicted. Every night we had 200—300 people in the audience. At the beginning of each performance, Paco would come out as the master of ceremonies wearing a tuxedo. He'd talk about this and that and he'd introduce the mariachi. Most of these people were not very sophisticated so he would convince them that the musicians were really movie stars. He would say, "Did you see the film *Zorro the Silver Fox*? Well, this is him—Zorro Plateado!" Or "You remember *Dracula*? This fellow played the young boy in that film."

The audience was in awe. They thought these guys were all stars! Many of them had only seen mariachis in the movies, so when the boys began to play, the audience would just go bananas.

After a few numbers, Paco would come out as Colilla, the clown. He and Rocha would do some funny stuff. Then he'd go off and come back as Nostradamos and he would do a big act predicting the future.

There was one thing that he could do only when there was some bare ground near the theater, but every time he did it, he got a standing ovation. He'd ask for a volunteer to be hypnotized and buried alive. Of course, the volunteer would be our boy, Juanito, who would be sitting out in the audience. He'd come up to the stage and, after a lot of gobbledygook, he'd go into a trance. Paco would have two men lay him on a board and carry him outside, followed by the whole audience.

Earlier in the day, they would dig a trench that was like a shallow grave. Paco would roll the boy up in a tarp and lay him in the hole. They'd cover him with dirt as if they were really burying him and Paco would tell the audience, "We'll come back after the show to revive him."

Paco would get back into his tux so that he could introduce the star attraction—me. I'd come out and sing for about half an hour accompanied by the mariachi. Then for the grand finale, we'd all go outside. They'd dig the boy up. He'd be absolutely stiff so a couple of guys would carry him up to the stage and lean him against a wall. Paco would come out with more hocus-pocus, snap his fingers, and say, "When I count to three, you'll come back to us. ¡Uno, dos, tres!" And the kid would wake up. The audience loved it.

The first time he did the stunt I was a little worried, but Paco told me his secret: "I always wrap the tarp real loose around him and there are pockets of air so that he can breath under the dirt."

We played Flagstaff, Gallup, and Grants. We were doing great, but then Paco's old Packard just gave up the ghost. We had to tow it to a little roadside garage and leave it there.

We couldn't wait for the car to be repaired because we had a big dance that night in Albuquerque. The tickets were already sold, so we could make some real bucks—if we could get there. Some of the boys took the Greyhound bus and the rest us went on in my car. We all made it, and the dance was a success.

We had to leave immediately afterwards because we were booked in Denver. I don't know how they did it, but Paco and the boys all got into my car. They started north and I took the bus back to pick up the Packard. It was about 3:00 A.M. when I got on the bus. I took a little nap, but then I had to get in the car and try to catch up with the gang.

I volunteered to go back for the car instead of sending one of the boys because I knew that the band could play the dance and Paco could do his act without me if they had to. I was the star attraction, but they could just say, "Lalo got sick and he can't be with us tonight." The crowd would already be there and they would have a good time.

I missed the performance. I picked up the car and I drove all day through the New Mexican desert. It was a two-lane road in those days, not a freeway. There were times when I wouldn't see a single car for hours. I wanted to get to that dance because it was so important, but the more I drove, the sleepier I got. To stay awake, I'd sing for awhile, then I'd scream and yell.

I was in the mountains somewhere in Colorado when, all of a sudden, I heard a horn blaring: "Beep! Beep! Beep!" I almost jumped out of my skin because I had dozed off. The oncoming driver honked because he saw me headed toward the steep drop-off on the right. He zoomed by and he probably never knew that he saved my life.

I was already off the road and headed for the cliff. As soon as I could, I found a safe place to park, and I thought, "If I don't make it to Denver, to hell with it. It's not worth losing my life."

Then I fell asleep right there in the car. I got to Denver about two or three hours late. I was exhausted, so I just fell into the bed and they played the job without me that night.

For three weeks, we went from town to town. When I came home, I had around $80,000. Paco got 20 percent of that. After I paid off everything, I had enough left over to buy a house in East Los Angeles.

Paco took his share and went to Denver where he went on the

radio with his own show, first one hour every morning, then two, then three. Eventually he got his own station. Later he ran for the state legislature and he won. And to think that he started with me at that little theater back in Calexico! All he needed was someone to give him a push, someone with a little faith in him.

The trip with Paco Sanchez was so successful that I wanted to do it again with my dance band. I met a young composer with a real gift of gab, Teddy Fregoso. He needed work, so I decided to hire him to set up another tour. I had seen him around town enough to know that I didn't want to trust him with my nice new Pontiac, so I sent along my friend, Yuca Salaz, as a driver. They took off with a list of cities and the names of the promoters.

Everything went fine until they were on their way home. About 40 miles from El Paso, Yuca got drowsy and Teddy persuaded him to let him drive. A few miles later, Teddy ran off the road and flipped the car. The boys didn't get hurt, but the car was ruined.

I had to buy another car, so I was mad at Teddy because he wasn't supposed to be driving. To show you how persuasive that guy could be, he talked me into letting him come with us on the trip as the master of ceremonies. He started talking the day we left Los Angeles and he never stopped. He had us in stitches all across the country.

Teddy went on to become a very popular disc jockey in Los Angeles and he got his own radio station above the El Capitan Theater in Hollywood.

After that, twice a year, I went on tour with my orchestra. They were good musicians and we had a good book, a good repertoire. In the forties and fifties, almost everyone who came to the dances was Mexican—not Mexican American. They were starved for Mexican music and we could play whatever they wanted: danzones, boleros, polkas, waltzes. For the younger people, we always included a couple of American pop numbers in each set. We packed the ballrooms wherever we played.

I learned to book my tours according to the way the crops were going. I would call the promoters to find out when the peak harvest would be, because the people moved to where the work was. They would say, "We're harvesting onions in June" or "We're picking cotton in September." Sometimes the farm workers themselves, the braceros, would direct us to where the action was at any particular time and we'd guide ourselves a lot by that because then they would have money to buy the tickets for the dances. Years later I used this same technique to book road dates in California.

At first we avoided Texas because we had heard that there was a lot of discrimination against Mexicans there. On the third tour, I booked some dates in West Texas and we stopped at a bar for a beer. There were a couple of young Mexicans outside. When we started in, one said, "You guys going in there? They're not going to serve you."

I said, "Why not?"

He looked at me as if I was crazy. "Because you're Mexicans."

I kind of shrugged my shoulders and said, "We'll see what happens."

All seven of us went in. The bartender looked at us kind of funny, but we sat down and ordered beer. He didn't act very friendly but he served us. Maybe he was a little intimidated because there were so many of us. He didn't know that musicians are lovers, not fighters.

When we finished, I took four bottles to the men outside. They said, "They sold you beer? They don't allow Mexicans in there."

"They did today," I said.

We never had any trouble getting a place to stay, but I had a friend, Pete Bugarin, who was also on the road with his band. He had a black sax player, Curtis Grey.

At one motel, the manager said, "I'm sorry, but we can't rent to him."

"Why not?"

"Well . . . he's colored."

Pete said, "No, he's not. He's Mexican like us. Hey, Grey! Say something in Spanish."

Grey didn't speak Spanish but there were a lot of choruses in the songs where they would all sing, so he said, "Sí, sí, sí. Yo quiero mambo."

And the motel manager said, "I guess it's okay." So they let him stay.

Someone told me that they saw a sign in Texas that said, "No Mexicans or dogs allowed," but I never saw anything like that. We never had any problems. Sometimes we did feel a little coldness, and we weren't really comfortable until we got into the Mexican neighborhoods where the ballrooms were.

Year after year we hit the same towns. We'd start in Flagstaff, go on to Gallup, up to Grants, Albuquerque, Santa Fe, and from there to the mining town Trinidad. Then Pueblo, Denver, Cheyenne, Scott's Bluff, and Grand Island. All the way to Omaha, then through Kansas, on to Denver, and south to repeat in Santa Fe, Albuquerque, Phoenix, and Tucson, and then back home. It was a long trip, but we were young and we had so much fun together.

So many stories stick in my mind. . . . The band traveled in my nine-passenger wagon. The guys would play cards in back and the one in the middle would have to hold a board on his lap. Once we went into a little cafe somewhere in Nebraska and they were arguing: "It's your turn to be the table."

"I was the table last time."

A man at the counter said to the waitress, "This nut thinks he's a table."

She said, "And the other one believes him!"

The boys loved to celebrate the Fourth of July, and fireworks were legal in a lot of places then. One Fourth we were in Kansas traveling along Highway 50 toward Colorado. I was driving and behind me they were throwing out little firecrackers—pop, pop, pop. Then there was an explosion and the wagon was full of smoke! Somebody had dropped a match into a box full of firecrackers! By a miracle, nobody was hurt.

I stopped the car and cleared out the smoke and they said, "Since we're stopped, we've got a couple of sky rockets to set off."

I agreed because I didn't want any more fireworks in the car. We were way out in the middle of nowhere with nothing around but dried-up cornfields, so they set up a rocket pointing straight down the highway. It swerved right into a field. And poof! All those dried cornstalks went up in flames!

We ran down the side of the road trying to put out the fire with our coats, but it got away from us.

I said, "Let's get the hell out of here before the police come," so we took off. It was twilight by then; when we looked back, the whole sky was lit up. We all gave a sigh of relief when we got across the border into Colorado.

You'd think that would be the end of it, but no way. That night in La Junta, before the dance, we were just hanging around outside the ballroom and Ray Lugo found a cherry bomb in his pocket. He lit it and rolled it over toward the others. When it went off, it sent up a rock that hit a boy standing nearby. The blood started pouring down his forehead. I told the guys to start without me and I drove the boy home wondering how I was going to explain it to his parents.

His mother came to the door. She looked at him and then at me. "You're Lalo Guerrero! What an honor! Come into the house."

I tried to tell her what had happened to her son but she just sort of brushed it off. "He'll be all right," she said, and she called her husband and sister to come in and meet me.

When I got back to the dance, I really laid down the law: "No more fireworks."

Now that I think about it, they were all a little weird. At the time, they seemed normal to me because that's how musicians are.

The weirdest was an Italian from Philadelphia named Charlie. I was going on a trip and, at the last minute, I had to find a trumpet player. A friend told me that Charlie was very good and he needed work, so I called him and told him, "Meet me at the Musicians' Union and have your clothes and horn ready."

I picked him up and we hit the road.

Charlie was maybe a little bit off in his cabeza. He told us that he had a worm that was eating through his brain so he had to wear a hat all the time because if he took it off the worm would move faster. And he was always showing up with big, long submarine sandwiches full of salami and bologna that he would pull out and eat on the bandstand when we took a break.

He was such a marvelous trumpeter that he became a big attraction. When he would get up and play these fantastic solos, the customers would stop dancing and stand around the bandstand. He was so great that I never told him to stop eating on the bandstand or to take off the hat, and the audience thought it was all part of the act.

Pete Alcaraz was my piano man. He had a booze problem. I don't know how many times over the years I said to him, "Pete, you're drunk again." He'd think a minute and say, "True," and go on playing. He knew that I wouldn't fire him because he was great. He played better drunk than most guys do sober. He'd just go crazy on the keys.

Pete was the exception to my rule: You can smoke or drink whatever you want, but you do it on your time. Not when we're working. People make mistakes when they're drunk or high.

Those long, flat highways got pretty boring and sometimes the guys would hand around a joint to pass the time. They were always bugging me, "Come on. You'll like it. Just one little toke, Lalo."

One day I got tired of the nagging, or maybe I was just bored, so I said "Okay." I stopped and let Rudy take over the wheel. They passed me the joint and I took a big drag. I didn't feel much of anything, but when we got to the job that evening I didn't sound good at all. My voice was very rough and raspy. The stuff affected my throat and my throat was my profession, so I said, "Nope, never again."

My mind sort of jumps around and "never again" reminds me of something that happened in Denver with my song *Nunca Jamás* (Never Ever). Some of my songs were written with a message that could help people understand some kind of pain and maybe learn to accept what had happened or maybe change it. In 1954, when I wrote *Nunca Jamás,* it was still very common among poor Mexicans that men would beat their wives. It was a real macho thing. Women usually didn't work outside the house so the husband was the sole support. Some of the men thought they could do whatever they pleased because they were sure the wife wouldn't leave. The woman had to accept it because, if the husband left, she would have a hard time scraping up a living for herself and the kids.

I saw it happen in my neighborhood, and that was when I was inspired to write this song. I tried to put myself inside the skin of that woman and to feel the desperation that she felt. The song was one of my favorites and people liked to dance to it, so I would sing it a couple of times every night.

We were booked in Denver at the Rainbow Ballroom the same evening as Trio Los Panchos. We would start at 8:00 and they would come in at 11:00 to play for an hour, and then we would continue until 2:00 A.M. or so. Los Panchos were from Mexico City and they were famous all over the Southwest as well as in Latin America.

That night was when I learned how the trio got its name. I had always thought that they were just three guys who happened to be named Francisco. Actually the name was given to them as a kind of insult back in the days when rednecks called every Mexican "Pancho."

When the trio came to New York, they didn't have a name. They were waiting backstage, getting ready to perform for the first time in this country, when the director looked around and said, "Okay. Who's on next?"

One of the technicians said, "Those panchos over there."

The director called for "The Panchos." They thought that it was funny and they started using that name.

The trio was hot and my band was popular, so that night in Denver the huge ballroom was packed. Los Panchos arrived in time to hear me sing several songs including *Nunca Jamás*.

Afterward they came over to me and said, "You sang a song tonight that we've never heard before."

One of them quoted the last three lines and I said, "I wrote that. The title is *Nunca Jamás*."

"We all liked it very much. When we get back to Mexico City, we'd like to record it." I didn't really believe that they would do it, but I had nothing to lose. I wrote out the lyrics and a lead sheet—that's the melody line with the chords up on top—and I gave it to them.

A few months passed. I was back in Los Angeles. One night after we finished at the Bamba Club, I went into Mariquita's with a couple of the boys in the band. On the juke box I heard Los Panchos singing my song. What a thrill!

Nunca Jamás was later recorded by two of the biggest stars in Latin music: Javier Solis and Jose Feliciano. I recorded it myself in 1965.

All these recordings missed the point. This is supposed to be a woman singing to her abusive husband telling him that he can hit her or beat her as long as he doesn't leave her, because without him she will die. When I wrote it I meant exactly that, but somehow it got romanticized.

It's still a standard in Mexico. Once in a restaurant in Mexico

City, I heard someone ask the mariachi, "You guys know the song about the wimp? You know where this guy tells his wife that she can beat him up if she wants to?"

Of all the songs I've written, the two that were first recorded almost by accident, *Canción Mexicana* and *Nunca Jamás,* are the ones that have been the biggest hits over the years.

To get back on the road in the fifties: we pulled along a little teardrop trailer for our clothes and instruments. One day on our way into Albuquerque, we were driving down a long hill. The boys in the back were playing cards as usual, I was driving, and Pete was in the front seat. Out of the corner of my eye, I saw him looking over to the side a couple of times, then he said, "Hey, Lalo, is that our trailer passing us?"

The damn trailer had come loose and it was going faster than we were! I honked my horn and yelled to warn the other drivers so nobody crashed. I had to chase that thing about half a mile before it finally went off the road into a ditch.

Pete just shook his head and said, "I thought that looked like our trailer."

More things happened to Pete. I think it was in Santa Fe; we had a real nice motel with a pool. He wanted to go swimming but he didn't have any trunks, so he put on some brand new undershorts that looked okay—maybe just a little too loose, but okay.

There were some nice-looking ladies sitting around the pool, so Pete decided to show off. He went up onto the springboard and dived into the deep end. Suddenly the ladies all started screaming and I heard Pete yelling, "Lalo, Lalo! Help me!" And then I saw his shorts floating on top of the water down at the shallow end of the pool. We all stood around laughing until somebody took pity on him and brought him a towel so that he could get out.

Santa Fe was my favorite city. Mayor Ortiz was a good friend of mine and I never found a kinder, friendlier, people than the New Mexicans. They loved us. The kids could recognize my wagon and they would come out on the street and run after us.

The kids had a little trouble with my name, so they'd yell, "Lalo's back! Here's Lalo and his garreros." Garrero means ragman.

When Lalo came to Santa Fe, it was fiesta time! The people were so hospitable. Every night after we'd play, we'd have an invitation to eat and drink at someone's house.

I have one very sad memory of Santa Fe, though. Frank Quijada, my drummer, was one of my original Cinco Lobos. He was blind in one eye and he looked strange because his blind eye was crossed. Most band leaders wouldn't hire him because he didn't look good on stage. But he was a very fine drummer. If a guy is a good musician, I don't care what he looks like.

When we recorded *El Bolerito de la Main* (The Shoeshine Boy), the only way that he could get the sound of the rag snapping was by taking his pants off and slapping his bare thighs. We kept making mistakes and we had to repeat it seven or eight times. When we finally all got it together, Frank had big red splotches on both his legs. That's the way he was. I could always count on him to go all the way no matter what we were doing.

Frank and I roomed together on the road. I tried to watch out for him because of his blind eye—I was afraid that he would trip or fall off the stage—and he tried to take care of me. It made him so happy when business was good and we sold out the club or the ballroom.

When he was in his thirties, he got cancer. We had to go on the road and he couldn't go with us. We were in New Mexico when his wife, Sarah, called me and said, "His last words were 'Lalo. Look! The place is packed, Lalo. Isn't it wonderful!'"

He died believing that he was in Santa Fe with me.

I'm not sure, but I think that my band was the first one to go on the road in that area, and I wouldn't have done it except for Paco's experience with the circus. The idea caught on fast and pretty soon we started to meet up with other bands: Beto Villa and Mike Orneles from Texas, Pete Bugarin from Phoenix, Phil Carreon out of L.A. We were playing the same towns at different times. To make it on the road, you had to have a name, you had to have records, and the records had to be out there so that people knew who you were and what kind of music you played.

Beto was probably the best known of all of us. He was from a small town in south Texas where they use a lot of accordion and saxes, more like an orchestra than a band. The jukeboxes everywhere were full of his music. Up north, my music was as popular as his, but no way could I compete with him in Texas. He was the king of the polka. I am not a great polka fan, but when I was following Beto somewhere, I'd have to throw one in now and then because people demanded it.

Our paths would crisscross so we might meet two or three times on a tour. We got to know each other's voices. I'd be in a room in a motel and I'd hear some guys come in. I'd say "Beto? Is that you, Beto?"

And he'd yell back, "Lalo? Is that you? Where are you, man?"

We'd get together for a drink and to trade stories about the places we'd been playing and the places we were headed for. Then we'd all go to bed because we had to leave the next morning for the next town. What a life! What great memories!

The Fifties

During the fifties, I appeared in several films. I never thought of myself as an actor, but I was tall and slender with sleek black hair not quite Indian, not quite Spanish—an Anthony Quinn type. I guess some directors liked my face, because they would call me up every now and then. I have been a movie fan ever since I was a little kid, so I felt very fortunate to get to meet a lot of the big stars and to work with them.

In *His Kind of Woman*, I'm playing my guitar in a little cafe in a border town and Jane Russell is singing "Five little miles from San Berdoo. . . ." Robert Mitchum walks in and goes up to the bar.

All of a sudden the director yelled, "Cut! Cut! Cut!"

Mitchum turned around and said, "What's wrong?"

"Look. You're coming into this place where this beautiful woman is singing. You wouldn't just walk in looking straight ahead. The natural thing to do would be to look at the girl."

"Oh—I don't know about that. Did you notice the ass on the guitar player?"

Everybody on the set—the grips, the lighting men, the script girl, even the director—was on the floor laughing.

But Jane got real angry. She thought that was very disrespectful. To her, not to me, even though I was the butt of the joke. Or my butt was anyway. She stomped her foot and walked off the set.

So the director said, "Take a break, everybody."

I went off to the side and sat down to tune my guitar. Bob Mitchum strolled over and he said, "Hey. I want to apologize. I hope that you didn't get upset. With that little joke?"

"Naw, of course not," I said.

To tell the truth, I had been a little embarrassed at the moment when he said it, but he was so quick, his timing was so good, that it was really funny.

He said, "You know what? I play a little guitar myself."

I said, "You do? You want to try mine?" So he sat down next to me and played a few chords. And then Jane cooled down and we went back to work.

I was on the set with Mitchum for about a week and a half, so I got to know him pretty well. He was a nice guy and quite a comedian. I had a lot of fun with him.

Another part that I enjoyed was in *Bolero* with Nina Foch and George Raft. I was an admirer of Carlos Gardel, the Argentinean tango interpreter, and one of the reasons I got the part was because I knew a lot of tangos. George was quite a dancer, especially when it came to the Latin rhythms. It was a joy to watch him and Nina dancing together.

I was doing fine in California, but I still wanted to record in Mexico. In the mid-fifties, I went to Mexico City again to knock on doors and try to get my songs published. This time I took Margaret and the boys, and we got a little apartment.

One of the newspapers asked for an interview. I was really pleased because I thought that the Mexicans had finally taken notice of me and the interview was going to be something positive, but they used it to put me down. They wrote some terrible articles referring to me as a pocho, a Mexican who forgets his language and his heritage and tries to act like an American bigshot. One article referred to me as "this Texan who spits out of the side of his mouth and wears a cowboy hat." It was a lie. I never wore a hat. And I don't even know how to spit very well.

I wasn't getting anywhere musically, but I did meet a lot of the local musicians and composers. They were all boozers and party animals, so I hung out with them having a ball.

After several weeks of this, Margaret told me, "That's it. You're not getting anywhere and you're out drinking every night. I'm going home. If you want to stay, stay. I'm taking the boys whether you come with us or not."

She was right; I was wasting my time. By the time I got my shoes on, she had packed up the car.

It's a little spooky, but the next day when we were about halfway home, we heard on the car radio that there had been a huge earthquake in Mexico City. The apartment house where we had been living was completely destroyed. We missed getting killed by just one day, thanks to Margaret.

At that time there weren't any American-born performers who had made it big in Mexico. Later Andy Russell did, and Vickie Carr, and Selena. On the whole, though, Mexican performers have been treated better in the United States than Mexican Americans have been treated in Mexico.

My Life with Pancho Lopez

I was the matchmaker when Davy Crockett met Pancho Lopez in 1955. Like a lot of things in my life, this happened by chance.

Manuel Acuña and I recorded for Colonial Records at Jimmy Jones' studio in Pasadena. In the mid-fifties, Jimmy met Paul Landwehr, a very sharp businessman with some money to invest and an interest in the recording business. Jimmy called me and asked if I would be interested in joining them in starting a new recording company.

So we formed Discos Real. The name had a double meaning. In English "Real" means real, actual. In Spanish, it means "royal," and we had a crown on our label. I was in charge of Artists and Repertoire because I knew about music and I knew how to find talent; Jimmy had the studio and was a sound engineer; and Landwehr was in charge of sales and bookkeeping.

We planned to record in Spanish because I had had some hits with Imperial Records in Spanish, but I'd never had any luck with recording in English.

At that time Walt Disney's Wonderland Music Publishing had the hottest record out, *The Ballad of Davy Crockett*. You heard it everywhere—on the radio, on the streets, in elevators. You couldn't get away from it.

Then something happened that led to my making a lot of money, crossing over into the English-language market, and getting my own nightclub.

One day on my way to work, I heard some little Mexican boys in my neighborhood singing "Pancho, Pancho Villa, la, la, la, la," to the tune of *Davy Crockett*. They didn't know any words after that, but they sure were cute.

Right then I decided to write a Spanish version of *Davy Crockett*. I knew that I couldn't use the name of Pancho Villa because he is still kind of a hero to some Mexicans, so they would be offended. And the people who don't admire him—both Americans and Mexicans—find him despicable.

So I took one of the most common names in Mexico and I invented Pancho Lopez, "nació en Chihuahua en mil nueve ciento seis" (born in Chihuahua in 1906). It was a Mexican-type humorous song about a kid who was a combination of Pecos Bill and Super Baby. When he was four he could shoot out the eye of a louse at thirty yards, at six he fell in love, at seven he married, at eight he went off to fight in the Revolution, at nine he was dead. The moral was "no viva la vida con tanta rapidez" (don't live life so fast). The thing took off among the Spanish-speaking people all over the southwestern United States. Then it made the Top Ten in almost all the countries of Latin America.

It was such a big hit in Mexico that they made a feature film with Luis Aguilar playing *Pancho Lopez*. I never got a penny for that. It still burns me up to think that, even when it played in San Diego, the producers never got in touch with me. They didn't even offer me a free ticket!

The song did so well that I took a demo recording in to Al Sherman, a distributor in Hollywood. He didn't speak Spanish but he listened, and when I got to the chorus, "Pancho, Pancho Lopez," he cracked up and said, "That's great. You write that in English and I promise you, I'll sell a million records."

Writing a parody is harder than most people think—especially if the parody is in a different language than the original. You have to be completely bilingual and bicultural. You have to understand the original version of the song or story or whatever, and you have to somehow make it mesh with the new version. To be funny, it has to be different but recognizable. I had never written a parody in English, and I wasn't sure that I could make it work. But he said, "You write it and sing it, and I'll sell it."

So I recorded it in English. "Born in Chihuahua in 1903 . . . "

and on and on. In the end, son of a gun, he decides to follow the sun and ends up in Los Angeles as "King of Olvera Street."

Pancho Lopez (English version)

> Born in Chihuahua in 1903
> On a serape under a tree.
> He was so fat he could almost not see,
> He could eat 12 tacos when he was only three.
> Pancho, Pancho Lopez, he came from old Mexico.
> When he was seven he could shoot his gun,
> Ride on his burro till the day it was done.
> But when there's work to do, Pancho he run,
> He go out a-grinnin' to sleep in the sun.
> Pancho, Pancho Lopez, you lazy son of a gun.
> Come the revolution and Pancho he get sore,
> He go with Pancho Villa to fight in the war.
> But Pancho he don't want this risky chore,
> So he went back to Chihuahua and he sleep some more.
> Pancho, Pancho Lopez, he lie in the sun and snore.
> When he wake up, his sleeping all done,
> The wetback movement had just begun.
> So he packed his guitar the son-of-a-gun,
> And he came to California to follow the sun.
> Pancho, Pancho Lopez, he swim across the Rio Grande.
> Old Pancho he worked 'til he almost dropped.
> Out in the fields he'd pick up the crops.
> So he went to Olvera Street and he open up
> A taco stand and his troubles they stop.
> Pancho, Pancho Lopez, the King of Olvera Street.
> So if you're ever in Los Angeles,
> Go to Olvera Street and there he is,
> Selling his tacos and his beans with cheese.
> Old Chihuahua was never like this.
> Pancho, Pancho Lopez, the King of Olvera Street.

Al loved it. He passed it along to a disc jockey, Alan Ameche. As soon as it went out on the air, other stations picked it up. All across the country, people started clamoring for it and the records sold faster than hot tortillas.

But there was one little hitch. We had never gotten clearance to use the music. So one day Paul got a call from Wonderland: "We would like to see you in our office regarding *The Ballad of Pancho Lopez.*"

Paul told Jimmy and me and we said, "That's it. We're done. They're going to make us take it off the air. They'll sue us. We are finished."

A couple of days later the three of us went over to the Wonderland office in Burbank. We checked in at the lobby and, what really shook us up, they took us right into the office of Walt Disney. Mr. Disney was sitting behind his big walnut desk, and there were three men standing behind him.

He said, "Come on in, gentlemen." He stood up to shake hands and he introduced the other men—a couple of attorneys and the head man of Wonderland Music. Then he said, "Please be seated."

He got right down to business. "I want to congratulate you on your wonderful success with *Pancho Lopez* but, as you know, that music is our property." We all just nodded.

"Now, you know that you didn't get any clearance to use our music." We all shook our heads. We had decided that I would be the spokesman because, after all, I was the culprit who wrote the thing.

So I said, "Yes sir, we realize that but we really didn't expect to sell more than a few thousand copies. And we thought that nobody would ever know about it, including you."

His mouth twitched just a little bit like he was going to smile. Then he said, "Mr. Guerrero, I want to congratulate you. You wrote a very clever lyric. (Coming from Walt Disney, what a compliment!) But that music is our property. There are two ways that we can work this out. We can go to court. . . . "

I glanced at my partners and they weren't even breathing. I thought to myself, what the hell is he going to take? We didn't have anything except the company we had just formed. Maybe he had thought of that, too, and that's why he said what he did. "Or . . . we can split the proceeds. We get 50 percent for the music and you get 50 percent for your lyric."

I couldn't believe my ears. Real fast, I said, "We'll take it."

I didn't have to consult my partners. They were ecstatic; I could see it on their faces.

We went straight over to another office and their lawyer drew up a contract. We signed it right then and there.

The Ballad of Pancho Lopez was my first big hit in English. It sold three quarters of a million records and it reached number three on the Latin charts for the entire country. Everywhere I played I shared the billing with Pancho. Sometimes I even wore a serape and sombrero with my suit. The merchants in Olvera Street gave me a fabulous fiesta for putting them back on the map with Pancho's taco stand. I sang that song on national television on the Tonight Show with Steve Allen, the Art Linkletter Show, Peter Potter's Platter Party, and The Al Jarvis Show. Pancho and I even got written up in Time magazine.

My partners and I split our share three ways, and we all did very well. In fact, from that one record, I made enough money to buy my nightclub in East Los Angeles.

Pancho Lopez was written mostly just for fun and partly to spoof Davy Crockett and to hint at how my people felt about that episode in American history. I just got tired of all the hullabaloo. And I guess a lot of other people did, too, because that record shot up like a skyrocket.

Funny thing, when I was in San Antonio a few years ago, I visited the Alamo for the first time. On the wall I found a list of the names of the men who were defending the fort. There were quite a few Mexicans inside, including several Guerreros.

I don't sing Pancho Lopez much anymore. I wrote it in Spanish and I was singing for our own people. Comical, silly songs are a Mexican tradition, so people just laughed and enjoyed it.

But twenty years after it came out in English, some of the Latino organizations that fight discrimination found it offensive. Editorials showed up in several newspapers saying that the lyrics are degrading to Mexican Americans because I sing about him swimming across the Rio Grande and picking the crops.

It's okay to laugh about things like that in the family, so to speak, but in English maybe it does come out racist, so I just don't perform it in public anymore.

In my own defense, I want to say that I sing about what I see, and what I wrote about Pancho Lopez was the truth in many ways. He didn't want to fight in the Revolution; he didn't believe in it. He came across the border to work in the fields. Once he got over here, he didn't like the hard work so he went to Olvera street—where I started my musical career in L.A. And he was smart enough to open his own taco stand. So I don't think it was degrading at all; my parents came over here to get away from the Revolution and to find work.

Humor is always changing. Over the years, some of my songs have offended different groups: Chicanos, gays, women. I have never intended any malice or meaness, but I've never worried much about being politically correct. I just find humor in everything. As far as I can tell, the only acceptable joke these days is: Two people are standing on a street corner and neither one says anything.

You know that original *Ballad of Davy Crockett* was pretty silly and disrespectful; I wonder if any Texans ever protested against it.

I Go into the Nightclub Business

When Jimmy, Paul, and I formed Discos Real, we planned to release records in Spanish because all of my hits had been in Spanish. The English version of *Pancho Lopez* did so well that I recorded other parodies and comical songs in English: *Tacos for Two; Hey, Mabel; Adios to Mexico City;* and *Do You Believe in Reincarnation?* All of these were very popular and we had some other artists who sold well: Gloria Becker, the Don Ralke Trio, Daniel Rodriguez, and Blanca del Mar.

Paul liked attending recording conventions and rubbing elbows with executives from RCA Victor, Decca, and all the other big labels. While Jimmy and I were busy with the production end of the business he was flying to meetings all over the United States, and once he even went down to South America. He kept reporting that sales were great, and we figured that he knew what he was doing.

Paul's rule was "No wives at business meetings," and usually it was just the three of us. I don't remember why, but I happened to bring Margaret along for one of our sessions. Margaret was very sharp and she had a lot more business sense than I did; it took her about two minutes to figure out that Paul was having a ball on company funds. She didn't say anything there, but she said plenty when we got home. After I told her that she didn't know anything about the music industry, I called up Jimmy and we decided to ask Paul for a rundown on the expenses. As soon as we saw how little there was in the bank account, we dissolved the company.

The year before, when I'd told Manuel Acuña that I wanted to form a label with Paul and Jimmy, he'd said, "Go ahead. Try it." Now I had to call him to see if he wanted me back. He did, and we continued to work together for years after that.

The downfall of Discos Real discouraged me for a while, but a few months later I was ready for another business venture. In 1957, I was playing with my band at a club out on North Broadway. The owner and his wife worked at the club. They were quite a bit older than I was, and they treated me like their son.

On Sunday we had two hours between the matinee and evening dances, so they'd put me to bed in a little room in the back and make me take a siesta. Then they'd wake me up and feed me dinner.

I thought that they were so nice to me because they really liked me. I was wrong. This was right after I struck gold with *Pancho Lopez,* so I was in the chips and they knew it.

One day the boss said to me, "Let's open a club together." It sounded like a good idea, but I've always been a lousy businessman. I said that I knew about playing in clubs but nothing about operating one.

"That's okay. I know all about running nightclubs," he said. And he talked me into going into a fifty-fifty partnership with him. We found a place in East Los Angeles called Torrey's Inn. We did some remodeling and opened Lalo's in 1958.

We had a grand opening with searchlights like they have for big Hollywood premiers. What a party! In those days everybody paid with cash, so the register got full and so did the little strongbox. We had a couple of rooms in the back with some beds to rest on between shows, and that night so much money came in that we laid it out under the mattresses.

Night after night the people kept coming. As we got more successful and started bringing in more and more money, my partners started giving me a bad time. That sweet old man and that sweet old lady who had treated me so nicely became just the opposite! When they saw all that money, they got greedy; they wanted me out. They started treating me worse and worse.

People would come looking for me in the daytime and say, "May I speak to Lalo Guerrero?"

"Who?"

"Mr. Guerrero."

"Never heard of him," or " I think there's a guy here by that name cleaning the toilets."

Finally I couldn't stand it anymore. But we had that fifty-fifty contract so I couldn't force them to get out, and they couldn't force me to get out.

My partner got really strange, paranoid. One day I went into in the office and he pulled out a revolver. "You're trying to take my club away from me. I'll kill you first!"

He was actually frothing at the mouth like a mad dog. That scared the hell out of me. This guy was out of his skull. And with a gun on me! He said, "You'll take this club away from me over my dead body, but I'll kill you first. I swear I'll kill you. If you want out, I'll buy you out."

Sometimes I have trouble making decisions, but this was not one of those times. I said, "Okay. Buy me out."

He offered me about what I had put in at the beginning, and I took it. I just wanted out of there with my skin intact.

He thought that he would continue to rake in the dough. Somehow he didn't count on who was bringing the people in: me—the guy whose records were being played on the radio everywhere.

I took my band down the street to the Paramount Ballroom, and my fans followed me.

The old club kept going down, down. Before a year was up my former partner was drowning. Finally he sold the club to a couple of friends of mine. They were real nice people and I wished them well, but I knew that it was just a matter of time. I knew what the people wanted, who the people wanted, and I was it.

Elvis, the Martian, and the Three Little Squirrels

Meanwhile my records were selling great—especially the humorous songs in both English and Spanish. Over the years, I've listened to a lot of different kinds of music and different kinds of comedy, and it's all up there in my head waiting to be tapped. Sometimes I like to take totally unrelated stuff and make it work together, or I give the lyrics a little tweak just to make people laugh.

After *Pancho Lopez,* I wrote *Tacos for Two,* a parody of *Cocktails for Two,* about a romantic rendezvous Mexican style. Tennessee Ernie Ford had a hit record, *Sixteen Tons,* about a coal miner. Ernie did my version on his TV show, dressed up like a washerwoman scrubbing "sixteen pounds of dirty old clothes." Dolly Parton sang, "Please release me; let me go," and I had a car sing, "Please regrease me, change my oil." Kenny Rogers sang *Lucille,* about a woman who is leaving her husband, and I sang *Lucila,* about a woman that I wanted to leave me.

I was asked to perform at an event in the Palladium Ballroom where an old friend of mine, Ricardo Montalban, was the guest of honor. Ricardo used to do commercials for Cordova cars and, as a surprise for him, I wrote *Cordova* to the music of *Granada.*

When I started to sing, at first he looked kind of puzzled, kind of serious. Then he smiled a little. And he really broke up when I got to:

"There's ladies that would go to Hades to drive a Mercedes,

And there's men that rejoice 'cause they have a Rolls Royce in their eighties,

But I'm wild ova' my brand-new Cordova that I bought from Ricardo Montalban."

I can "mexicanize" anything. I made Davy Crockett into Pancho Lopez and Elvis Presley into Elvis Perez:

"When he plays the guitarra, he don't sing *Guadalajara,*
All he sings is rock 'n' roll."

For that song, I combined rock and roll with ranchera and wrote both English and Spanish lyrics. The English version was popular here, and the one in Spanish was a hit in Latin America, Spain, and Portugal.

In April 1959, *Elvis Perez* and my calypso song *Lola* both made the Top Ten in Montevideo. And I didn't even know anyone in Uruguay. That week in New York City, *Elvis Perez* was #2 on the Latin American charts. In August 1959, *Lola* was #2 in Buenos Aires and *Elvis Perez* was #8. What pleased me most, after so many years of rejection, was that Elvis and I made it to #2 in Mexico City!

My records were popular in a lot of places that I didn't know about at the time: Cuba, Chile, Peru, Argentina, El Salvador, Uruguay, and Colombia. Communications were not as good as now, so they could get away with a lot and I didn't get the royalties that I should have. I really didn't give a damn about the money; I did it for recognition. I was making my money with personal appearances.

Sometimes I didn't even know who was recording my stuff. *Ya Supe Lupe* was a hit for Trio Los Calaveras (The Skulls). Nobody knew it was mine until I went to the publishing house in Mexico City and asked why I wasn't getting any royalties for it.

These songs were all written just for fun, but later I sometimes used humor to make a statement when I saw something that wasn't right in our society.

In 1959, I had a major hit that I stumbled onto through another lucky accident. This led to me finally getting to record in Mexico.

In 1957, the Russians jumped way ahead of us when they sent up Sputnik. We launched our own rockets and all you heard on the news was space, space, space. That sparked an idea in my mind: Wouldn't it be something if a Martian came down to Earth? What would he say about our world? Were we bugging them with all that noise from our rockets? That was going around in the back of my head for several weeks. The more I thought about it, the funnier it got.

Then one day, I was in Jimmy Jones' studio for a recording session. At that time we had just started to record on tape. At one point, Jimmy put it on fast forward and this little high-pitched voice went YYYYYYYYYY. It sounded to me exactly like a little Martian. I said, "Hey, man! You know when you ran the tape real fast, my voice went way up. Is it possible to leave it at that level?"

He was sort of thinking out loud. "Not with this tape machine. I don't have any way to control the speed. But I might be able to find a way. . . . "

I said, "I wish you would. I have an idea for a song."

A couple of days later, when I had to go back for another session, Jimmy said, "I found it, Lalo! I found it!"

I had been busy performing, writing, finishing up a couple of other records, and I had forgotten all about our previous conversation. So I said, "What'd you find?"

"Remember what you asked me about controlling the speed? I found a way to do it." Then he showed me a little knob on top of his machine.

So I went home and wrote the words and the music for *El Marciano* (The Martian). He was a little green man with one big eye in the middle of his forehead and he spoke Spanish. At that time there was a popular song that said, "Los Marcianos llegaron ya. Llegaron bailando cha cha cha." (The Martians have arrived and they came in dancing the cha cha cha.) My Martian says that he wants to clear up certain matters: "We don't dance the cha cha cha, there's no rabbit on the moon, and if you don't quit sending those noisy rockets up here we're going to come down and whip both the Russians and the Americans."

That song immediately became a hit all over Latin America. It quickly climbed to the top ten in Peru, Columbia, Argentina, and Mexico.

But where it was a real smash was Cuba. It flew right to the top of the charts. Someone sent me a newspaper from Havana with the headline *Un Marciano en la Tierra* (A Martian on Earth). I got an offer to appear at a club in Havana, and I was thrilled. Havana was a real swinging town in those days with lots of action—gambling, show girls, and all that wonderful music.

I had my contract, my ticket, and my passport, but I didn't get to go. Just a week or so before I was to leave, the revolution exploded and everything was canceled. I missed it by just that much.

At the time I thought that the Cubans liked it because it's a cute little song. But Castro and his buddies were coming into power and anti-American feelings were getting stirred up all over Latin America, so maybe they thought, "This guy is really telling off the Americans!"

When I wrote that lyric, it never entered my mind that someone might think that it was a political statement. Over the years, quite a few of my songs have been interpreted in a way very different than what I meant them to be—sometimes to my benefit, sometimes not.

The Martian was laid to rest, but I still had the little voice in my head. I thought that it would be fun to use it to write something in Spanish for children. For years, trios had been very popular in Mexican music, so I asked Jimmy if we could do three little voices. He said that he could, and I wrote *Las Tres Ardillitas* (The Three Little Squirrels).

I didn't want to give the squirrels any common names, so I picked out three that are unusual and kind of comical—with all due respect to people who have these names: Pánfilo, Anacleto, and Demetrio. Pánfilo was the naughty one. On these records sometimes I'm talking to myself, because in my normal voice I'm "The Professor"; with the speeded-up tape, I'm Pánfilo. Over the years, the other two squirrels were played by different people.

For several years, in the early sixties, I recorded songs for Las Ardillitas in Los Angeles on the Colonial label. Then, in 1966, Manuel Acuña sent a couple of records to EMI Capitol de Mexico as demos. They loved them, so they signed me up. After all those years of banging on doors, I finally got to record in Mexico City . . . as a squirrel.

After that, once or twice a year every year for twenty years, I went down to Mexico City and recorded an LP album. In the summer the songs were about manners, good behavior at school, respecting your parents, just all kinds of advice and fun. For several years we also put out an LP of Christmas music in the fall.

Some people don't take children's music seriously, but it is very important. My little squirrels teach them right from wrong, what to do and what not to do, with humor and a happy melody.

Each album had ten songs. Usually I wrote seven or eight of them. For about a dozen of the songs, I wrote the lyrics and my son

Mark wrote the music. He is a talented songwriter and he also did all the charts for the rock and roll numbers. Mark has been recording with me since he was a teenager and, for three or four years, he was the voice of Demetrio.

From the beginning my little squirrels were popular in Mexico and, in April 1960, *Las Tres Ardillitas* were #4 in Cuba. I bet some of those guys played them over and over listening for some hidden political message.

It's just amazing how many different ways I can get into trouble. At almost the same time that my squirrels began singing in Mexico, Alvin and the Chipmunks became very popular here. I really don't know who was first. At one point I got a letter asking me to cease and desist, but my lawyer wrote back that little voices for animals had been used for years in movie cartoons so nobody has any exclusive right to them. I guess they agreed, because I didn't get any more letters.

After twenty years, Capitol dropped the series, but since then they have released some of the songs on CDs. Now the grandchildren of the children who heard them more than forty years ago are listening to Las Ardillitas. And in many places where people don't know my popular songs, they still enjoy Pánfilo, Anacleto, and Demetrio.

Lalo's Again

Back in Los Angeles I packed them into the Paramount Ballroom every night, but my old club kept going down. After several months, the owners called me: "We're just not making it here. We need you. Will you come work for us?"

"No, but I'd like to have my club back. How much do you want?" They gave me a good deal and I took it—without a partner this time.

I changed the name back to Lalo's. The artist Carlos Almaraz was a friend of Dan's; he painted my ardillitas dancing on the walls. On October 27, 1960, we rented the searchlights again and had another grand opening. The club had a capacity of 400 and we had to turn people away that night. The next day the Los Angeles *Times* called it "East L.A's newest, largest, and finest night club."

Everything was going so well in my life. And then I did something incredibly stupid and I lost Margaret.

The club was very successful, but it was a lot of work and sometimes I'd get tired of the routine. I couldn't take off for weeks anymore, but I could get away for a few days now and then. I'd bring in a substitute band and I'd take my boys for a short tour out of town. Margaret would stay in Los Angeles and be in charge of the club. And that was the beginning of the end of my marriage, and it was all my fault.

I never wanted to do anything to ruin my marriage because Margaret was too important in my life. For years, she had worked hard along with me to get to where we were. The problem was the ladies. It's an occupational hazard for any musician. Some women are drawn to the spotlight.

My downfall was just one woman, and it was the biggest mistake of my life.

Whenever we were in Fresno, we played at the Rainbow Ballroom. There was this attractive girl who used to come up to chat with me whenever the band would take a break. She was pretty and she was young—in her twenties. I liked her friendliness and I looked forward to talking to her. We'd stand right up there in front of the stage with people all around us.

This happened three or four times; then one night she really came on to me. I'd had a few drinks; I usually don't drink when I'm performing, but I did that night. So it happened.

The next morning, I went back home and that was that. Except that she showed up in Los Angeles. In those days we didn't use the word "stalking," but that is what she did. She called me; she hung around wherever I was working. I tried to tell her that I wasn't interested, but she wouldn't leave me alone. She'd get really upset, really emotional. Finally we had a big scene and I didn't see her for months.

Then one day I got a summons to appear in court. I was faced with a paternity suit. And that's how Margaret found out about it. Of course, she was broken-hearted. Before I went to court, Margaret told me, "If you win, we'll stay together, but if you lose, I want a divorce."

At that time there was no such thing as DNA testing. They used blood tests. And it happened that all three of us—me, the woman, and the little girl—all had Type A blood. Along with about 80 million other Americans.

I fought as hard as I could, and spent as much as I had to for the lawyers and the fees, but I still lost. Margaret was angry . . . hurt . . . humiliated. So she divorced me.

She had suffered so much with me. We went through so many bad times together and, when the good times came, I went and botched it up. She didn't deserve it. She was a good wife to me, a good mother to my sons, a good woman.

At first, I couldn't believe that Margaret would divorce me. I thought that as soon as she cooled off and she saw that I regretted what I had done, she'd forgive me. For two years I kept begging her, but I had hurt her too much.

All during the trial and the divorce proceedings, I continued to perform at my club night after night. The band, the bartenders, and other people who worked there knew what was going on, but we never talked about it. Every night I had a whole club full of happy people but, sooner or later, I had to go back to my empty apartment. I had never lived alone before. I was so lonely.

From the beginning, Lalo's was a huge success. It was not luxurious but it was classy. There were always a lot of girls in their prettiest dresses and young men in their suits and ties. It was a party that went on and on for twelve years.

We were in the barrio of East Los Angeles. We didn't get the Hollywood crowd like we had at the Bamba Club, but Latino stars often showed up. Among others, Mexican actors and musicians like Tito Guizar and Trio Los Panchos would drop in whenever they were in town.

I had a lot of different acts: El Piporro, a comic composer and singer; Paco Miller, a ventriloquist, with his two dummies, Don Roque and Titino; José José, a very fine singer; Mariachi Vargas de Tecalitlan. One group, Los Churumbeles de España, would play and dance at the same time. Some great orchestras: Carlos Campos, Luis Arcaráz . . . when they played, the place was packed. You couldn't get in the door.

My own musicians were a great bunch, and I was real good to them. There was a little room where they could play cards on their break and have a drink if they wanted, as long as they didn't get sloshed. The only one who got sloshed all the time was Pete. He could get by with it because he was such an incredible pianist. If he could have stayed sober, he could have worked with a symphony or one of the big bands like Benny Goodman's.

After twenty years, some of my original Cinco Lobos were still with me as the nucleus of my orchestra. The joke around town was, "If you want to get into Lalo's band you have to wait until someone dies." We worked together so long that we got really tight because we knew each other's touch on the notes, the length of the notes, the feeling of the music.

One thing that drew people to my place was our repertoire. I was always on top of the latest styles of music—everything that was being played on the radio. Over the years, I worked with two very talented musicians: first, David Lopez, and later, Pete Alcaraz. I could go to them and say, "I want this song and this one," and they'd write out the charts for the whole band.

In those years, I got the chance to live out some of my boyhood dreams. I can be pretty persistent when I really want something, no matter how many doors get slammed in my face. I love Mexican music but I also wanted to perform American music. In the thirties, forties, and fifties, I tried to break out of the Mexican American, Spanish-language box that the music industry kept shoving me into. But I couldn't do it. The only other way that I could record American music was to write my own Spanish lyrics to American rhythms and melodies. For example, the Anglo market had never accepted me as a crooner, so I wrote Spanish lyrics for songs that were popular in English, like *Llorar* after Johnny Ray's *Cry*. I also wrote my own music in the same style, like *Llegaste Tarde* (You Arrived Late). So I could croon to my heart's content.

At Lalo's, we played whatever people wanted to dance to: mambo, cha cha cha, polka, swing, or rock and roll. They could make requests and dedicate songs to their boyfriends or girlfriends. It really was like a big house party. Everybody knew each another; at least they did by the end of evening. To this day, couples come up and tell me how they met at my place. There were other clubs in the East Los Angeles area, but mine was the most popular.

When my dad and my mom came over from Tucson to visit me, Papá spent every night at the club. He loved to play poker. The minute we broke for intermission, he would make a dash to the back room. The musicians always acted surprised. "Oh, Mr. Guerrero. You wanta play cards?"

"Of course. That's what I came for." Twenty minutes every hour every night.

Just one night we made him stay out front. That was when he and my mom celebrated their sixtieth anniversary at the club. We had a big cake for them, and they danced *The Anniversary Waltz*. When it was over, they came up to the bandstand and I embraced them both. They were so proud of me that night, and I was so proud of them.

Every Sunday afternoon our matinee dance began at 3:00. For the first hour, we broadcast a radio program from the club. It was a teaser, and by 4:00, the place was usually full. We played until midnight so it was a long, long day.

My sign-off theme was *Nuestro Amor* (Our Love). When I'd give the signal to the boys they'd all heave a sigh of relief, but there would be some groans from the dancers who never wanted the party to end.

In the Fields

Life kept going on. Every so often I'd get restless, so I would pack up the station wagon and take my band up north for a few days. The majority of the people who came to the dances were Mexican Americans or Mexicans who had come up to California when they were quite young, so they were a little more sophisticated than the people we saw on those earlier trips east.

Some had already moved on to other types of jobs, but the majority still worked in the fields. They harvested everything from apricots to zucchini. They'd tell me when the melons were going to be ripe around Bakersfield, when the tomatoes would be ready around Ventura, and when the plums would be picked in the Sacramento Valley. Just like on my earlier trips, I'd take that into account in deciding where I would book the band. The field workers followed the crops, and so did I.

When we played in the San Joaquin Valley around Bakersfield and Tulare, I noticed one young man who was there for every dance. He'd hang around the bandstand to talk to me at the breaks. He was very intelligent and he gave me advice on the dates and places where I would find the action in the fields and orchards. For a long time I knew his face but not his name; he was just one of the guys.

A few years later, everybody in California knew Cesar Chavez. When I first met him, I don't think that he had the slightest intention of doing what he did later on. At that time, everybody in the fields seemed happy as far as I could tell; of course, I only saw them on payday.

In the early sixties, Cesar started organizing the workers to improve the situation for the people in the fields. He joined with another hero of our times, Dolores Huerta, to organize the United Farm Workers of America.

In 1968 the workers picking table grapes around the little town of Delano went on strike. In the big farming areas all over California, from the Sacramento Valley, down the San Joaquin Valley, out in the Coachella Valley, and all along the coast, there was a strong sentiment of support for Cesar Chavez and the people in Delano.

The field workers also had the total support of the Mexican Americans in the cities, because it was our people who were suffering. We hadn't known that they were working under such terrible conditions—inadequate housing, no sanitary facilities, very low pay. Many Anglos joined us in the boycotts of table grapes and lettuce and of big companies like Gallo, Safeway, Coors, and Nestle.

I assisted with some fund raisers for Cesar's work and wrote *El Corrido de Delano* (The Ballad of Delano) to let people know what was happening there.

We all did whatever we could. Luis Valdez, who later used my music in *Zoot Suit,* formed El Teatro Campesino (The Farm Workers' Theater). A group of actors toured around the countryside using the back of a truck for a stage. They performed very funny skits about the big growers and the workers and the things that were happening every day. Their shows really helped keep up the morale of the strikers.

At a rally in Delano, in 1968, I was introduced to Robert Kennedy; I got to shake his hand, but I never had a chance to really talk to him. Not long after that he was assassinated.

When I went to Washington in 1991 to receive the National Endowment for the Arts Heritage Award, I sang the corrido that I wrote about Robert Kennedy. I had a hard time getting the words out because I got so choked up. He was such an intelligent young man with a wife and children and his whole life ahead of him. President and Mrs. George Bush were there. When we went through the reception line later that night, the President told me that my song was "a very beautiful tribute to a great man."

We Mexican Americans were never the same after World War II. The young men who had been in the services felt like they had a right to everything this country has to offer, and they were supported by many of the Anglos who had served with them.

There was more intermarriage between Anglos and Latinos. During the war, a lot of boys from the East were stationed at Davis

Monthan Air Force Base near Tucson. For them, Arizona was a very exotic place. Some of them liked the city and the people so much that they decided to stay. My sisters Connie, Terry, and Mona all married Anglos.

Real changes in society come very slowly, but we were ready to listen to Cesar when he appeared on the scene. His motto was "Sí se puede" (Yes we can). He showed us that we could make things happen if we stuck together. We began to hear about "Brown Power" and "La Raza" (The Race).

Meanwhile the war in Vietnam had become more and more unpopular. Then statistics came out showing that Mexican Americans were being drafted and killed at a very high rate compared to their numbers in the total population. This led to rallies and demonstrations in barrios all over the Southwest.

On August 29, 1970, thousands of antiwar demonstrators gathered in Laguna Park in East Los Angeles. Most of them were young Latinos, but there were also Anglos and blacks. It started as a peaceful march, but people got all worked up. As far as I remember that's the first time I heard the word "Chicano" used as a battle cry. They were raising their fists and yelling "Viva la raza" and "Somos Chicanos."

Then the police came and it got really rough. Everybody started running. Ruben Salazar, the KMEX-TV news director and a reporter for the Los Angeles *Times,* was there to cover the story. A few blocks from the park he ducked into the Silver Dollar Bar and was accidently killed by a tear gas canister that was shot into the room. Another life wasted. For him I wrote the corrido *La Tragedia del 29 de Agosto* (The Tragedy of August 29th).

Papá's Dream

In spite of all the very sad and serious events of those years, I have a lot of happy memories.

One Christmas, I think it was 1962 or '63, I got a call from the sheriff's department of East Los Angeles: "Would you be our Santa Claus this year?" I was really pleased, because I have always liked performing for children. Besides, Santa Claus was my hero when I was a kid and I held on to him until I was practically grown up. So I said yes, and they got me a real nice suit, beard and all. They saved money on the padding because I was pretty chubby at that time.

They roped off an area in the park behind the sheriff's station and they brought me in by helicopter. There were cops all around to keep the kids back until we landed. Just as I stepped down, the kids broke loose and came rushing at me. They poured across the field in hordes—thousands of them—all screaming. Or maybe it only looked like thousands. Anyway, there were a lot of kids. I thought that we were going to have a riot.

One good-looking young man came up with a little boy in his arms. The boy said, "Papá, Papá! Santa's here."

Then he got a closer look at me and he turned around and said to his father, "This guy ain't Santa. He's a Chicano."

He was only three or four years old but he was no dummy. He was looking for that white dude with the cherry nose. Santa Claus is white all over the world . . . except in East Los Angeles. They got used to a brown Santa there, because I had so much fun that I played Santa every year after that.

It was about then that Mark decided to follow in my footsteps. When he was twelve, I took the family to Mexico for Easter week. Our car broke down in Ensenada and the mechanic told me that it was going to take several hours to fix it, so we started walking around town.

Mark saw a music store and he said, "Dad, will you buy me a guitar?"

We went inside and he picked out the kind that he wanted—a small acoustic guitar, because he wasn't very big. The tag said twelve dollars, but I did a little bargaining and got it for eight.

I showed him a chord, and he strummed a while, and then he said, "Teach me another one." I taught him a few more chords while the car was being worked on. By the time we were driving home, he was playing and singing *La Bamba*.

A few months later he got an electric guitar and formed a band called Mark and The Escorts. They played surf music, rock and roll, and rhythm and blues. When the Beatles came on the scene, they started doing some of their songs. They performed in my club several times and went on one tour with me and my band. It kind of embarrasses Mark to remember this, but on a couple of occasions they even performed wearing Beatle wigs.

At that time, all across the country, a lot of young Americans were forming bands. We seemed to have one in every garage in East L.A. One group, later called Los Lobos, was made up of boys a little younger than Mark, just out of high school at that time. They knew me and they admired me from the time when they were real young kids. One of them, Cesar Rosas, was the nephew of David Lopez, one of my original Cinco Lobos. The others, David Hidalgo, Louis Perez, and Conrad Lozano, were all from the neighborhood.

They needed a place to rehearse, so they asked me if I would let them use my club. During the day nobody was around but the janitor, so I said okay. They didn't bother anybody and I really didn't pay much attention to them.

In 1988 Philip Sonnichsen decided to produce an LP album of my parodies, and he hired two of those boys, David and Conrad, to back me up. After that we played a few gigs together, but then we kind of lost touch until 1994 when Lieb Ostrow, the owner of "Music for Little People," wanted to put out a bilingual CD for children called *Papa's Dream*. He approached Los Lobos because they play classic rock and roll as well as traditional Mexican music.

The story is about a man who dreams that he takes his sons and his grandchildren on a fantastic trip to Mexico to celebrate his eightieth birthday in the town where he was born. They travel on the Wooly Bully blimp and have all kinds of adventures along the way.

Ostrow asked Los Lobos if they knew an older man who might be able to play the part of the grandfather. They said immediately, "We know just the man: Lalo Guerrero. We've known him since we were kids. He's a wonderful songwriter and he can write in English and Spanish."

Los Lobos played my children, and I loved working with them. They wrote some of the songs and I wrote some others. The grandchildren were a group called Los Cenzontles (The Mockingbirds) from a music school near San Francisco. The director of the school, Eugene Rodriguez, also wrote some of the lyrics.

We got a nomination for a Grammy but we got nudged out by an album from England. That was a little disappointing, but just being nominated is an honor.

Papa's Dream is used a lot in schools. The lyrics are mixed Spanish and English, and they are printed on the cover. Learning the songs helps the Spanish-speaking kids feel more comfortable with English, and it helps the others to pick up some Spanish and maybe gives them an appreciation of the language and the culture.

Lidia

I had been divorced for about ten years when Lidia came into my life. I knew a lot of girls and sometimes I would go out with one or the other. I was so lonely that, at one point, I even got into a very short-lived, very unfortunate marriage.

Like a lot of other events in my life, my meeting Lidia was the result of a lucky accident. One day she was downtown shopping on Broadway and, in this huge city of millions, she was all of a sudden face to face with an old friend from El Paso whom she hadn't seen for years.

She said, "Antonia?"

"Lidia, what are you doing here?"

So they took up their friendship again. Antonia was going steady with one of my bartenders, Alfredo, and one night she invited Lidia to come along with her to my club. And that is how I met the woman who became my wife and my right arm.

Lidia was tall, slender, young, and pretty. I noticed her right away, so I went over to where Alfredo was talking to the two girls and he introduced me to them. I got a little tingling of the heart, but I didn't say much of anything to her.

I told Alfredo after they left, "I like that girl. Would you do me a favor and ask your girlfriend to find out if Lidia would go out to dinner with me sometime?"

The girls came back the following Saturday. At the first break, I went over to say hello. I guess Antonia had told her what I had said to Alfredo because Lidia piped up, "Why did you ask Alfredo if I would go out with you? Why didn't you ask me?"

I said, "I was afraid of being rejected. If you turned me down, I'd just be crushed. So, how about it? Will you go out with me?"

Thank God, she said, "Yes."

She worked nights at a factory downtown. She didn't have a car and the city bus was really dangerous late at night, so sometimes I'd go pick her up and drive her home.

I liked her a lot, but I didn't know how much I cared for her until I had to go to Mexico City on a month-long business trip. That was when I realized how much I needed her, how much I loved her.

In Mexico City, I'd get together with my relatives. We'd have a few drinks and sing together with our guitars. I'd start a song that would remind me of Lidia and I'd burst into tears because I missed her so much.

Finally I said to myself, "This is the real thing. I love her enough to marry her." And then I thought, "I'd better tell her right now before some other guy beats me to her."

So I called her that same night and asked her to marry me.

When I got back from Mexico, I'd send a car over to the factory almost every night to bring her to the club to relax and be with me. If she got out late, and I couldn't get away, I'd call my friend Arturo. He was the sheriff, and he'd pick her up in the police car. The other women at the plant must have thought that she was a real big shot. Either that, or they wondered what she was getting busted for.

I enjoyed running the club, but I got tired of the same routine night after night. I started thinking about getting out of Los Angeles and going back to Tucson, my home town.

But I was 57, too young to retire, and I still liked the idea of having my own place. I turned it over and over in my mind and decided, "Maybe something smaller. A restaurant instead of a night-club."

The problem was . . . I didn't dare tell Lidia. I thought, "She likes the club so much. If I tell her that I'm going to sell it, she won't marry me." Maybe she was getting a little tired, too, because when I finally worked up my nerve to ask her, she agreed to go with me.

I didn't want to give her time to change her mind, so I sold the club and took off for Tucson.

I wanted to simplify my life. I was looking for a little Mexican restaurant with a few people to cook and serve, where I could entertain two or three hours every night by myself or maybe with a trio that could take over whenever I wanted to get away.

A real estate agent found me a place on Oracle Road that I could rent. It was very nice and just the right size.

And this shows you what a sharp businessman I am: I was so eager to open up that I immediately ordered a big neon sign. It was half built when the property owner found out that I was planning to serve beer. Alcohol was against his religion and he refused to give me the lease!

So that went down the drain. I could have a restaurant but no booze! What kind of Mexican restaurant doesn't have beer? I lost a lot of money on the half-built sign and the real estate agent's commission. I was so discouraged, I tucked my tail between my legs and headed back to California.

Palm Springs

I told you before that for years I've felt that the California desert was calling me.

When we got to the Coachella Valley where Lamberto and I had gone around peddling parrots more than thirty years earlier, I stopped to gas up. I guess Lamberto was kind of on my mind because I remembered that he was living in Palm Springs. I called him and he told me that his niece, Gloria Becker, had been looking for me.

I've known Gloria since she was a little girl. She's a singer; she recorded *Sixteen Pounds* for us on Discos Real back in the fifties. After that she became a booking agent.

So I called her. "Hey, Gloria! What's new?"

"Is that you, Lalo? I've been looking everywhere for you. Since you left the club, nobody knows where to find you. There's a beautiful new restaurant opening up near here in Rancho Mirage. The owners are looking for some good musicians. They know who you are and they'd love to have you there. It's called Las Casuelas Nuevas." (That means "The New Cooking Pots" but in this case the pots aren't new; the restaurant is.)

I said, "I don't know, Gloria. I'm headed back to check out the scene in Los Angeles, and I think I'd like to take another shot at Tucson next year."

"Just come over and meet them. They're great people and they already have a couple of restaurants here in Palm Springs."

I thought, "What the heck?" and made a little detour. Gloria introduced me to Mary and Florencio Delgado. Florencio and I really hit it off because he was originally from a mining town in Arizona. Later on he often called me "my old Arizona buddy."

The new restaurant wasn't quite ready to open, but the Delgados showed me the building. It was the Spanish Mission style with a patio, a tile roof, and adobe walls. And Gloria had told the truth; it was beautiful.

They said, "Stay a while. Try it for a few months and, if you don't like it out here in the desert, you can move on."

I knew that I would like the desert because I was born and raised in Tucson, and I didn't have any other real plans, so I agreed to stay for six months.

They paid me well, they treated me well, and the atmosphere was great.

Los Angeles is less than two hours away by freeway, so many Hollywood stars have second homes in Palm Springs. As soon as Las Casuelas Nuevas opened, a lot of celebrities became regular customers. Frank Sinatra, Red Skelton, Hoagy Carmichel, Dinah Shore, Phil Harris, Alice Faye, Bette Midler—they all came in fairly often. It was great performing for those fabulous stars that I had seen on the screen.

I had a stool with a spotlight on it in one corner of the bar. I played my guitar and sang, and the customers got to know me. When they came in, it was always: "Hi, Lalo. How're you doing?"

And sometimes someone would add, "When you have a break, come on over for a drink." So I got pretty well acquainted with the regulars.

Right from the beginning, I loved the Delgados and the restaurant. I wasn't sure that I wanted to give up my plans to get back to Los Angeles or Tucson but, by then, I had my second family with me: Lidia, her two kids—Jose and Patty—and her mother. At the end of six months I said to the Delgados, "I think that I'd like to stay a little longer. Could you give me a contract for another six months?"

"Sure, Sure."

At the end of the year, I said to Florencio, "You know, Lencho, if it's okay with you, I'd like to stay a while longer. Will you give me a contract for two or three years? Whatever you want."

And he said, "We don't need a contract anymore. You can stay as long as you like."

That was Florencio Delgado, a great man and a good friend. I worked for him and his family for 24 years. I think that may belong in the *Guinness Book of Records* for "The Steadiest Gig by a Solo Musician in One Place."

I have some great memories of those years, but the most wonderful experience of all was when Frank Sinatra kissed me.

My first meeting with Frank Sinatra was kind of a weird beginning to the friendship that we had later on. It was in 1975. I had been playing at Las Casuelas about a month or so. That night I was sitting at my usual place in the bar when he walked into the restaurant. He passed right by me on his way to the main dining room. I blinked and I thought, "Wow! That's Frank Sinatra."

I was thrilled, of course, when I recognized him. Frank was also the child of immigrants and he was just one year older than me. I had been a great admirer of his ever since I first heard him sing back in the forties.

That night he walked by, looking straight ahead, in a kind of arrogant way. He didn't even glance toward me, but I guess he heard me playing because a few minutes later a waiter came over and said, "Lalo, I have a message from Mr. Sinatra. He said, 'Tell your new singer that he is not ever to come to my table unless I send for him.'"

I had no intention of going to his table; I won't go anywhere to sing unless I'm invited. I assumed that he had been bothered by other musicians in other restaurants wanting to perform for him, so I told the waiter, "Tell Mr. Sinatra that Lalo says 'No problem.'"

Later the waiters told me that he was always unfriendly, kind of indifferent, kind of cold. But he only lived a few blocks away so he came in pretty often. Whenever he showed up, a little buzz would go through the room: "There's Sinatra." The other customers would look sideways out of the corner of their eyes, but they never bothered him and they never asked for an autograph. Maybe they were afraid of him. There were those rumors about his connections with the Mafia.

Sometimes he'd come in and sit at the bar with a friend or two and have a drink. After a while, he started calling me by my name. He'd say, "Hi, Lalo! How are you?" And I'd say, "Fine, Mr. Sinatra. How are you?"

He'd always call me Lalo and I'd always call him Mr. Sinatra. First because I had so much respect for him as an entertainer and second because he was a customer.

Then one evening he sent for me to come sing for his party. When I went over, somebody at the table said, "Sing *El Rancho*

Grande!" Somebody else said, "No. Do *Cielito Lindo.*" But Sinatra said, "I'm tired of that old stuff. Lalo, do you know anything by Agustín Lara?"

What a question! Did I know anything by Agustín Lara? I knew everything by Agustín Lara; he had been one of my heroes ever since I was a teenager. I sang *Solamente Una Vez,* which was popular in English as *You Belong to My Heart.* And then he asked for *Veracruz* and *Farolito.* The last one is about the little streetlamp on the corner where two lovers meet. When I turned to leave, he came over and shook my hand. And he left a crisp, brand new $100 bill in it!

He usually came in with friends, and some of them were pretty crazy. I think that he needed someone to make him laugh. Once he was with Jack Benny, who was celebrating his birthday—the thirty-ninth, as usual. One that was really wild was Don Rickles. He would have Frank in stitches all evening.

Another time, Milton Berle was with him. Mr. Berle called me over and asked, "Lalo, do you know *The Mexican Hat Dance?*" So I played it, and he got up and started dancing. And then he unsnapped his belt. He must have put weights in the cuffs of his pants, because they dropped straight down all the way to the floor. He acted like he didn't know anything had happened. There he was in the middle of the restaurant in his white shorts dancing with his pants around his ankles. All the other customers stared, and Frank was practically on the floor laughing.

The years went by and we traded little stories and comments and gradually got to know each other better. He had his eighty-first birthday on December 10, 1996. His wife, Barbara, asked me to play at his surprise party in a private room at the restaurant. We were all waiting there quietly; then we heard the whispers: "That's Sinatra." When he walked in, we all started singing "For he's a jolly good fellow. . . . "

When they lit all the candles on his birthday cake, it looked like a forest fire. I sang *Las Mañanitas,* the Mexican birthday song, and then we all sang *Happy Birthday.* After that he blew out the candles and the party continued.

Later he happened to be talking to a friend about an arm's length away from the corner where I was sitting and playing. The friend turned away for some reason, so I reached out and tapped him on the shoulder and said, "Mr. Sinatra, I didn't know that you and I were both Capricorns."

"Were you a December baby too?

"Yeah. I was born on Christmas Eve."

And he said, "That was my dear Dolly's birthday."

Everyone knew that Dolly was his pet name for his mother. I had heard that several years earlier he had chartered a plane to take her from Palm Springs to Las Vegas to see him perform. The plane crashed in the mountains and she was killed.

Tears started to come down from his eyes and, when I saw that, I got teary-eyed too. He embraced me very gently and very softly kissed me on the cheek. Then he turned away and walked off with his drink in his hand.

That was a beautiful moment that I will always cherish. To have a man of his stature do that, to let me see that human side of him. With that embrace, I felt that he wanted to tell me that he liked me and respected me. I think right then I knew the real Frank Sinatra, a great entertainer and singer, but also a man who knew how to love.

That night I could hardly wait for a break so that I could tell my friends. I ran into the kitchen and I said, "Hey, guess what! Frank Sinatra kissed me."

I thought they would be so impressed, but they all started teasing me. One waiter said, "Frank Sinatra? Did he kiss you on one cheek only? Are you sure that he didn't kiss you on both?" Because you know when a mafioso kisses you on both cheeks, you're gone.

I didn't care. If I had to name the two greatest highlights of my musical career, the first would be the National Medal of Arts and the second would be Frank Sinatra's kiss.

My So-Called Retirement

After I decided to sell my club in Los Angeles and wind down out in the desert, I got discovered all over again. My office is filled with awards that I've received in the past twenty-five years or so. I know that sounds like boasting, but I am very proud of what I have accomplished. In my wildest dreams, I never thought that I'd come this far. It gives me great pleasure to sit back and remember when I got a certain trophy or plaque. I think about what each one means and why someone thought that I deserved it.

When I was a little kid, I played the piano and sang just for fun, just for my own pleasure. I feel that I have been very lucky because, for my entire life, I have been able to earn my living doing what I love to do most. Along the way, I've met a lot of wonderful people and had a lot of fun. Getting any kind of official recognition is just the icing on the cake.

There's also a lot of self-satisfaction in sharing my music with others, watching a whole roomful of people dancing to my songs. You know, people can't live without music. I don't care what kind of music you like, you gotta have music.

And you gotta have laughter. I believe that your state of mind has a lot to do with your health. Music and laughter—that combination has kept me alive and singing for all these many years.

One of the awards hanging on my wall came about because sometime in the early seventies I met Philip Sonnichsen. He first heard my music when he was a teenager working in a record store in El Paso. Phil was the one who brought my zoot suit songs to the attention of Luis Valdez in 1978.

Phil is a musician, a writer, a teacher, and an ethnomusicologist. In 1975, the Smithsonian Institution sponsored the Festival of American Folklife. The theme was "Old Ways in the New World." Phil was asked to put together the Mexican American part of the music program, and he invited me to represent my generation and my kind of music.

The day before the actual festival, musicians from all over America were flown to Washington, D.C., and all of us were housed in a college dormitory. That evening we built a big bonfire outside and we all played music—all different nationalities. We didn't have any kind of program; we just did what we wanted to. We sat around the fire and sang until midnight. Nobody wanted to go to bed. It was such a beautiful feeling of brotherhood—of knowing that even though we were from different ethnic groups and different backgrounds, we were all the same, all a part of one great nation.

The next morning we went over to the Mall in front of the Washington Monument. The park is more than a mile long and it was filled with tents and stages. In each tent, there was a different kind of music: mariachi, jazz, bluegrass, country-western, German polkas, Scottish bagpipes. There was music all day long; it was like heaven. Every time I look at that certificate on my wall, I can hear the music again and I can relive that weekend.

It was in the seventies that some Latino newspapers started to refer to me as "the voice of our people" and an "activist." I'm not sure exactly how that happened, because I've never been militant. I do try to speak for my people—to explain how we feel about a situation and what we think should be done about it.

I have always written about real life, about what I see. Some things are serious and sad, and some are funny like *Felipe el Hippie* or *La Minifalda de Reynalda* (Reynalda's Miniskirt).

Sometimes people get confused and take the funny ones seriously, like *No Way, Jose*. For a while everybody was using that phrase, so I put it into a comical song. Next thing I know they're saying that it's a protest against the treatment of illegal immigrants. I wasn't protesting anything. I wrote that song because I like to write funny songs.

On the other hand, I know that there is a very fine line between comedy and tragedy, and I have written funny songs about very serious matters. I'm not much of a speaker. Since I was a teenager I've communicated through my music and I write about whatever I think is important. I tell the truth, but sometimes I present the problem in a humorous way. We call it "dorando la pildora" (sugarcoating the pill). When I write something like that, I hope that people will listen and laugh, and then maybe they'll think, "There's a lot of truth in what he's saying."

For example, back in the eighties, I noticed the lack of Latinos on prime-time television. I don't mean just in starring roles, but also as extras and in commercials. To me, it seemed to imply that the big TV networks didn't think that we were an important part of their audience. So I wrote a comical protest song, *No Chicanos on TV.* I sang it when I received my second Golden Eagle Award from Nosotros in 1989.

No Chicanos on TV (excerpt)

> I think that I shall never see
> Any Chicanos on TV.
> . . . It seems as though we don't exist,
> And we're not ever even missed
> And yet we buy and buy their wares
> But no Chicanos anywhere.
> . . . Edward James Olmos and Montalban,
> That's all we've got, son-of-a-gun.

They loved it there because Nosotros is the most important organization for our people in motion pictures and television. It was founded by Ricardo Montalban, and the organization works to improve the image of Latinos on the screen. Not long after that ceremony, the Los Angeles *Times* sent a reporter to interview me, and they ran an article with comments from just about every Latino in Hollywood. Almost all of them said that they had suffered from prejudice and discrimination at some time in their careers.

I hate to talk about stereotypes, but sometimes we Mexicans and Mexican Americans are just too passive. We're reluctant to fight for our rights or to try to change the system. When I wrote *Himno Chicano* (Chicano Hymn), some Anglos, and some really conservative Chicanos, commented that I was encouraging troublemakers, and they resented the title because in English it's sometimes called *The Battle Hymn of the Chicanos.* I just wanted to inspire my people to get out and vote, to become a part of the society, a part of the population that makes the laws in this country. I still sing it every year at election time.

Another thing that gets me up onto my soapbox is the importance of education. Mexican Americans often don't place a very high value on education. In Mexico, especially in the rural areas, youngsters may have to drop out to go to work and, even if they go to school, there may not be any jobs available when they graduate. Some of our people carry this same attitude across the border. I know that there are all kinds of reasons for the high dropout rate from high school, but often the parents don't realize how important it is for their children to stick with it and to get a diploma.

It hurts me to see young people making all kinds of excuses for wasting their time and just giving up. Whenever I perform in schools, I tell the students over and over again, "Make something of your life. Decide what you want to do, what you won't ever get tired of, and stick with it. You can be a carpenter, a writer, an attorney, whatever. Just find your dream and follow your dream. All of my life, I wanted to write music and play music. I wanted it so much that, even when times were really hard, I wouldn't ever think of leaving it. I did it; you can do it."

I wrote one of my most important parodies on this subject. I always prefer singing to talking, and I want to get through to parents as well as children. So I took Willie Nelson's *Don't Let Your Babies Grow Up To Be Cowboys* and came up with this:

. . . Mexican mamas, don't let your babies grow up to be busboys,
Don't let them pick lettuce and them other crops.
Let them be doctors or lawyers or cops.
Mexican mamas, don't let your babies grow up to be busboys,
Send them to school que aprendan ingles,
So when they grow up they will be a success.

I'll sing about anything. One of my songs starts like this: "Aqui le vengo a cantar, no de la mosca casera" (I didn't come here to sing about the housefly). I wrote it when the California Department of Agriculture asked me to help get the message out about the problem of the medfly and the fruit fly. I was chosen because I am one of the best-known Chicano entertainers and one that the Mexican Americans trust. They travel back and forth across the border and they often bring mangos and oranges from home. Sometimes they think that the American customs officials are trying to trick them and steal their fruit because they know that the fruit from Mexico is tastier than that in the American supermarkets. So I tell them all about the flies and the tiny larvae that hatch in the fruit and the damage they can do to the fields and orchards. The campaign was so effective that now I've teamed up with Mark to write about the invasion of the fire ants. Since many Latinos work on farms, they are more aware of these pests than the city folks.

One of the most active Chicano organizations, MEChA (Movimiento Estudiantil Chicano/Chicana de Aztlán), found me some way or the other and they kind of adopted me. Their goal is to improve conditions in the barrios and to encourage more of our young people to go to college. For several years, they invited me to perform at colleges and universities all around the country: Yale, Stanford, Harvard, the University of Texas. Once I even got cast as Diego Rivera in a play at Antioch College in Ohio! It was great being on those beautiful campuses, and I've always enjoyed performing for young people.

I've met three presidents, but the first one was a real surprise. In 1980 Lady Bird Johnson and First Lady Rosalyn Carter threw a party to celebrate the fifteenth anniversary of the National Endowment for the Arts. Mrs. Johnson founded that when she was the First Lady, and she stayed involved even after her husband was out of office. All of the people who were invited were artists—painters, composers, basket weavers, saddle makers. Some of the great music legends were there: Bob Dylan, Theodore Bikel, Burl Ives—and me.

I really enjoyed talking to Burl Ives, because I had admired his style and his songs for years. And, of course, I had seen him as Big Daddy in *Cat on a Hot Tin Roof*. He told some neat stories; I just wish that I could remember them.

Mrs. Johnson went up to the bandstand, and we were all standing around getting ready to listen to whatever she had to say when I heard a kind of murmur behind me. I turned around and here came

President Carter wearing that big smile of his.

The room was packed, but we sort of opened up an aisle so that he could walk right down through the middle of the crowd. He stopped to shake a few hands—including mine. Then he went up to the bandstand and made a little speech telling us how wonderful we all were.

That was the same year that the Smithsonian declared me "a national cultural treasure." It's a great honor, but I don't feel I've done anything to deserve it. I've never done anything except to live my life, write my music, and sing my songs.

In a frame on my wall, I have a letter that I received from President George Bush in 1991. It says, "The National Endowment for the Arts Heritage Fellowship is presented to artists who draw from the traditions of their forebears and in turn enrich our American heritage. It is a tribute to your work, and it reflects both the uniqueness of our country and the diversity of our culture . . . may your achievements inspire younger Americans to preserve and to build upon those same traditions."

I went to Washington to receive that award. We had a special program where each recipient performed or talked about himself and his work. As I told you before, that's when I sang the corrido that I wrote about Robert Kennedy. Charles Kuralt was the moderator, and the great blues singer B.B. King was on the same program. One of the things that I love about this business is the kind of people that I get to hang out with. I've been a blues fan ever since those nights that I stood glued to the back window of The Beehive, so spending some time with B.B. King was an incredible thrill for me. And I got to shake hands with the President, too.

Some of my late-blooming rediscovery was because of my son Dan. After Dan graduated from East Los Angeles Junior College, I encouraged him to go on to UCLA or USC to get his degree. I wanted him to be a lawyer or a doctor, but he had it in his head that he wanted to go to New York City to act in musical comedies.

I really tried to get him to change his mind because show business is so insecure. Dan could sing and dance, but I know many, many good entertainers and writers who never got the breaks that they needed. It's a matter of luck. You have to be in the right place at the right time and catch the attention of the right people.

Dan was just as stubborn as he had been as a baby. He said, "I want to go now, Dad. If I finish college first, I'll be too old. Just let me go; if I can't make it in New York, I'll come back and go on to school."

He finally wore me down and I agreed, so he went. He got some good parts on Broadway and he went on tours with several big musical productions. He even played the White House for President Nixon. I'm sorry to say that I never got to see him perform. I was on the road much of the time, and so was he.

Twenty years later, in 1982, he came back to the West Coast. He got into television as a producer and director. He has produced shows for PBS, NBC, Univision, Telemundo, Showtime, and HBO, so he's done okay. Maybe better than "okay," but I don't want it to sound like I'm bragging about my kid.

He has all kinds of connections in Hollywood—in theater, film, and television. I'm sure that, directly or indirectly, many of my awards happened because of Dan. People who might have forgotten all about me met him or saw his name somewhere and they thought of me again.

One award on my shelf, The Feathered Serpent, brings back so many memories. I received it when Luis Valdez' Teatro Campesino celebrated its twenty-fifth anniversary in 1990. Paul Rodriguez was the host that night. The plaque on the statue says that they honor me for my music, my humor, and my creativity, but also because I have been "an inspirational maestro who has dedicated his life to the definition and enrichment of the Chicano experience in America."

The ceremony was a reminder to all of us who had been there of the struggles of the workers in the fields, of Cesar Chavez, Dolores Huerta, and Robert Kennedy. And we were also reminded how the dedicated performers in the Teatro Campesino helped keep up the morale of the workers as the strikes went on and on.

In 1992, I was voted into the Tejano Music Hall of Fame in San Antonio. That plaque says, "For his many contributions to the world of Latino music." I've never thought of myself as a Tejano, but I wrote a lot of Texas-style, norteño music. Several of my songs, like *El Tex Mex*, *El Güiri-güiri* (The Chatterbox), and *La Minifalda de Reynalda*, were big hits in Texas.

That award gave me the opportunity to visit San Antonio again. It is one of the most beautiful cities in America. It's very green with lots of trees and parks. A river runs right through the center of the city, with great restaurants and clubs on both sides. In the evening, you can take a boat on the river and just float along through the music from mariachi to jazz to rock and roll to flamenco.

The people are very cordial and friendly, and there are a lot of Mexican tourists around. In fact, I bet that General Santa Ana would have liked one sign that I saw there. It said, "Bienvenidos a nuestros visitantes de México" (Welcome to our visitors from Mexico). It was at the entrance to a big shopping mall right next to the Alamo.

There were some other special events in 1992. To commemorate my sixty years in music, the City of Palm Springs gave me my own "Golden Palm Star" on the Walk of Stars. You can see it at 368 North Palm Canyon Drive, right in front of the original Las Casuelas Restaurant, where the Delgados got their start when they came to Palm Springs in 1958.

My old friend and fellow Arizonan Lencho Delgado had died a few months before. At the dedication ceremony, I said, "I selected this spot for my star because I want it to be a tribute to Mr. Florencio Delgado, who was my boss for many years and who was also a dear, dear friend."

On the same day that the star was dedicated, I got another very special honor. The College of the Desert wanted to raise some money to set up a scholarship in my name and, a couple of months earlier, they had called Dan up for advice or something. I think that they got more than they bargained for.

Dan never does anything in a small or simple way, and he decided to produce an extravaganza to celebrate my life and my music. He called it "Lalo and Amigos."

The 1,200 seats of the McCallum Theater of the Performing Arts were filled that night. Just about every Chicano in Hollywood was there, plus some others: Eddie Olmos, Paul Rodriguez, Carmen Moreno, Cheech Marin, Little Joe Hernandez, Don Tosti, David Valdez, Gloria

Becker, and Richard Montoya, Ric Salinas, and Herbert Singuenza of the comedy team Culture Clash showed up. Jose Hernandez and his Mariachi Sol de Mexico came over from Los Angeles, and Mariachi Campanas de America came from San Antonio. My old friend Ricardo Montalban could not make it because he was in New York City, but he sent me a congratulatory letter that I still treasure.

The whole program was all my music except for one song that wasn't by me, but it was about me. Mark wrote it as a tribute, and it was beautiful.

Dan put me in the best seat in the house—a box seat up on the side. During the evening, those celebrities came out onto the stage one by one. Then he or she would look up and say something nice about me, and I'd answer back.

Cesar Chavez was there that night. Before the show, he told Dan that he didn't know what to say, and Dan told him, "Just say what you feel, what's in your heart."

So Cesar talked about how he first heard my songs on the radio when he was a boy working in the fields with his parents. There were only about fifteen minutes of Spanish programming each day. When it came on, everybody would stop work and gather round to listen. He said, "With his music, Lalo has chronicled the life of the Hispanic in this country better than anyone else has done."

When he spoke, I had tears in my eyes because he was such a special person. I've always thought that there should be a statue of Cesar in Tijuana or Mexico City. He was an American, born in Yuma, but many of those workers that he struggled for were from Mexico.

All that evening, I felt like I had died and gone to heaven. I just couldn't believe that so many of my friends had come all the way out to the desert to take part in the show. It was incredible; I have accomplished a lot in my life, but to get recognition like that from my fellow artists was a wonderful, wonderful feeling.

At the end of the program, I went down onto the stage to get the applause and the accolades and the vivas from the audience.

Another friend who was there that night had also heard me on a radio out in the fields. Paul Rodriguez says that when he was a boy up near Bakersfield, his family used to listen to my music while they were out picking apricots or tomatoes or whatever. His parents liked the romantic songs and he loved the funny ones.

In the early nineties, Dan was the producer of Paul's TV show, and I was a guest on it a couple of times. Then the big shots at the network decided that they wanted more comedy. To make it work, Paul needed a cohort—a pal, a straight man. Dan says that Paul looked at him and said, "Your dad would be perfect."

I became Paul's sidekick—like Ed McMahon for Johnny Carson. We had a lot of fun on that show. Once Paul interviewed a three-month-old baby. And one time he and I dressed in drag to play a couple of cleaning ladies called Las Comadres. That term is kind of hard to define because it means a woman friend, an old lady, a godmother, a gossip . . . anyway, you get the idea.

Another time, Paul decided that he wanted to sing my romantic ballad *Nunca Jamás*. That was pretty funny, but I still am not sure whether he was clowning on purpose or he really is the world's worst singer. I think that it was that same show when our special guest was my little dog, Osito. Osito played the piano while his mother sang. She's not a very good singer, even for a dog, but she's a little better than Paul.

For me, one of our most memorable guests was the Mexican violinist Olga Breeskin. She has a great figure and she came on wearing a tight dress that really showed it off well. She leaned over to straighten my tie, and immediately my glasses got all steamed up.

I've always been a boxing fan, so another guest that I'll never forget was a very young Oscar de la Hoya. He seemed so shy and modest that it was hard to believe that he had won an Olympic gold medal just a few months before.

We had the great composer, guitarist, and vocalist Jose Feliciano. He has a tremendous sense of humor. He's constantly telling jokes; every time there was a moment's break, he'd go into a story.

I had met him twenty years earlier when we were both guests on some TV show. When I arrived at the studio, he was backstage in his dressing room. I knew his music, but I didn't know if he knew anything about me.

The stage manager took me back and yelled, "Jose, do you know Lalo Guerrero? He's going to perform with you."

Jose yelled back, "Do I know Lalo Guerrero? Are you kidding?" And he started to sing *¡Ay! Lucho.* That was a funny song that I wrote as a tribute to the Chilean singer Lucho Gatica. Lucho put a lot of emotion into his voice, almost sobbing at times. In my song, I exaggerated that emotion even more. And Jose embellished my delivery. It was really funny. He told me later that there was a radio station in New York City that was always playing my songs.

Jose was born in Puerto Rico. He was five years old when the family moved to New York City. He has been blind since birth, but he told me that when he was a kid he could roam all over New York by himself just by using his senses of hearing and smell. When he started traveling away from his home town, he got a guide dog, and it was there in his dressing room.

For the show, Jose sat on his stool and his dog lay down at his feet. After he sang *Sin Ti* (Without You), the camera moved across to me and I sang *Nunca Jamás.* Then I walked over to join him and we did a duet, *Tú Solo Tú* (You, Only You).

When we finished the song, everybody applauded and Jose said, "We did pretty good, Lalo."

I said, "Yeah, Jose. We did great," and I stretched my hand out to him. He was looking straight forward toward the audience and he didn't notice my hand. So I said, again, "Thank you, Jose," and held out my hand.

We had played and sung so beautifully a few minutes before that I actually forgot that the man was blind. In my defense, I have to say that he wasn't wearing dark glasses, but there was that guide dog lying right on the floor beside him. The cameraman kept pointing at my hand; the stage hands were cracking up. Even the audience was starting to laugh.

I finally caught on, and for the third time, I said, "Thank you, Jose." Then I took his hand and shook it. I was so embarrassed; I felt like a dodo, like a fool. When I think back to it, it was a compliment to Jose. To me, the most important thing about the man is his music, not his blindness.

A lot of what Paul and I did on the show was just for fun, but we had some serious thoughts wrapped up in the humor. I remember that

Sinbad, the black comedian, was a guest at a time when there had been some serious problems between the black gangs and the Mexican gangs in Los Angeles. He made a kind of bitter joke that he felt right at home on Paul's show because it seemed to him that young blacks and young Chicanos had a lot in common. They were both spending their energy fighting for the bottom spot on the totem pole.

The original concept was that the program would be in Spanish except when we had guests who didn't speak Spanish. However, a lot of us who grew up in this country kind of slide back and forth between the two languages. For a running joke, Paul had a big cue card made saying "Mas español" (More Spanish).

One day, Paul decided that he wanted me to sing one of my most popular parodies, *There's No Tortillas*. It's a subject that is very dear to my heart and is set to the tune of *O Sole Mio*.

There's No Tortillas

I love tortillas, and I love them dearly,
You'll never know just how sincerely,
I love the corn ones y también de harina,
But when my wife calls out from la cocina,
"There's no tortillas, there's only bread,"
There's no tortillas, and I feel so sad.
My grief I cannot hide, there's no tortillas for my refrieds.
Without tortillas, there'd be no burritos,
Without the corn ones, there'd be no Doritos.
I love to hold them—tenderly enfold them.
Oh how I dread to eat with bread, believe me.
Ya no hay tortillas, ya solo hay pan,
Ya no hay tortillas, son-of-a-gun!
My grief I cannot hide,
There's no tortillas for my refrieds.

When Paul asked me to sing it on the show, I said, "Okay. But you know it's mostly in English."

He said, "Have a Spanish version by tonight." And I did.

One of our guests was Cheech Marin. He grew up in Los Angeles, so his Spanish, like Paul's, includes a lot of "Spanglish." Cheech is such a funny guy; sometimes he uses the wrong word or the wrong pronunciation and you don't know if he has done it on purpose or not.

That day he said something that I totally agree with: that we should be interested in preserving our culture and not worry so much about the language. Cheech said that he could speak English and still feel muy Latino.

The year 1996 was big for me. I was approaching my eightieth birthday, so I decided that it was really time to retire. The Delgados gave me a nice sendoff from Las Casuelas Nuevas and I settled back to relax. But somehow, as soon as I left my job at the restaurant, the word spread that I was available and people started calling me for all kinds of events. Now I play at schools, because I love performing for kids and they like my comic songs. And I perform for senior citizens in retirement homes. We remember the old times together, and I sing the songs from the thirties and the forties when I was in my prime and so were they. I perform for charities like the Red Cross or the Braille Institute, or a fund raiser for a friend who's down on his or her luck. I'm glad that I now have the time to do some of these things; it's very gratifying for me.

Also in 1996, I got to be a calendar boy. That year the theme for the Miller Brewing Company calendar was "Hispanic Music Greats." According to the certificate on my wall, the honorees were chosen "not only for their musical contributions but also for their generosity with their time and talents and sense of humanity."

As you might guess, there were twelve of us. Miller flew us to New York and gave us a great party with lots of beer. I had had a beer or two when I thought that I saw the great Cuban singer Celia Cruz across the room. I love her music, so I yelled out her trademark: "¡Azucar!" (sugar). Only I got confused and said "sabor" (taste) instead.

I went over to embrace her and she looked at me kind of funny and said, "¿Sabor?" I realized that I was hugging some woman that I didn't know.

She seemed like a real nice lady, and I didn't want her to know that I had thought that she was someone else, so I said, "Hi. I'm Lalo Guerrero."

She said, "I know. I saw you on TV with President Clinton."

A few minutes later she was introduced as the Puerto Rican singer Ruth Fernandez.

There was another Puerto Rican at the party, Tito Puente. He was easy to recognize with all that white hair. In L.A., we used to say that he and Barbara Bush went to the same hairdresser.

I first met Tito in San Francisco sometime in the sixties. I was in town with my band and we had played the night before at the Casanova Ballroom. Tito's orchestra and another one were booked into the Sailors' Union of Pacific Hall. They were scheduled to have a "battle of the bands." The other group got involved in an accident over in Oakland, and the promoter managed to get in touch with me.

At first I didn't want to go. My band against Tito's? We were really good but compared with what he had, there just was no comparison. He had fourteen musicians and they were all great. I just had seven, because that was all that would fit into my old van.

Finally they talked me into it. I'd never even met the guy, and there I was competing with him. Of course, it really was no competition, but Tito acted so friendly to us that I didn't mind. He made us feel that we were doing them a favor, and I guess we were. The audience was expecting two bands; they just weren't expecting us.

It turned out to be a good show. Our styles were very different. Tito was New York–Puerto Rican and they played mambo, salsa, Caribbean type rhythms; we were more into romantic ballads and swing. Nobody complained or asked for his money back, so I guess we did okay.

The next day after we played with Tito, I loaded my band and our instruments into the van and started for home. We didn't get far. I headed straight up Powell Street. And that is pretty much straight up. Just as I got to the signal at the top of the hill, it turned red. I stopped, and right then my van died.

There was a whole string of cars behind us, the cable car was coming, and I couldn't get the van started. The drivers were honking and yelling; the conductor was ringing his bell.

I couldn't do anything until finally a cop came and made them give me some space. I let the van roll back until I had the hind wheels up against the curb. The other cars could go around us, but we were stuck until AAA sent out somebody to give me a boost. I said to the guys, "That's it. I think I'm going to dump this car in the bay."

And right then I thought of Tony Bennett and I wrote *I Left My Car In San Francisco*. Another funny song about a very serious subject.

After that, my path crossed Tito's now and then at a fiesta or a big party like the Miller party. He was always friendly and funny; we laughed a lot together.

I didn't get a trophy of any kind from Miller, but I did get a dozen calendars and a nice jacket that actually fit.

The National Medal of Arts and Other Honors

The most important award of my life came in 1996. And that brings us back to where we started this story.

In April, I got a phone call. The lady told me that she was calling from Washington, D.C., and she asked me, "Can you keep a secret?"

Of course, I said yes. Then when I found out what it was all about, I wanted to jump up and down and shout it from the rooftop. After that I got the official letter from the White House saying that I had been chosen to be one of the twelve recipients of the 1996 National Medal of Arts.

That medal was established in 1985. It had already been awarded to people like Bob Hope, Helen Hayes, Harry Belafonte, Gene Kelley, Cab Calloway, and Ella Fitzgerald, and now my name is on that list.

The presentation ceremony was on January 9, 1997, at the Andrew Mellon Auditorium, not far from the White House. There were twelve of us and we represented different facets of the arts. Robert Redford was one of the recipients; he's even better looking in person than he is on the screen. Edward Albee, the great playwright, was there, and children's author Maurice Sendak, and Stephen Sondheim, who wrote those fabulous lyrics for *West Side Story*. There were people from the opera, the ballet, and the theater.

Lionel Hampton was sitting right next to me. In spite of the fact that just a day or two before he had had a fire in his home that destroyed many things that were very dear to him, he didn't seem depressed. I was kind of babysitting him. He was almost ninety years old, and he'd doze off from time to time while the president was talking, so I'd nudge him in the ribs with my elbow. He'd look up at me and give me that beautiful smile of his.

It was an incredible feeling to be there with all those famous people. I guess my sons thought so, too, because they were in the audience and later Dan told me, "I looked up to that stage and I said to Mark, 'Migawd, he's the only one I never heard of!'"

The President introduced each recipient and told what he had accomplished and why he or she was deserving of this honor. Then he and Mrs. Clinton would walk over to that person, who would stand up. Mrs. Clinton would put the medal around his neck and they'd take a photograph.

When it was my turn, he said the honor was "for a distinguished music career that spans over sixty years, two cultures, and a wealth of different musical styles. With humor, passion, and profound insight, he has entertained and enlightened generations of audiences, giving powerful voice to the joys and sorrows of the Mexican American experience."

Actually, I don't remember all of that because I was busy trying to keep Lionel from falling off his chair. I heard the speech later on videotape.

After Mrs. Clinton gave me my medal, it looked like she was going to walk away. Well, I wanted that picture bad; they weren't going to get away from me! I reached out and kind of pulled her toward me, right up against my ribs, and I said, "You are going to take a picture with me, aren't you?"

She started laughing and so did the President. That's when the President made his "salsa" remark. The audience laughed, and that was the only laugh the whole morning.

Later, in an interview for NBC, somebody asked me, "When you were sitting there after you got your medal, you looked so solemn. What were you thinking about?"

Immediately I remembered what had been going through my head. "What am I doing here? How did I get here?"

That's the first time in my life that I really felt that I was an American! I knew that I was an American because I was born in this country, but I never felt like an American. I felt like a Mexican who happened to be born in the United States of America. Sitting on that stage in that beautiful hall with the gold medal around my neck, I thought—I finally made it; I really am an American. And that was an incredibly beautiful feeling.

Later we returned to our hotel to get all dressed up in our tuxedos for dinner in the White House dining room. President and Mrs. Clinton were there, as well as the medal recipients and their guests. We were split up so Dan, Mark, and I were at three different tables. I know that made my sons a little nervous. They love me and they look after me, but they're always afraid that I'm going to do something that I shouldn't.

I've forgotten what we had for dinner, but we didn't have enchiladas or tacos—not even any nachos. Whatever it was, it was delicious. All they served to drink was champagne. I prefer margaritas but, just to be polite, whenever the waiter came by with a tray, I'd take a glass.

One of the girls at my table saw Robert Redford coming across the room and she said, "Oooh—I'd love to talk to him."

So when he walked by our table, I stood up and I said, "Mr. Redford, can I speak to you for a minute?"

"Oh, certainly."

I introduced myself and he said, "I saw you at the ceremony today. It's a pleasure to meet you, sir."

I said, "I'm happy to meet you, too, but actually I stopped you because this young lady is a fan of yours and she's dying to speak to you."

He said, "Why, it's my privilege." He talked to her for a few minutes, and she just melted.

After dinner the marine band played. They looked great in their red coats and blue pants. They played the wonderful songs of the forties and fifties, and they sounded just like the old Glenn Miller band.

I danced with this girl and that girl. One of them was Tish Hinojosa, the fabulous Tejano singer. Talking to her brought back the memory of the night a year or two before when we both sang in a concert at the Temple of Music and Art in Tucson.

When I was young, the Temple was where they presented all the great classical orchestras and opera singers from all over the world. It was uptown, and usually I couldn't afford a ticket. I don't remember how it happened, but when I was about fifteen, I got to go there to hear the great Mexican tenor José Mojica. I wasn't performing yet, but I had the bug already; I was born with the bug.

It seemed like a huge theater and I was way up in the balcony. From there, José looked to be about eight inches tall, but that beautiful voice of his filled up the whole hall. That evening, I sat there listening so hard that I could hardly breathe.

All those many years later, I became an artist worthy of performing in the Temple. I was thrilled to the bone to be on that stage. I looked up at the highest balcony and I thought, "I was sitting way up there and José Mojica was here. Now I'm down on the stage and maybe there's some youngster up there watching who'll be standing here someday."

Back at the White House, Bill and Hillary were out there dancing with the rest of us. Every time a waiter came by with a tray, I'd point and he'd hand me a glass. I wasn't drunk, but I was feeling no pain and having a great time.

I always get real friendly when I've had a few drinks, and as a musician, it bothered me that everybody just seemed to take the band for granted. Between songs, I went over and said to the bandleader, "I have to tell you what a great band this is. You're really something."

He smiled at me and said, "Thank you, sir."

The boys had been keeping an eye on me, and maybe I was a little unsteady on my feet by then, because Dan came up to me and asked, "What were you doing over there with the band?"

"I was just telling them how much I'm enjoying their music. That's all."

A few minutes later Mark came over to check up on me. I saw Mrs. Clinton standing by herself and I decided to pull his leg a little, so I said, "That's a shame. Nobody is dancing with Hillary. I'm going to go right over there and ask her."

He grabbed hold of my arm and said, "No, you're not!"

"Yes, I am. She's just standing there. It's not right."

He said, "This is the last time that I am ever coming to the White House with you." Mark says he doesn't remember saying that, but I remember it . . . I think. I never did get to dance with Hillary.

All evening, I know that my sons were shaking in their boots for fear I'd do something I shouldn't. But I was celebrating. I felt like I was really somebody! From morning to night, that was one of the happiest days of my life. The high point for me came toward midnight, when I looked over and saw that the President and the First Lady were about an arm's length away from me, as big as life. I couldn't hold it in any longer, I had to go over to them.

I said, "Mr. President, I want you to know that I'll treasure this medal for the rest of my life and I'll always be grateful to you and Mrs. Clinton."

He shook my hand and then he put his arm around my shoulder and gave me a little hug. She smiled and said, "You're very welcome, Mr. Guerrero."

They danced away. Two more songs and it was all over; they left us and went upstairs. It was quite a night!

It was partly because of the publicity around the Medal of Arts and partly because of some connections of Dan that I got to go to Paris. There was a Latina from L.A. living in Paris. This woman, Roxanne Frias, was a TV and radio producer, and she had the idea of introducing the Parisians to Chicano music.

The government of France brings in musical groups from different countries to perform at La Cité de la Musique. They were already planning a three-day American Music Festival with black, cajun, and country-western groups, so Roxanne explained to the director that Chicano music is also American music and she thought that we would sort of round out the program.

He agreed with her, so she started to work on the project. She knew about me and my music because she grew up in Los Angeles. Somehow she tracked down Dan, and they worked together for almost a year to make it happen.

I had never been to Europe, so I was very excited and a little bit nervous about being in a place where I didn't speak the language and didn't know the customs. It turned out that I traveled with quite an entourage. Mark went along to act as the musical director and to back me up with his guitar. Roxanne had also asked him to perform a couple of his own songs. We took one more musician, Lorenzo Martinez, who plays the guitarron, a Mexican bass guitar. Dan came along to coordinate whatever needed coordinating. And the *Los*

Angeles Times decided to send a reporter to document the whole trip.

Flaco Jimenez and his band were on the same program with us. I had met Flaco, but I didn't know him very well. I knew his music, of course. Flaco's music has a Texas country feeling and ours has more of a California urban feeling. Roxanne knows that these are two very different styles, and that's why she invited both of us.

As soon as we got to Paris we had a radio interview, and then we went out sightseeing. The one place that I really wanted to see was the Cathedral of Notre Dame, so that was our first stop. On the outside, it was so beautiful, and I'd seen so many pictures of it that it was hard to believe I was looking at the real thing. As soon as we stepped through the door, the boys took off in all different directions. I just sat down on the closest pew and looked around trying to convince myself that I wasn't dreaming, that I was really there.

Then I spotted a huge painting of the Virgin of Guadalupe, the patron saint of Mexico. You always see her in Mexico and in the United States where there are a lot of Mexicans, but I couldn't imagine what she was doing in Paris. I went over and I knelt down in front of the painting to say a little prayer. At the bottom of the frame, I saw a plaque that said, "Donated to the Cathedral of Notre Dame by the Mexican Community of Paris."

"Wow!" I thought. "There's Mexicans in Paris." So I rounded up the guys and said, "Come over here. You gotta see this."

They were as surprised as I had been. "Mexicans in Paris! We didn't expect to find even one, and there's a whole colony of them."

That evening, about sixteen of us, our group and Flaco's, went out in front of the hotel and asked a cabby if he knew where to find the Mexican part of town. He said, "Oui, Monsieur."

We climbed into three cabs and off we went! The first place we hit was ¡Ay, Caramba! It was filled with piñatas and Mexican flags. A five-piece mariachi was playing *Cielito Lindo*. Everybody was eating nachos and tacos, and there were huge pitchers of margaritas; I felt like I was back in East L.A.

It didn't take them long to figure out that we were from out of town. Someone came up and said, "You're not the musicians that are going to be at La Cité de la Musique?"

I said, "Yes, we are."

The place went crazy. "Who's Lalo Guerrero?" "Is Flaco Jimenez here?" They sent us some drinks and they got me up to sing with the mariachi and they got Flaco to play the accordion. What a party!

After that, we checked out a place called El Tex Mex. When Flaco walked in, they thought it was the Second Coming! We got home about two in the morning and we had to be at rehearsal the next day at 1:00. We had a short night but it was worth it; we had a blast.

The next day on our way to rehearsal, we went to the Louvre. We were in too much of a hurry to look up the Mona Lisa, but we did have lunch there. We got to see the Eiffel Tower and the Arch of Triumph. From my hotel window, I could see the Seine; I really wanted to take a cruise on the river, but we never had time.

The concert was the following night. La Cité is one of the most important and most beautiful concert halls in Paris. They bring in the best musicians from all around the world. The house was packed. Maybe a quarter of the audience was Latino, although that word usually means just people from Latin America. I guess that I should call this group "Hispanic." Besides all the Mexicans, South Americans, and Central Americans, we also had a lot of Spaniards.

In the introduction, Roxanne Frias defined the word "Chicano" to the audience as "an American of Mexican heritage." It was kind of strange to think that in America we are sometimes treated like foreigners, but to the French we were Americans playing American music.

My biggest worry about performing in France was the language. Sometimes you don't have to understand the words to enjoy music, but our lyrics, mine and Mark's, tell a story and they are all in Spanish and English. Dan was worried about that, too, so he sent Roxanne some notes about each song and she translated those into French. They printed programs in Spanish and English on one side and in French on the other side.

The audience loved us. They were dancing in the aisles when I played *Chicas Patas Boogie*. It swings in any language. Mark's *Oh, Maria* was a hit because it's a polka and polkas are universal. And he sang *On the Boulevard*. Most of them probably didn't know much about Whittier Boulevard in East Los Angeles, but at least they could understand the word "boulevard" because it's French. They laughed at my parodies and they sat very, very still when I sang *Barrio Viejo*.

Then they gave us a standing ovation. I was very gratified that they appreciated the music that means so much to me. The translation in the program helped, but I think that it was the feeling of the music, the emotion, that really made the connection. After the show, we were surrounded by people who came over to embrace us and to thank us for the wonderful evening. I felt like I should be thanking all of them; it was a tremendous experience.

One spinoff from these events was that Mark and I were invited to perform at the beautiful Getty Museum in Los Angeles. Their theater is very classy—small and intimate.

For the Getty, Mark decided to recreate the program that we had done in Paris. He put together a six-piece band that we called The Second Generation Band because most of the musicians were second-generation Chicanos about Mark's age. I had performed by myself for so many years that I had almost forgotten how much fun it is to work with a band.

We had two performances that were sold out weeks in advance. In fact, we were such a success that we were invited to perform at colleges and universities all over Southern California and, for a while, I was busier than I had been before I retired.

On one shelf back in my office, I have an ALMA that I received in 1998. ALMA stands for American Latino Media Arts; the award was established by the National Council of La Raza, the largest Hispanic civil rights organization in the country. Besides recognizing achievements in the arts, they also try to encourage positive and accurate portrayals of Latinos in film and television. "Alma" in Spanish means "soul" or "spirit," and this award is like a Latino Oscar.

The emcee that night was Jimmy Smits, and I was thrilled to meet him in person because he is such a fine actor.

They had asked me to perform Barrio Viejo at the ceremony. The lyrics are in Spanish but, just a day or two before the event, someone decided that I should do the song in English because the ceremony was going to be broadcast nationally on ABC. I was actually putting the finishing touches on the lyrics while I was waiting backstage. I was a little nervous and I would probably have been even more nervous if I had known that I was going to get an award that night!

In 1998, I received the Mexican Cultural Institute Lifetime Achievement Award. The presentation was in Los Angeles by the Mexican Consul, José Angel Pescador, who was representing President Ernesto Zedillo that night. The award is special because Mexico is a very special place to me. I love the country and the people, and it was my parents' homeland. I think that I was the first American composer to have so many of my songs played by bands and mariachis there. *Canción Mexicana, Nunca Jamás, La Minifalda de Reynalda* . . . most people probably don't even know that those songs were written by a pocho.

Mexico has given us so much beautiful music that I've always wanted to give something back. For that reason, it has bothered me that I have been so unappreciated in Mexico as a performer. I really enjoy contemplating that award. I'm not even sure why they finally decided to recognize me, but I am very happy that they did. I wish that my mother could have been in the audience that night.

Another award that I like to look at was from the Bilingual Foundation for the Arts. A few years ago, I wrote some music for a play they staged in Los Angeles. It was adapted from a Mexican novel about the Revolution, *Los de Abajo* (The Underdogs). In 1999, they presented me with their lifetime achievement award. It's in the shape of an angel and she, or maybe he, is standing up on the shelf watching over me.

Maybe an angel had something to do with an honor I received that was not for anything that I have done; it was like winning the lottery. My picture was chosen to go on the big memorial wall in Tucson.

It wasn't put there because of who I am. The artist, Stephen Farley, said that he designed that wall to give recognition to the pioneers, the ordinary people who helped make the city what it is today. On it he used photographs taken by street photographers in downtown Tucson in the thirties and forties. The photos were not of famous people—just people who had lived and shopped there. Many of them were Mexican Americans because our barrio was right there.

One afternoon, in 1935, I think, Greg Escalante and I were walking down the street together when a photographer snapped our picture. He gave us a ticket, and later Greg and I went in and we each bought one.

Dr. James Griffith, who was the director of the Southwest Folklore Center over at the University of Arizona, had a copy of the photograph in his archives. Steve found it there.

He didn't know me from Adam and, even if he had known me now, he couldn't have recognized me in that photograph because I was only 19 or so. I was six foot one and weighed about 135 pounds.

When he picked it out, Jim Griffith said, "Don't you know who that is? That's Lalo Guerrero. He's a famous songwriter and he just got an award from the president."

"Really? This kid?"

Later, when I met Steve, I said. "Man, I'm sure happy to be up there, but how in the heck did you ever pick me?"

"It was your outfit. I saw those white shoes and the draped pants with the little suspenders. And you young guys were walking along real cool. I knew I had to have that one."

The odds must have been 10,000 to one that that picture ended up in the archives and that Steve found it. My whole career has been that way.

I'm glad that my picture is on that wall. It lets young people who pass by know that a boy from a poor Mexican American family in the old barrio could accomplish what I did as a musician and a composer. I got all those awards, I met three presidents, and I have had a wonderful, wonderful life. If I did it, that means that any young person can do it if he has a dream and if he'll stick with it.

Here in my own valley, I have been honored many times. Not long ago, they named a street for me in Cathedral City. That's the highest honor any city can give you. It's an important street: City Hall stands on Avenida Lalo Guerrero, so my name is on all the official stationery. And I'm in good company in that neighborhood, just a few blocks from streets named for Frank Sinatra, Bob Hope, Dinah Shore, and Ginger Rogers.

In Los Angeles, in Arroyo Seco Park, they are building a music school that will be named for me. I love music and I love children. All kids are full of creativity just trying to get out; it's so sad when they die with their music still locked up inside them. What a wonderful memorial that will be! Better than all the medals and statues put together.

Dan and I made a trip to Tucson together recently and went to see my old neighborhood. In my song I wrote that it was dead and buried, but it's being resurrected and it's marvelous to see it coming back to life. Maybe I'll have to write a new ending for *Barrio Viejo*.

Encore: Back in the seventies, Mark enrolled in Chicano Studies at Cal State L.A. Some people think that the word "Chicano" was invented at that time, but actually it was used in Sonora even before the Revolution. When I was young, I often heard my mother say, very proudly, "Soy pura chicana, pura chicanita" (I am pure Chicana). Sometimes Mark would talk to me about what he was learning about Mexican history and culture. It reminded me of how proud my parents were to be Mexican and how they taught me to feel that same pride in my heritage. So I would like to leave one last song with you: *El Chicano*.

El Chicano

Yo soy chicano señores,	Gentlemen, I am a Mexican American,
nací al lado americano.	I was born on the American side of the border.
Para México soy pocho,	To Mexicans, I am a "pocho,"
no me aceptan mis hermanos.	My brothers do not accept me.
Los güeros me discriminan,	The whites discriminate against me
como si fuera extranjero,	As if I were a foreigner
a pesar de que esta tierra	In spite of the fact that this land
fue de México primero.	Used to belong to Mexico.
Este pais es mi tierra,	This country is my country,
México es la de mis padres,	Mexico is that of my parents.
pero la sangre que llevo	And the blood that flows in my veins
es la de Benito Juarez.	Is that of Benito Juarez.
Yo soy purito chicano	I am pure Chicano
de raza que no se raja.	Of a race that never gives up.
Mi madre nació en Sonora,	My mother was born in Sonora;

mi padre fue de la Baja.

Mis padres me inculcaron,

su cultura desde chavo.

No es mi culpa haber nacido

a otro lado del Bravo.

Me da mucho sentimiento
que en México no me quieran,
porque a México lo quiero,
como si fuera mi tierra.
Como Emiliano Zapata
y tambien Francisco Villa,
yo soy revolucionario
en este moderno día.
Unidos a César Chávez,
los México Americanos,
luchamos por la justicia,
para todo los Mexicanos.
Por mi educación bilingue,

hablo chicano y gabacho.

Y se despide este pocho

hasta luego, ¡y ahi lo watcho!

My father was from Baja
California.
From the time that I was a
child,
My parents taught me the
culture of their homeland.
It was not my fault that I was
born
On the other side of the Rio
Grande.
It hurts me very much
That I am not liked in Mexico
Because I love Mexico
As if it were my own country.
Like Emiliano Zapata
And also Francisco Villa,
I am a kind of revolutionary
In this modern era.
United with Cesar Chavez,
We Mexican Americans
Struggle for justice
For all Mexicans.
Because of my bilingual
education,
I speak both Spanish and
English,
And so this pocho bids you
farewell
For now, but I'll see you
later!

Afterword by MANUEL PEÑA

The Mexicans of the Southwest are historically among the most musically creative regional groups in the Americas. For example, in the development of the influential narrative ballad known as corrido, the Mexican Americans were in the forefront, composing their share of corridos even before they became popular in Mexico itself. Hispanics of the Southwest also forged a culturally rich wind ensemble that was a hybridized version of the American swing band and the urban Mexican orquesta. And the Texas-Mexicans were principally responsible for the creation of the epochal conjunto, the accordion-based ensemble known more generally as norteño.

The people of the Southwest were involved in yet more musical innovation. Existing on the conflict-ridden cultural border that divides North and Latin America, they seemed destined to forge ever-new forms, and they were active in synthesizing musically the many crosscultural influences that historically have swept through the Southwest. They thus crafted their own regional varieties of the myriad styles and genres they encountered, whether these be of American or Latin American origin. For example, Mexican American artists created their own conjunto/country-western hybrid, they invented Latin rock, and they forged intricate syntheses of American swing-jazz and Afro-Hispanic styles known generally as tropical (rumba, cumbia, mambo—what later morphed into salsa). Always, of course, whether it be the cumbia or swing-jazz, the Mexican Americans injected their own bicultural spin on the genres they adopted.

The collective creativity of the Mexican Americans understandably has been made possible by the work and talent of many individual creators. However, prior to the advent of the mass media in the early part of the twentieth century, these individuals tended to remain submerged in the anonymity of a collective folk tradition. The mass media revolutionized the notion of tradition, and the whole process of music-making was irrevocably changed. Beginning in the mid-twenties, when the large American recording labels (RCA Victor, Columbia, Decca, Vocalion, Brunswick) arrived in the Southwest, individual names began to surface and attain renown. Most important, these individuals became the recognized initiators of innovation and change. Individual fame replaced collective anonymity.

At that time, the most popular of the various traditions was the vocal, both in the form of solo and duet singing, and it was this music that the major labels exploited most extensively. Thus, some of the best known and enduring names from that era were vocalists. In Texas we hear of singers such as Los Trovadores Regionales, Los Hermanos Chavarría, Eva Garza, and one of the most recognized musical names in the Southwest, Lydia Mendoza, whose historical renown has but one parallel in the region—that of Lalo Guerrero.

The major labels also recorded a few vocal trios in Texas and California—singers of the canción romántica (romantic song) in a style launched in Mexico in the 1920s. One Mexican-styled quartet recorded by the Vocalion label in 1937 was Los Carlistas, which included a young man, 20 years of age at the time, whose name would be the only one to challenge that of Lydia Mendoza as an enduring icon of musical creativity among the Mexican Americans of the Southwest. I refer to the venerable Lalo Guerrero. Of course, Don Lalo could not have known in 1937 that for the next six decades he would remain one of the beacons of Mexican American music. As he confided to me in one of several discussions we had over the years, "When the band took a break, we would come on, with the three guitars, singing Mexican songs. That's how I got started, very young, about 18, in the big-time clubs of Hollywood. I think the Anglo patrons saw us as an exotic form of entertainment, but we loved it. At 18 we were on top of a whole new world."

But his experiences with Los Carlistas were only the beginning for Lalo, the Hollywood nightlife being but one of the myriad musical influences to shape the remarkably eclectic career of the young singer.

Guerrero's role as Mexican America's most enduring male performer is justly attributed to his prolific output as both singer and composer of songs. As a singer, first with Los Carlistas and later as a soloist, Don Lalo early on carved out a leading role unmatched by anyone (save, perhaps, his female counterpart, Lydia Mendoza). Guerrero sang every type of song imaginable, from folk-inspired country songs known as rancheras to the most sophisticated and romantic of boleros—not to mention American foxtrots, swings, and one of his specialties, humorous novelty songs (many bilingual). Endowed with a strong resonant voice and an engaging stage presence, Don Lalo continued over the decades to capture the imagination of his people on both sides of the border. As would befit a son of the bicultural Hispanic Southwest, Don Lalo's hits ranged from canciones rancheras such as *Canción Mexicana* (his own composition) and boleros like *Nunca Jamás* (also one of his compositions) to humorous songs such as the bilingually amusing *There's No Tortillas* (another Guerrero composition, based on the aria *O Sole Mio*).

While Don Lalo justifiably gained fame as a singer, a most important asset in his artistic arsenal has been his presence as a composer. Hundreds of songs have sprung from his creative imagination, again, running the gamut from ranchero to sophisticated, and from Mexican-Latino styles to American. *Canción Mexicana* and *Nunca Jamás* are two songs that enjoyed long and widespread popularity, not only as performed by Don Lalo, but as recorded by such greats as El Trío Los Panchos, Lucha Villa, and many others. Don Lalo also composed a treasury of American swing-styled tunes, beginning with his creation of the Mexican American-styled boogie in the 1940s. In this genre are included the historically important *Vamos a Bailar* and *Marihuana Boogie,* two songs that not only took the Mexican Americans by storm, but marked some of the first examples of music composed in a bimusical style, incorporating both Mexican-Latino and American sensibilities.

In the 1950s, Lalo Guerrero became widely known, both in Mexico and the United States, with his songs for Las Ardillitas, in a style patterned after the Chipmunk songs that hit the American market at the time. Humorous and lighthearted, they were early harbingers of the torrent of humorous music Don Lalo would unleash beginning in the 1960s, when the aforementioned *There's No Tortillas, Tacos for Two, I Left My Car in San Francisco,* and *The Gay Ranchero,* to name but a few, blazed their way into the hearts of audiences everywhere in the Southwest and beyond.

Lastly, Don Lalo amply displayed his sense of ethnic allegiance and social consciousness with the numerous corridos he composed, addressing such critical issues as discrimination (as in *El 29 de Agosto*, about the Chicano Moratorium in Los Angeles in 1969, and the death of newspaperman Rubén Salazar) and, especially, the plight of farm workers and the efforts of Cesar Chavez and the United Farm Workers of America (as in *El Corrido de Cesar Chavez*).

As would befit the man who stands as the epitome of Mexican American musical creativity, Lalo Guerrero was instrumental in building an orquesta style unique to the Hispanic Southwest. This ensemble, which is historically the most reflective of the Mexican Americans' protean efforts to negotiate their bicultural identity on a conflictive border, was subjected by Don Lalo to the kind of intensive elaboration of which only he was capable. As did his orquesta counterpart in Texas, the legendary Beto Villa, Lalo Guerrero synthesized the myriad disparities present in the Southwest between Mexican and American as well as between ranchero (country) and what people referred to as "jaitón" (from the English "hightoned," or "high class"). In other words, Don Lalo's orquesta "traía de todo," as people would say—it had everything. As Don Lalo himself told this writer in an interview, "When I played [with my orquesta], I very much liked the bolero, and, since I was a romantic singer, I used to do a lot of those. I also played danzones; I loved danzones. I always started my set with a danzón. And then I'd play music that was popular at the moment, such as a porro colombiano like *María Cristina*. When the cha-cha hit, I would play that as well, and then the mambo, when that was in vogue. But since I played in that area [the Southwest] where the people were very much accustomed to Beto Villa's polkas, I incorporated into my repertoire several of his polkas, and some from Mexico."

But Don Lalo went one up on his peers in the orquesta tradition, including the influential Beto Villa. In connection with his invention of the Mexican American Boogie, he also developed a thoroughly unique, bimusical orquesta sound that synthesized the boogie version of big-band swing and the Afro-Hispanic sound that eventually came to be known as salsa. The result was an arresting synthesis that perfectly mirrored the biculturalism of Mexican Americans as expressed in their speech, dress, and even culinary habits. In this manner, Lalo

Guerrero became an icon of the orquesta tradition in the Southwest, thus adding to his already immense stature as a leading exponent of song and composition.

It is simply impossible to find in the annals of Mexican American music an artist with the depth and breadth of Don Lalo Guerrero's genius. In a career that spans more than sixty years, Guerrero's expansive spirit of creativity has touched on almost all aspects of musical culture as it develops in the crucible of border conflict that marks the course of Mexican American history. Don Lalo was not only a participant in the artistic expression of that conflict, he was a bold innovator whose creative power encroached on every one of the multiple traditions that were present in the Southwest and which he helped to develop—the canción, in its many guises; the corrido; the orquesta; and even the conjunto.

As a trailblazer, then, Lalo Guerrero has had no peer in the history of Mexican American music. But what is equally important in assessing the impact of this son of the Southwest (he was born in Tucson in 1916) is his legacy as a committed member of his community. Don Lalo has always been, above all, a man of unassailable integrity and genuine humility, someone whose good faith we can accept without reservation. Moreover, as a product of the working-class Mexican American barrio, he has always maintained a deep and abiding love for his gente—his people—a love that comes through often enough in the most poignant of his canciones, not to mention his indefatigable work for the many causes of Mexican American civil rights. In short, Don Lalo will stand for a very long time as a lofty example—musical and human—for those who may want to follow in his mighty footsteps.

Don Lalo Guerrero's is an epic life, one that embodies the hopes, disappointments, and triumphs of his people, the Mexican Americans. Bits of that life have been revealed in a multitude of venues, from newspaper articles to books on the music of the Hispanic Southwest. But as Don Lalo himself has put it, "A lot of words have been written about me—'about' me, but not 'by' me." Now, in this book and in his own words, Lalo Guerrero has finally set out to tell his story, and the history of Mexican Americans will be that much richer for his efforts.

Discography of LALO GUERRERO'S MUSIC
Compiled by Mark Guerrero

Introduction

Aside from the hundreds of titles that were recorded by my dad, many of his songs were recorded by other artists throughout the decades. For example, *Canción Mexicana* was recorded by the ranchera diva of the 1930s and 1940s, Lucha Reyes, as well as by her counterpart of the 1960s and 1970s, Lola Beltran. *Nunca Jamás* was recorded by the internationally famous trio Los Panchos; the legendary Mexican balladeer of the 1960s, Javier Solis; and the great Jose Feliciano. My father's ranchera/rock and roll song *La Minifalda de Reynalda* was a hit by the 1960s Mexican rock group Los Johnny Jets.

Vocalion Records (1939) was the first label for which my dad recorded. He was 21 years old and a member of a quartet called Los Carlistas, which formed in his hometown of Tucson, Arizona, in 1937. They were signed to the label by producer Manuel S. Acuña.

Imperial Records (ca. 1946–50) was owned by Lew Chudd. Mr. Chudd later went on to record top American rock and roll and rhythm and blues artists such as Fats Domino and Ricky Nelson on this label. On the Imperial label, my dad sang and wrote songs in many genres and introduced songs done in the pachuco dialect called "Caló." At times he recorded Spanish-language versions of many American hit songs first done by artists such as Frankie Lane, Johnny Ray, Mario Lanza, Patti Page, Louis Jordan, and Louis Prima. He also recorded songs in Spanish and Caló using blues, swing, and what was later called rock and roll as his medium. The songs that are listed as "tropical" are in a style that is today called "salsa."

Real Records (1955–56) was a company that was started and owned by my dad, businessman Paul Landwehr, and recording engineer Jimmy Jones. The records were released on 78 rpm as well as the 45 rpm format. Lalo's biggest seller, *Pancho Lopez* (the English-language version), was released on this label.

L&M Records (1956–57 and ca. 1972) was a label owned by my dad and his producer, Manuel S. Acuña, "L" signifying Lalo and "M" for Manuel. They reunited after my dad's association with Real Records. This list was difficult to do because there is no written record of L&M recordings available. All I could do was list the recordings I have. In the mid-fifties my dad recorded songs such as his classic *Pancho Claus* and *Elvis Perez* for L&M. The label was revived for a short time in the early 1970s.

There is no list available of all the titles my dad recorded for RCA; therefore, the best I could do is list the 45 and 78 rpm records I have.

Colonial Records was the label with which my dad recorded the greatest number of songs. It was owned by Manuel S. Acuña, who produced all the recordings. Las Ardillitas, the three singing squirrels, were introduced on Colonial Records in the early 1960s. My teenage band, Mark & the Escorts, recorded several songs with my dad during this period, including his big hit *La Minifalda de Reynalda*. All the records were in the 45 rpm format, and every year or so Manuel would release an album containing a collection of the singles.

This discography is organized by record labels listed in chronological order, with titles in alphabetical order under each label category. Each line is set up in the following manner:

the title of the song
an asterisk (*) if it was written by Lalo Guerrero or a
    plus sign (+) if he wrote only the lyrics
the matrix number that appeared on the record
the style of music
the musical group that backed him on the recording.

If any of the above information is not available, the category is left blank. I obtained this information from the records themselves (from my own or my dad's collections), from various lists, and from my dad's recollections.

Information on obtaining Lalo's CDs can be found on the

Internet at www.markguerrero.com. Or write to Mentor Productions, P.O. Box 1148, San Clemente, CA 92674.

Lalo's Definitions of Styles of Music Used in This Discography

banda: 2/4 or 3/4 time music that originated in Sinaloa, Mexico, featuring a tuba and crash cymbals, influenced by oom-pah music played by German immigrants

bolero: a slow, rhythmic, romantic song

calypso: tropical rhythmic music that originated in Jamaica and the Bahamas in the 1940s

cha-cha: tropical rhythmic music and dance that originated in Cuba in the 1950s

corrida: 2/4 polka-style song (not a story song like a corrido)

corrido: a song that tells a story about a person or an event

cumbia: 2/4 time rhythmic music that originated in Colombia in the 1960s

huapango: a style from southern Mexico using rhythmic strumming of the guitar

mambo: tropical rhythmic music and dance that originated in Cuba in the 1950s

merecumbé: tropical rhythmic music and dance that originated in the Caribbean in the 1950s

norteña: 2/4 time polka-style music that originated in northern Mexico, featuring an accordion and influenced by German immigrants

pachanga: tropical rhythmic music and dance that originated in the Caribbean in the 1960s

pachuco: a Chicano subculture with its own slang called caló

paso doble: two-step music and dance that originated in Spain

polka: music in 2/4 time that originated in Bohemia and was taken to southern Texas and northern Mexico by German immigrants

porro: Columbian cumbia, a style of music and also a dance

ranchera: Mexican country music that can be waltz, polka, or slow 2/4 time

rhumba: tropical rhythm and dance that originated in Cuba in the 1930s samba: tropical rhythmic music and dance that originated in Brazil in the 1940s

shotis: a style of music and dance that originated as a German polka ("schottisch") in the nineteenth century

son huasteco: a style of strumming similar to huapango from Caribbean gulf states such as Tamaulipas, Tampico, and Veracruz

tropical: Caribbean rhythmic music and dance that today is called "salsa"

Vocalion Records (1939)

As a member of Los Carlistas Quartet: Jose "Yuca" Salaz, Soledad "Chole" Salaz, Gregorio "Goyo" Escalante, and Eduardo "Lalo" Guerrero

Los Abonos, corrido
El Aguador* (MLA-327), huapango (first record, B side)
Anímese Mi Chata, comic
Así Son Ellas* (MLA-329), fox trot
Cuestión de una Mujer* (MLA-328), fox trot
De Que Murió el Quemado* (MLA-326), corrida
He Sabido* (LA 1736-B), ranchera
Las Morenas, corrida
Qué Estás Pensando, corrida
El Rosál, ranchera
Los Rumores, corrida
Si Señora, Soy Ranchero, huapango
El Serrucho* (LA 1741-B), corrida
Ya Vine, ballad

Imperial Records (ca. 1946–52)

As a member of Trio Imperial: Jose Coria, Mario Sanchez, and Lalo Guerrero

Amor Ranchero (DI-118), corrida
Balajú (DI-44), son huasteco
La Boda de Los Pachucos* (DI-439), comic
El Borrachito (DI-290), comic
Borracho Busco un Amor (DI-232), ranchera

Borracho y Enamorado* (DI-554), ranchera
El Bracero* (DI-438), corrido
El Burro de tu Padre (DI-551), huapango
El Caimán (DI-46), porro
Caminito de Chihuahua (DI-231), corrido
Las Comadres Pachucas* (DI-291), comic
Corrido Mexicano* (DI-136), corrido
La Cotorrona (DI-442), corrida
La Desabrida* (DI-532), comic
Los Dos Carnales* (DI-215), pachuco/corrido
La Gallinita* (DI-531), comic
El Hijo de Juan Charrasqueado* (DI-161), corrido
El Jaliciense (DI-499), corrido
Juan Charrasqueado (DI-133), corrido
El Lavaplatos (DI-293), corrido
Maldita Suerte del Pachuco* (DI-289), corrida
La Mancornadora (DI-87), ranchera
Me Gusta Jugar Parejo (DI-443), ranchera
Mi Saxofón (DI-498), comic
Mi Pueblo Natál* (DI-61), son huasteco
Mi Ranchito (DI-45), ranchera
El Mojado* (DI-891), corrido
El Mosquito* (DI-552), comic
La Morenita (DI-117), corrido
Las Mujeres* (DI-295), corrida
Mujeres Apachucadas* (DI-292), comic
Nuestro Idioma* (DI-214), corrida
La Nueva Generación* (DI-135), corrido
Olvidarte Jamás (DI-88), fox trot
Pa' Luego Es Tarde (DI-199), corrida
Pa' Mí Es Igual* (DI-43), corrida
El Pachuco* (DI-163), pachuco/corrida
El Pachuco y el Tarzán* (DI-216), pachuco/corrida
El Pachuco, el Tarzán y el Charrasquedito* (DI-294), pachuco/corrida
El Pachuco Guaino* (DI-440), pachuco/corrida
La Pachuquilla* (DI-90), pachuco/corrida (first pachuco song)
El Piscador* (DI-889), ranchera

Por la Senda Triste (DI-583), bolero
El Presidiario 13* (DI-162), corrido
Por una Carta (DI-534), ranchera
El Renegado (DI-60), ranchera
Siempre Trais a tu Mama (DI-164), corrida
Las Suegras (DI-89), huapango
Te Madrugue (DI-444), corrido
Ten Cuidado* (DI-437), corrido
Tengo un Grano en la Nariz (DI-441), comic
El Tímido* (DI-584), comic
El Tirilongo* (DI-501), pachuco/comic
El Tránvia* (DI-585), comic
El Trenecito* (DI-201), ranchera
Tu Libertad (DI-533), ballad
El Velorio* (DI-890), porro
La Vida del Soltero* (DI-296), corrida
Virgencita Milagrosa* (DI-134), ballad
La Viuda Negra (DI-586), comic
Y Nada Pasó (DI-200), comic
Ya Hallé Mi Saxofón (DI-553), comic
Ya Me Voy para Korea* (DI-888), corrido

Lalo y Elena
Chicana (DI-575), corrida (with Los Costeños)
Chollas (DI-620), polka (with Los Costeños)
El Conquistador (DI-578), polka (with Los Costeños)
Contestación a Que Te Ha Dado Esa Mujér (DI-576), ballad (with Los Costeños)
Contestación a Por Ultima Vez (DI-541), ballad (with el Mariachi México del Norte)
Elena (DI-539), polka (with Los Costeños)
Me Lleva el Tren (DI-577), comic (with Los Costeños)
Mi Güerita (DI-544), polka (with el Mariachi México del Norte)
La Respingona (DI-621), comic (with Los Costeños)
Yo Soy el Bato* (DI-540), corrido (with el Mariachi México del Norte)

Lalo Guerrero (solo)

Acuerdate de Mí (DI-791), fox trot (with la Orquesta de Manuel S. Acuña)

Al Compás de Este Vals+ (Tennessee Waltz), (DI-766), waltz (with la Orquesta de Lalo Guerrero)

El Alacrán (DI-848), porro (with el Conjunto Maraclave)

El Alfabeto+ (Rag Mop), (DI-665), swing (with sus Cinco Lobos)

Apiadate de Mí (DI-988), ranchera (with el Mariachi Cardenales)

Aquella Vez (DI-376), bolero (with la Orquesta de Manuel S. Acuña)

Así Como el Sol+ (Lucky Old Sun) (DI-659), ballad

Así Te Quiero Ver (DI-481), bolero (with la Orquesta de Manuel S. Acuña)

El Aventurero (DI-435), bolero (with la Orquesta de Manuel S. Acuña)

El Barzon (DI-360), corrido (with el Mariachi México del Norte)

*Bésame Más** (DI-830), fox trot (with la Orquesta de Lalo Guerrero)

El Bolerito de la Main+ (Chattanooga Shoe Shine Boy) (DI-666), swing (with sus Cinco Lobos)

*La Borrachera** (DI-633), ranchera (with el Mariachi Imperial)

La Burrita (DI-461), corrido (with el Mariachi México del Norte)

El Burrito (DI-661), comic (with el Mariachi Imperial)

Cananea (DI-738), corrido (with el Mariachi El Prado)

Canasta Uruguaya (DI-826), corrido (with el Mariachi Estrella de Jalisco)

La Canción de los Dos (DI-375), bolero (with la Orquesta de Manuel S. Acuña)

Canta Corazón (DI-878), ballad (with el Mariachi de Francisco Rodriguez)

*Cantineando** (DI-695), ranchera (with el Mariachi Imperial)

Chicas Patas Boogie+ (Oh Babe) (DI-755), pachuco/swing (with sus Cinco Lobos)

*Los Chucos Suaves** (DI-537), pachuco/rhumba (with sus Cinco Lobos)

El Cochinito (DI-943), comic (with el Mariachi de Juan Navarrete)

Contestación a Mentira+ (DI-808), bolero (with la Orquesta de Manuel S. Acuña)

Contestación a Prieta Linda (DI-650), ranchera (with el Mariachi Imperial)

Contestación a Tú Solo Tú (DI-647), ranchera (with el Mariachi

Imperial)

*Continuación de la Cosa** (DI-788), rhumba (with sus Cinco Lobos)

Convéncete (DI-607), fox trot (with la Orquesta Tropical de Manuel S. Acuña)

Copa Tras Copa (DI-879), ranchera (with el Mariachi de Francisco Rodriguez)

*Corazón Burlado** (DI-512), ranchera (with el Mariachi México del Norte)

Corazón Corazón (DI-982), ballad (with el Mariachi de Juan Navarrete)

*Corrido de Enrique Bolaños** (DI-542), corrido (with el Mariachi Imperial) (tribute to the Mexican boxer)

La Cosa+ (The Thing) (DI-767), march/comic (with sus Cinco Lobos)

Cosita Linda (DI-828) bolero (with el Conjunto de Luis B. Hijar)

La Culebra Pollera (DI-846), comic (with el Mariachi de Francisco Rodriguez)

De Nada Me Valió (DI-827), ranchera (with el Mariachi Estrella de Jalisco)

*De Que Murió el Quemado** (DI-463), corrida (with el Mariachi Imperial)

Despierta Corazón (DI-277), bolero (with la Orquesta de Manuel S. Acuña)

El Desventurado (DI-605), bolero (with la Orquesta de Manuel S. Acuña)

Díme Corazón, ranchera

Dinero Robado (DI-464), corrido (with el Mariachi Imperial)

Dos Almas y un Solo Corazón (DI-505), bolero (with la Orquesta de Manuel S. Acuña)

Ella (DI-739), ranchera (with el Mariachi El Prado)

*Ella y Yo** (DI-769), ranchera (with el Mariachi Imperial)

En Ti (DI-485), fox trot (with la Orquesta de Manuel S. Acuña)

Enamorado (DI-373), bolero (with la Orquesta de Manuel S. Acuña)

Eso Quisimos (DI-606), fox trot (with la Orquesta de Manuel S. Acuña)

La Fea (DI-809), comic

Flor Deshojada (DI-486), bolero (with la Orquesta de Manuel S. Acuña)

Florecita (DI-276), bolero (with la Orquesta de Manuel S. Acuña)

La Flota de Los Borrachos (DI-944), comic (with el Mariachi de Juan Navarrete)

Frío en el Alma (DI-179), bolero (with la Orquesta de Manuel S. Acuña)

Hipócrita (DI-604), bolero (with Manuel S. Acuña y Su Orquesta
   Tropical)

*El Hombre Gordo** (DI-921), blues shuffle (with sus Cinco Lobos)

La Que Se Fue (DI-812), ranchera (with el Mariachi Estrella de Jalisco)

*El Lavadero** (DI-510), corrida (with el Mariachi Imperial)

*Llegaste Tarde** (DI-919), fox trot (with sus Cinco Lobos)

Llorar+ (Cry) (DI-918), ballad (with sus Cinco Lobos)

*Malagradecida** (DI-697), ranchera (with el Mariachi Imperial)

*Mambito** (DI-642), mambo (with sus Cinco Lobos)

*Mambo Guajiro** (DI-645), mambo (with sus Cinco Lobos)

*Mambo Mambo** (DI-643), mambo (with sus Cinco Lobos)

*Mambo No. Cero** (DI-756), mambo (with sus Cinco Lobos)

*Manzanita** (DI-644), tropical (with sus Cinco Lobos)

*Marihuana Boogie** (DI-535), pachuco/blues (with sus Cinco Lobos)

Me Pagas Mal (DI-989), ranchera (with el Mariachi Cardenales)

La Media Naranja (DI-849), porro (with el Conjunto Maraclave)

Mentira (DI-178), bolero rítmico (with la Orquesta de Manuel S. Acuña)
   (first solo record, B side)

*Mi Burrito** (DI-500), comic (with el Mariachi Imperial)

Mi Chavelita (DI-543), ranchera (with el Mariachi Imperial)

Mi Corazón Llora (My Heart Cries for You) (DI-787), ballad (with la
   Orquesta de Manuel S. Acuña)

Mi Gusto Es (DI-511), ranchera (with el Mariachi México
   del Norte)

Mi Vecina (DI-985), comic (with el Mariachi de Juan Navarrete)

Mía (DI-790), bolero (with la Orquesta de Manuel S. Acuña)

Millones de Mujeres (DI-503), bolero (with Manuel S. Acuña y Su
   Orquesta)

*Mis Cinco Novias** (DI-829), swing (with sus Cinco Lobos)

*Montuno** (DI-569), tropical (with sus Cinco Lobos)

La Mula Bronca (DI-359), corrida (with el Mariachi México del Norte)

*Muy Sabroso Blues** (DI-536), blues (with sus Cinco Lobos)

Ni Tú, Ni Yo (DI-984), waltz (with el Mariachi de Juan Navarrete)

No (DI-876), bolero (with el Mariachi de Juan Navarrete)

No Llores (DI-436), fox trot (with la Orquesta de Manuel S. Acuña)

No Mas por Tí (DI-1003), ranchera (with el Mariachi Chapala)

No Me Vuelva Enamorar (DI-275), bolero (with el Mariachi Imperial)

No Te Aflijas Morena (DI-504), comic (with el Mariachi Imperial)

No Vuelvas (300-B), bolero (with la Orquesta de Manuel S. Acuña)

Noches de Angustia (DI-847), ranchera (with el Mariachi de Francisco Rodriguez)

La Novia Perdida (DI-945), ballad (with el Mariachi de Juan Navarette)

Nube Gris (DI-942), ballad (with el Mariachi de Juan Navarrete)

Para, Para la Rumba* (DI-538), rhumba (with sus Cinco Lobos)

Pecadora (DI-177), bolero (with la Orquesta de Manuel S. Acuña) (first solo record, A side)

Pobre Corazón (DI-696), ranchera (with el Mariachi Imperial)

Pobrecita (DI-1002), ranchera (with el Mariachi Chapala)

La Polka* (DI-920), polka (with sus Cinco Lobos)

Por Eso Me Ves Borracho (DI-771), ranchera (with el Mariachi Imperial)

Por Que Presumes (DI-983), ranchera (with el Mariachi de Juan Navarrete)

Prieta Linda (DI-631), ranchera (with el Mariachi Imperial)

Prisionero (DI-502), bolero (with Manuel S. Acuña y Su Orquesta)

Que Si Que No (DI-568), comic (with sus Cinco Lobos)

Quien Será Mi Rival (DI-736), bolero (with el Mariachi Imperial)

Los Resbalones+ (Slipping Around) (DI-660), swing (with sus Cinco Lobos)

Se Fue y Me Dejo* (DI-570), blues (with sus Cinco Lobos)

Se Llama Lupe (DI-513), corrido (with el Mariachi México del Norte)

Se Mi Amor+ (Be My Love) (DI-807), ballad (with la Orquesta de Manuel S. Acuña)

Separación (DI-374), bolero (with la Orquesta de Manuel S. Acuña)

Si Dejaras Que Te Amara+ (Let Me Love You) (DI-789), ballad (with la Orquesta de Lalo Guerrero)

Si No Vuelves (DI-488), bolero (with la Orquesta de Manuel S. Acuña)

Si Yo Fuera Rey+ (If I Were King) (DI-786), ballad (with la Orquesta de Lalo Guerrero)

Siempre Siempre (DI-877), ballad (with el Mariachi de Juan Navarrete)

El Soldado* (DI-831), corrido comico (with sus Cinco Lobos)

Solo Tú* (DI-567), fox trot (with sus Cinco Lobos)

Soñando Esperare (DI-278), bolero (with la Orquesta de Manuel S. Acuña)

El Sonorense (DI-462), corrido (with el Mariachi Imperial)

Sufre Como Sufro (DI-768), bolero (with el Mariachi Imperial)

La Tamalada+ (Saturday Night Fish Fry) (DI-648), swing (with sus Cinco Lobos)

Tenochtitlán (DI-630), corrido

Tiro de Mulas+ (Mule Train) (DI-646), ranchera (with el Mariachi Imperial)

Tonto Corazón* (DI-698), ranchera (with el Mariachi Imperial)

Tu Injusticia (DI-770), bolero (with el Mariachi Imperial)

Tú Solo Tú (DI-632), ranchera (with el Mariachi Imperial)

Tú Vendras a Buscarme (DI-487), bolero

Un Amor+ (My Love) (DI-754), bolero (with la Orquesta de Lalo Guerrero)

Vamos a Bailar* (DI-757), swing (with sus Cinco Lobos)

Vendras a Buscarme (DI-487), bolero (with Manuel S. Acuña y Su Orquesta)

Vengo a Pedirte (DI-603), fox trot (with Manuel S. Acuña y Su Orquesta)

Vuelvame a Besar (DI-180), bolero (with la Orquesta de Manuel S. Acuña)

Ya No Puedo Quererte (DI-662), waltz

Ya Volvió el Soldado Raso* (DI-737), corrido (with el Mariachi Imperial)

Yo Se Que Es Imposible (DI-806), fox trot (with la Orquesta de Manuel S. Acuña)

Real Records (1955–56)

A Donde Tú Vayas+ (Whither Thou Goest), waltz (with el Sexteto Real)

Adán y Eva+ (Adam and Eve), bolero

Adios to Mexico City*, bolero (with the Don Ralke Trio)

Aguanta Corazón, ranchera (with el Trio Melodico)

La Carreta*, comic

Dime Quien Te Dijo, corrida

Do You Believe In Reincarnation*, 6/8 rock ballad (with the Don Ralke Trio)

Espinita (213-B), bolero/mambo (with la Orquesta Real)

Every Tower, comic

Hey Mabel*, swing (with the Don Ralke Trio)

I Would Rather Cha Cha, cha-cha

I'll Never Let You Go (1301-B), bolero (with el Trio Melodico & the Song Sirens)

Madre Mía (217-A), bolero

Mentiras Tuyas* (224-A), corrida

Message from Garcia, comic

Mickey Mouse Mambo (Micky Mouse Club Theme), comic/mambo

Muy Agradecido* (217), bolero (tribute to Pedro Vargas)

My Rosita from Texas+ (The Yellow Rose of Texas)(1302-A), parody

Pancho Lopez+ (The Ballad of Davy Crockett) (Spanish) (218-A), parody

Pancho Lopez+ (The Ballad of Davy Crockett) (English), parody

Pancho Rock*, rock and roll

Poor People of Juarez+ (Poor People of Paris), parody

Porque*, ballad

Puñalada Trapera, ranchera (with el Trio Melodico/el Mariachi Real)

El Ranchero Sonorense, ranchera

Rock & Roll Rita*, rock and roll (with the Don Ralke Trio)

Señor Sueño* (Mr. Sandman), bolero/mambo (with la Orquesta Real)

El Schotís de Carlota*, schottische/comic

Tacos for Two+ (Cocktails for Two), parody

Take Me Out to the Bullfight+ (Take Me Out to the Ballgame), parody

Te Adoro*, cha-cha

To You My Love, pop

Tormento de Traición, ranchera

Tu*, bolero

Ya Supe Lupe*, ranchera (with el Mariachi Real de Mexicali)

L&M Records (1956–57 and ca. 1972)
45 rpm singles (ca. 1956)

Christmas In Mexico* (LM-1004), waltz

Elvis Perez* (LM-1001), corrido/rock/comic

Lola* (LM-1001), calypso (ca. 1956)

Lola* (Spanish version), calypso (1957)

Pancho Claus* (based on poem "'Twas the Night before Christmas") (LM1001), comic

Pound Dog+ (Hound Dog) (LM1002), rock and roll

45 rpm singles (ca. 1972)
Gringo+ (Ringo) (LM1010), parody
One Tamale+ (Hello Dolly) (LM1009), parody

45 rpm EP (ca. 1972)
*Elvis Perez** (EP-001), corrido/rock/comic
*Mario from the Barrio** (EP-001), ballad
*Pancho Claus** (third version) (EP-001), comic
Tacos for Two+ (Cocktails for Two) (second version) (EP-001), parody

RCA Victor Records (ca. 1958)
A Mi Modo (E2FB-7057), ranchera
Allá en mi Rancho Bonito (E2FW-7058), ranchera
Amarga Verdad (E4FW-4520), bolero
Cita con la Muerte (E4FB-4523), ranchera
*Embustera** (E2FW-7055), ranchera
Hay un Momento (E4FB-3015), ranchera
La India Bonita (E3FB-0125), waltz
Mentiras (E4FB-3016), bolero
Muchos Besos (E3FW-0123), bolero (with el Mariachi Reyes de Chapala)
No Debes (E3FB-0124), bolero
*Nunca Jamás** (E4FW-4521), bolero
Por Querer a una Mujer (E4FW-0126), ranchera (with el Mariachi Reyes de Chapala)
Ricordate Marcelino (L&M-1003-B)
*Sabado en la Noche** (E4FB-4522), ranchera
La Tortolita (E2FB-7056), ranchera
Tu Vida y la Mía (E3FW-3017), bolero
Tula, Tulita, Tulona (E4FW-3018), ranchera

Colonial Records (ca. 1960–72)
45 rpm singles
El Aguila Negra (CR-690), ranchera (with el Mariachi Los Camperos)
Al Pie de un Laurel (CR-604), ranchera (with el Mariachi Los Camperos)
*La Ardillita Gringa** (CR-603), comic (with Las Ardillitas)

*Las Ardillitas en Navidad** (CR-613), comic (with Las Ardillitas/el Trio Los Naipes)

Ay! Cosita Linda (CR-365), merecumbé (with el Cuarteto Casino)

*Ay! Lucho** (CR-371), comic/corrida (with el Mariachi Reyes de Chapala) (tribute to Chilean singer Lucho Gatica)

Azul, Pintado de Azul+ (Nel Blue Dipinto Di Blue) (CR-431), bolero

Las Bicicletas y El Sube y Baja (CR-705), polka

El Bikini de Tia Trini+ (Itsy Bitsy Teenie Weenie Yellow Polka Dot Bikini) (CR-598), parody (with El Mariachi Los Camperos de Jose G. Frías)

*El Borlote** (CR-963), polka

*El Brujo** (The Witch Doctor) (CR-411), comic (with el Mariachi Los Reyes)

*El Burro Norteño** (CR-734), ranchera (with el Mariachi Los Camperos)

Busco una Novia (CR-799), ranchera (with el Mariachi Occidental)

El Caballo Blanco (CR-597), corrido (with el Mariachi Los Camperos de Jose G. Frías)

*El Camino del Amor** (CR-951), ranchera (with la Orquesta de Lalo Guerrero)

*Canción Ranchera** (CR-534), ranchera (with el Mariachi Los Reyes)

*El Carro del 64** (CR-824), comic

*Carta a Santo Clos** (CR-1010), comic (with Las Ardillitas)

Carta de un Bracero+ (CR-812), comic

Carta de un Soldado (CR-980), ranchera (with el Conjunto Arellano)

*El Cartero** (CR-846), comic (with el Mariachi Estrellas de México)

*El Celoso** (CR-1084), comic (duet with Mimi Reyes)

Chon el Bisco (CR-825), comic

*Chuy el Chueco** (CR-754), twist/ranchero (with el Mariachi Los Vaqueros)

Cinco Robles (CR-324), waltz (with el Mariachi San Juan)

*Clases de Música** (CR-666), comic (with Las Ardillitas)

Cobarde (CR-458), ranchera (with el Mariachi Los Reyes)

Contestación a Y+ (CR-665), bolero (with el Mariachi Los Camperos)

El Correcaminos (CR-664), corrida

*El Corrido de César Chávez** (CR-1068), corrido (with el Mariachi Chapultepec)

*El Corrido de Delano** (CR-979), corrido (with el Conjunto Arellano)

El Corrido de Magdalena (CR-380), corrido (with el Mariachi de Meña Villa)

El Corrido de Pedro Infante* (CR-344), corrido

La Cosa+ (The Thing) (CR-1103), march/comic

Cuando Alguien se nos Va (CR-773), bolero

Cuando Crucé la Frontera* (CR-1037), comic (with Los Hermanos Arellano)

Cuando Llegue a Juarez* (CR-1085), ranchera (with el Conjunto de Cuco Rodriguez)

Cuando Me Muera por Ti* (CR-702), bolero (with la Orquesta de Lalo Guerrero)

Cuatro Espadas (CR-402), ranchera (with el Mariachi Aguila)

Cuatro Suspiros (CR-1046), ranchera (with el Mariachi Los Reyes)

Cuentos de Pánfilo* (CR-1011), comic (with Las Ardillitas)

Cumbia de Las Ardillitas* (CR-953), cumbia (with Las Ardillitas)

De Torreon a Lerdo (CR-703), polka

Delirio de Amor (CR-704), instrumental waltz (with la Orquesta de Lalo Guerrero)

El Día Que Te Cases (CR-298), ranchera

Dulce Madre (CR-487), bolero

Echame a Mí la Culpa (CR-370), ranchera

El Paso+ (CR-557), country-western

Elvis Perez* (second version) (CR-310), ranchera/rock and roll (with el Mariachi de Meño Villa)

En la Cantina (CR-906), bolero (with el Mariachi Los Camperos)

Esposa (CR-1073), bolero

Era Noche Buena+ ('Twas the Night Before Christmas) (CR-952), comic (with Las Ardillitas)

Eres Como la Baraja (CR-586), comic/ranchera

Las Estampillas* (CR-780), comic/ranchera (with el Mariachi Occidental)

Estilo Norte* (CR-413), polka/ranchera (with el Mariachi de Meño Villa)

Felipe el Hippie (CR-1079), comic/rock (with Mark & the Escorts/el Conjunto de Los Hermanos Arellano)

Feliz Año Nuevo* (CR-379), ranchera

Feliz Cumpleaños (CR-624), waltz (with el Mariachi Chapala)

Feliz Navidad* (CR-594), comic (with Las Ardillitas)

*El Feo** (CR-891), ranchera (with el Mariachi Los Camperos)

*La Flaca** (CR-997), ranchera (with el Conjunto de Los Hermanos Arellano)

Gema (CR-442), bolero (with el Mariachi de Los Reyes)

*El Gordobés** (CR-907), comic (with el Mariachi Los Camperos)

*Los Greñudos** (CR-937), rock (with Mark & the Escorts)

*El Güiri Güiri** (CR-443), comic/ranchera (with el Mariachi Los Reyes)

Guitarzán+ (CR-1092), comic (with Mark Guerrero & Nineteen Eighty-Four)

*Homenaje a Roberto Kennedy** (CR-1072), corrido

*Homenaje a Ruben Salazar** (CR-1115), corrido (with el Conjunto de Los Hermanos Quezada)

*El Hotel del Dolor** (CR-603), ranchera (with el Mariachi Los Camperos)

Idolo de Oro (CR-735), ranchera (with el Mariachi Los Camperos)

Juan Manuel+ (Charlie Brown) (CR-503), comic (with el Mariachi de Meño Villa)

Ladrón de Amores (CR-1038), ranchera (with Los Hermanos Arellano)

Lágrimas de Amor (CR-418), bolero

Lágrimas de Borracha (CR-1054), corrida (with el Conjunto de Los Hermanos Arellano)

Lamento del Soltero (CR-1089), comic (with el Conjunto de Los Hermanos Arellano)

*Llegó Muy Crudo el Greñudo** (CR-798), comic (with el Mariachi Occidental)

*Lola** (second version) (CR-374), calypso

*Los Angeles** (CR-488), ranchera

*La Luna** (CR-625), comic (with El Mariachi Chapala)

Malas Jugadas (CR-988), ranchera (with el Conjunto de Los Hermanos Arellano)

Maldita Suerte (CR-319), ranchera (with el Mariachi de Meño Villa)

Marcario el Carnicero+ (Mack the Knife) (CR-542), comic

Me Caís como Anillo al Dedo (CR-335), ranchera (with el Mariachi Reyes de Chapala)

*Me Gusta el Cha Cha** (CR-701), cha-cha (with la Orquesta de Lalo Guerrero)

Me Quedé sin Plata (CR-988), corrida

Mentira (second version) (CR-1015), bolero

Los Metales de Tijuana (CR-987), samba

Mi Cielo Eres Tú (CR-386), bolero

Miguel Aveces Gemía*, corrido (with el Mariachi Los Reyes)

La Minifalda de Reynalda* (CR-1053 and EP CO-100), corrida/rock/
comic (with Mark & the Escorts/el Conjunto de Los Hermanos
Arrellano)

Las Morenas (CR-1026), ranchera (with el Mariachi Los Camperos)

La Mujer* (CR-345), ranchera (with el Mariachi de Meño Villa)

Mujer Cualquiera (CR-790), ranchera (with el Mariachi Los Camperos)

Mujeriego* (CR-467), bolero

La Mula Bronca (CR-964), corrido

Mundo Loco* (CR-1045), ranchera (with el Mariachi Los Reyes)

Muy Agradecido* (CR-755), bolero (with el Mariachi Los Vaqueros)

Navidad (CR-1065), ballad

Navidad en el Bosque* (CR-1117), comic (with Las Ardillitas)

Navidad Estilo Americano* (CR-884), comic (with Las Ardillitas)

Navidad Norteña* (CR-1066), norteña (with Las Ardillitas/el Conjunto
de Los Hermanos Arellano)

No la Dejo de Querer (CR-855), ranchera (with el Mariachi Los
Camperos)

No Nací Pa' Soldado* (CR-974), ranchera (with el Mariachi Colonial)

No Pidas Mas Perdon (CR-585), bolero

No Pierdas Este Disco (CR-533), bolero (con el Mariachi Los Reyes)

Noche Buena* (CR-881), comic/bolero (with Las Ardillitas)

Nunca Jamás* (second version) (CR-1012), bolero

Ojo por Ojo (CR-394), ranchera

Olé* (CR-652), comic/paso doble (with el Mariachi Los Camperos)

Oye Mi Amor (CR-311), ranchera

Pa' Que Sientas Lo Que Siento (CR-299), ranchera

Pa-Pa-Pa-Pachanga* (CR-700), pachanga (with la Orquesta de Lalo
Guerrero)

El Pajaro Cu-Cu* (CR-854), comic/corrido (with el Mariachi Los
Camperos)

Palomita Morenita (CR-412), ranchera (with el Mariachi Los Reyes)

Pánfilo* (CR-574), comic (with Las Ardillitas)

Pánfilo Baila Twist* (CR-725), twist (with Las Ardillitas)

Pánfilo en Orbita* (CR-802), comic (with Las Ardillitas)

*Pánfilo en Texas** (CR-1119), comic (with Las Ardillitas)

*Pánfilo para Presidente** (CR-667), comic (with Las Ardillitas)

Peregrino de Amor (CR-761), ranchera (with el Mariachi Occidental)

Pobre Bohemio (CR-504), ranchera (with el Mariachi de Meño Villa)

*La Pollera Rota** (CR-950), cumbia (with la Orquesta de Lalo Guerrero)

*Las Posadas** (CR-813), comic

*Las Posadas con Las Ardillitas** (CR-880), comic (with Las Ardillitas)

Prieta Linda (CR-691), ranchera (with el Mariachi Los Camperos)

Que Agüite (CR-325), ranchera (with el Mariachi San Juan)

*Que Vuelvan Los Braceros** (CR-916), corrido (with el Conjunto de Los
   Hermanos Arellano)

Quiereme (CR-1093), bolero

Ranchero Rock+ (CR-396), ranchera/rock (with Los Satelites)

Recuerdame (CR-414), ranchera (with el Mariachi de
   Meño Villa)

Regalo de Navidad (CR-612), ranchera (with el Trio Los
   Naipes)

El Rock de Las Ardillitas+ (Twist and Shout/Roll Over Beethoven) (CR-
   885), comic/rock and roll (with Las Ardillitas/Mark & the Escorts)

Rock n' Roll del Niño+ (CR-643), rock and roll (with Los Satelites)

*Rock n' Roll Rock** (CR-351), rock and roll

Sabrás que te Quiero (CR-385), bolero

*Santo Clos y Las Ardillitas**, comic (with Las Ardillitas)

*Se Acabaron Las Parrandas** (CR-772), corrida

Seis Canciones (CR-653), bolero (with el Mariachi Los Camperos)

Señor San Antonio (CR-304), ranchera (with el Mariachi Aguila)

*Señora Gonzales** (CR-936), rock/corrido (with el Conjunto de Mark
   Guerrero)

Soldado Raso (CR-973), ranchera (with el Mariachi Colonial)

Sigue Mujer Tu Camino (CR-344), ranchera

*Si Hay Santo Clos** (CR-763), comic (with el Conjunto Los Cristales)

Si Yo Pudiera (CR-573), ranchera

*La Televisión** (CR-468), comic

*La Tragedia del 29 de Agosto** (CR-1114), corrido (with el Conjunto de
   Los Hermanos Quezada)

La Tamalada+ (Saturday Night Fish Fry) (second version) (CR-762), swing (with el Conjunto Los Cristales)

*El Tartamudo** (CR-457), comic (with el Mariachi Los Reyes)

*Te Deseo Amor** (CR-847), bolero (with el Mariachi Estrellas de México)

Te Me Olvidas (CR-364), bolero (with el Cuarteto Casino)

Te Odio y te Quiero (CR-509), bolero (with el Trio Los Naipes)

Tequila+ (CR-395), mambo rock (with Los Satelites)

*El Tex Mex** (CR-1102), corrida/country-western (with Mark Guerrero & Nineteen Eighty-Four)

El Timido (CR-790), comic (with el Mariachi Los Camperos)

*Tin Marín de Do Pingue** (CR-350), rock and roll

*Todo Tiene Su Contra** (CR-401), ranchera (with el Mariachi Aguila)

Torero (CR-417), cha-cha (with el Conjunto Colonial)

*El Transplante** (CR-1067), ranchera (with el Mariachi Chapultepec)

*Las Tres Ardillitas** (CR-541), comic (with Las Ardillitas)

*Las Tres Ardillitas en Navidad** (CR-164), comic (with Las Ardillitas)

Tu Orgullo y el Mío (CR-1025), ranchera (with el Mariachi Los Camperos)

*El Twist de Luis** (CR-724), twist

El Ultimo Tiro (CR-558), ranchera

Un Clavo para mi Cruz (CR-305), ranchera (with el Mariachi Aguila)

*Un Marciano en la Tierra** (CR-464), novelty (with el Mariachi Los Reyes)

Un Nuevo Amor (CR-917), ranchera (with el Conjunto de Los Hermanos Arellano)

Una Puñalada (CR-463), ranchera (with el Mariachi Los Reyes)

La Vampiresa (CR-872), comic

*Ven Corazón** (CR-642), 6/8 rock (with Los Satelites)

*El Venadito Samuel** (CR-1065), rock (with Las Ardillitas/el Conjunto de Los Hermanos Arellano)

*Vestido Cruel** (CR-318), bolero

Viciosa (CR-432), bolero

Virgen Morena (CR-890), ranchera (with el Mariachi de Los Camperos)

*Viva Becerra!** (CR-510), corrido (with el Trio Los Naipes) (tribute to the Mexican boxer)

*La Voz de la Conciencia** (CR-873), comic

*Ya Llegó la Navidad**, comic (with Las Ardillitas)

*Ya Supe Lupe** (CR-1088), ranchera (with el Conjunto de Los Hermanos Arellano)

*Ya Viene la Navidad** (CR-1116), comic (with Las Ardillitas)

33-1/3 rpm LPs

The following were collections of Colonial singles included in the above list:

Los Exitos de Lalo Guerrero (ALP-1000)

Lalo Guerrero Canta sus Exitos (CLP-1000)

Lo Mejor de Lalo Guerrero (CLP-1002)

El Burro Norteño (CLP-1004)

Que Vuelvan Los Braceros (CLP-1008)

Homenaje a Roberto Kennedy

Columbia Records (Argentina) (ca. 1960)

Torero (8185) (composed of licensed Colonial recordings)

Discos Torre (Distributed by Capitol México) (ca. 1965)

La Minifalda de Reynalda (N-19066) (composed of licensed Colonial recordings)

Cap Latino (Distributed by Capitol Records) (ca. 1969)
45 rpm singles

*The Burrito** (6887), rock and roll (with Mark Guerrero & Nineteen Eighty-Four)

La Cosa+ (The Thing) (third version) (6913), march/comic

Pancho Claus+ (6887) (second version), comic (with Mark Guerrero & Nineteen Eighty-Four)

*El Tex Mex** (6913), corrida/country-western (with Mark Guerrero & Nineteen Eighty-Four)

33-1/3 rpm LP

La Celosa y el Celoso (ST-19019) (composed of licensed Colonial recordings)

Discos Clave (ca. 1970)
45 rpm singles

*Ema, la del Autocinema** (115), comic/norteña (with el Conjunto de
Los Hermanos Quezada)
*En tu Casa no me Quieren**, rock
*El Güero Aventao** (103), comic/corrida
*Juana, Tacha y Chona**, cumbia
*Navidad en el Bosque** (101), comic (with Las Ardillitas)
*Las Pantimedias** (1103), comic/corrida
El Remate (115), comic/norteña
*Ya Viene la Navidad** (101), comic (with Las Ardillitas)

Discos Rex (1973)
33-1/3 rpm LP
Las Ardillitas de Lalo Guerrero (R-557)
*Las Ardillitas en la Escuela**, *Las Ardillitas en el D.F.**, *Que Bonito Es el Rock 'n' roll**, *Agapito el Sapito**, *Los Diez Perritos, Ay Mama mi Ardilla**, *Amor Chiquito, Volver Volver, Volvera el Amor, Ilusión de Primavera, Domingo Maravilloso, El Chile Verde, Juan Charrasqueado*

Discos Gas (1977)
33-1/3 rpm LP
Las Ardillitas de Lalo Guerrero (ING-1126) (with Las Ardillitas)
*Feliz Navidad, Clases de Ingles**, *Ya Casi Es Navidad** (the remaining seven songs were previously released, six on Discos Rex and one on Colonial Records)

Capitol Pops EMI (1976)
33-1/3 rpm LP
Oigo una Banda (POP-383):
*Oigo una Banda**, ballad/banda
*Enamorado de Ti**, bolero
*No Me Gusta Dormir Solo**, corrida
Porque Te Quiero, No Lo Se, bolero
*Ya**, bolero
Con Todo el Corazón, bolero
No Me Quedó Llorando, bolero
*Mayo y Diciembre**, bolero
A Pesar de Todo, rock ballad

Vamos a Bailar*, bolero

Latin International Records (licensed by EMI Capitol México) (1977)
> 45 rpm singles

El Chicano* (DLI-1124-B), corrido
Los Ilegales* (DLI-1124-A), ranchera

Ambiente Records (1981)
> 45 rpm singles

(with Mariachi de Jose Hernandez)
Fernando el Toro (45-AMB-001), comic (written by Mark Guerrero)
Olé Fernando* (45-AMB-001), comic

> 33-1/3 rpm LPs

Parodies of Lalo Guerrero (AMB-100) (with David Hidalgo and Conrad
Lozano of Los Lobos):
> *Lucila+* (Lucille)
> *The Gay Ranchero+* (Las Alteñitas)
> *No Way José**
> *Elvis Perez** (third version), comic/corrida/rock (Mark Guerrero on
> bass and guitar)
> *Tacos for Two+* (Cocktails for Two) (third version)
> *There's No Tortillas+* (O Solé Mio)
> *Cordova+* (Granada)
> *Pancho Lopez+* (The Ballad of Davy Crockett) (second version)
> *Pancho Claus+* ('Twas the Night Before Christmas) (third version)
> *Don't Drink the Water+* (Zacazonápan)
> *You're Impossible+* (Somos Novios)
> *I Left My Car In San Francisco+* (I Left My Heart In San Francisco)
> (Philip Sonnichsen on piano)

Capitol Pops (EMI), (1970–95)/Las Ardillitas de Lalo Guerrero
> 45 rpm single

El Violín*/La Risa* (8166), (1978)

33-1/3 rpm LPs

Las Ardillitas en Navidad (POP-084) (1970) (compilation of Colonial singles)

Las Ardillitas en Navidad, Vol. 2 (POP-254) (1973) (compilation of Colonial singles)

Navidad Alegre (POP-362) (1975)
> *Campanitas de Navidad*, Como Santa Claus No Hay Dos*, Cuando Llegue la Navidad, Los Venaditos de Santa Claus*, Fiestas de Diciembre, Navidad Alegre, Vi a Santa Claus Besando a mi Mama*, Carta Navideña, Arbolito de Navidad, Poupourri Navideño*

Hablando con Los Animales (POP-285) (1974)
> *Hablando con Los Animales*, La Situación, Tiro de Mulas+ (Mule Train), La Cosa+ (The Thing), Zacazonápan, El Telefono Carpintero, Topilejo, Mi Ranchito*, La Tierra Prometida, El Agente Viajero*

Blanca Navidad (POP-423) (1976)
> *Blanca Navidad+ (White Christmas), Los Dientes de Pánfilo*, La Caperucita Roja, La Navidad del Niño Pobre*, El Mundo de Navidad*, Noche de Paz+ (Silent Night), Las Pesadilla de Pánfilo*, Blanca Nieves y los Siete Enanos, La Muñequita de Navidad*, El Reno de La Nariz Roja+ (Rudolph the Red Nosed Reindeer)*

Las Mananitas con Las Ardillitas (POP-406) (1976)
> *Las Mañanitas, Los Gustos*, Mamita Bonita*, El Higado, Despedida de Solteros, Mañanitas Tapatias, La Hormiga*, Quinceañera*, Mi Tatarabuelo, El Hustle de las Ardillitas+*

Las Ardillitas de Lalo Guerrero (POP-433) (1977)
> *La Tamalada*, La Sra. Clos*, Navidad*, Tarjetita Navideña, Yo No lo Creo (Si No lo Veo)*, Navidad Comercial, El Día Mas Feliz del Año*, Tres Regalos de Navidad, Posadas Navideñas, Se Aproxima la Navidad**

Quico y Las Ardillitas de Lalo Guerrero (SL EMN-736) (1977)
> *En la Escuela*, Somos Amigos*, Cumbia de Quico*, Por Eso Digo*, Cancioncita Loca*, Quico El Buen Chico*, Trabalenguas*, Pastel de Cumpleaños*, Quico el Astronauta*, Lección de Ingles**

Feliz Navidad les Desean las Ardillitas de Lalo Guerrero (POP-447) (1978)
> *Nueve Días de Posadas+, El Burrito de Navidad*, Deletrea N-a-v-i-d-a-d*, Sonidos de Navidad*, La Canción de Navidad+ (Winter Wonderland), Santo Clos Esta en Dieta, Cartas a Santo Clos*, Donde Vive Santo Clos*, Felicitaciones de Navidad*, Fiesta Navideña**

Las Ardillitas de Lalo Guerrero en Navidad (POP-476) (1979)
Hay Que Bonito Es la Navidad*, La Piñata*, Las Barbas de Santo Clos, Mañana Es Navidad*, Los Santos y Santo Clos*, Por Que Lloras Nina*, Tamborcito de Navidad+ (Little Drummer Boy), *El Venadito Cojo*, El Mundo sin Navidad*

La Discoteque de Las Ardillitas de Lalo Guerrero (POP-465) (1979)
Marcelino Pan y Vino, Gasolina*, Disco Jalisco*, Que Bonitos Son Los Niños, Eres Naco*, El Arca de Noe*, Fiebre del Lunes*, La Higiene*, Tengo Diez Años, Dos Cuerdas Tiene mi Guitarra Mark Guerrero Band on songs 2, 3, and 7

Las Ardillitas de Lalo Guerrero (POP-489) (1980)
Super Mama*, La Alacancía*, El Ritmo del Reloj*, El Trenecito, El Sapo y La Rana, Vamos a la Feria, El Chapulín y la Hormiga*, Cuando Sea Grande*, El Chicle*, A Contar*

Las Ardillitas de Lalo Guerrero (POP-507) (1980)
Amorcito Loco+ (Crazy Little Thing Called Love), *Navidad en Jalisco*, Felicitaciones*, Señor Santo Claus (Los Juguetes)*, Viva la Navidad*, Navidad Tropical*, Gaspár, Melchór y Baltazár*, No Cabe por la Chimenea*, Mi Arbolito*, Los Chiquitines**

Las Ardillitas de Lalo Guerrero (POP-545) (1981)
Santo, Santo, Santo Clos*, Lo Que No Quiero para Navidad*, Rock de Los Cascabeles+ (Jingle Bell Rock), *Apurate Navidad*, La Primera Navidad+* (Oh Little Town of Bethlehem), *Señas de Que Viene Navidad*, Santo Clos Traenos Juguetes*, Hay Gusto en Navidad, Mamacita Donde Esta Santo Clos, Navidad, Navidad+* (Deck the Halls)

Las Ardillitas de Lalo Guerrero (POP-540) (1981)
Azotalo el Latigo+ (Whip It), *Quisiera Ser Superman*, El Caballito*, El Gato y el Raton*, Toñito el Atun*, La Marea Está Alta+* (The Tide Is High), *Popeye el Marino+* (Popeye the Sailor Man), *Mi Perrito, Vamos a Silbar*, Hoy Cumpliste un Año Mas** (Mark Guerrero Band on songs 1 and 6)

Country Al Estilo De Las Ardillitas de Lalo Guerrero (POP-559) (1982)
El Pizarrón*, Soy un Cowboy, El Güero Aventao*, El Vaquero Enamorado, Lulu Belle*, El Pequeño Panda de Chapultepec, El Vaquero Urbano*, El Tex Mex*, Gringo+ (Ringo), (Mark Guerrero Band on songs 1, 2, 5, 7, 8, 9, and 10)

20 Exitos Navideños de Las Ardillitas de Lalo Guerrero (POP-564) (1982)
    E.T. (El Extraterrestre)+, Pobre Santo Clos, En esta Navidad*, La La
    La Llego Santo Clos*, Ahi Viene Santo Clos*, Feliz Navidad Tohui*
    (song 1, music written by Mark Guerrero; the remaining fourteen
    songs on this LP were previously released)

Pánfilo el Rey del Rock (POP-589) (1983)
    *Pánfilo el Rey del Rock+, Me Picaron las Abejas, Quiero Tocar en la
    Orquesta, Carly+, Juegos de Video+, Rockanroleando en México+, Las
    Olimpiadas, E.T. (El Tortero)*, Ejercicios Aerobicos+, En El Rancho de
    mi Tío* (songs 1, 5, 6, and 9, music written by Mark Guerrero)

Aleluya! Es Navidad (POP-656) (1984)
    *Queremos Rock para Navidad+, Super Santo Clos+, La Computadora
    (de Santo Clos)+, El Niño Jesus+, Santo Clos Tiene Tos, Aleluya! Es
    Navidad+, Noche Buena en mi Pueblo*, Dulces y Caramelos, No Quiro
    Nada para Navidad,*, Pobre Arbolito** (songs 1, 2, 3,and 4, music
    written by Mark Guerrero)

Regalo Musical Navideño (110-795349-1) (1990)
    Cascabel+ (Jingle Bells), *Campanitas de Paz+* (Silver Bells), *Ya Viene
    Santo Claus+* (Santa Claus Is Coming To Town), *La Canción de
    Navidad+* (Winter Wonderland) (the remaining six songs on this LP
    were previously released)

Mensajes y Locuras (110-796702-1) (1991)
    Sonrie, Tin Marín De Do Pingue*, Super Mama*, Pánfilo El Catrin (The
    Dude)+, *El Trompo Bailador, Papa o Mama*, El Sapo+, Papa No
    Fumes+, El Día del Maestro*, El Himno de Los Niños** (songs 4 and 7,
    music written by Mark Guerrero)

    Compact Discs

Los 14 Exitos de Las Ardillitas de Lalo Guerrero (216-799403-2) (1992)
    (compilation of previously released recordings)

La Navidad con Las Ardillitas de Lalo Guerrero (0779938223) (1994)
    (compilation of previously released recordings)

Una Nueva Navidad con Las Ardillitas de Lalo Guerrero (7243 8 36378 2
    9) (1995)

El Rap de Navidad* (the remaining nine songs were previously
    released)

Southwind Records (ca. 1993)
La Loteria+ (SW-102), comic (one side of 45 rpm single)

Music for Little People (1995)
Papa's Dream, Los Lobos with Lalo Guerrero (9 42562-2) (1995) (Lalo
  Guerrero, narration and vocals; lead vocal on *De Colores* and
  Cielito Lindo, and wrote additional lyrics to *Route 90, Cielito Lindo,
  De Colores,* and Las Mañanitas Tapatias)

Sounds of Sancho Records
Tacos for Two (Lalo Guerrero's Greatest Parodies), (SOS-11982) (1998)
  Mexican Mamas Don't Let Your Babies Grow Up To Be Busboys+ (Mamas
  Don't Let Your Babies Grow Up To Be Cowboys), *No Chicanos On TV**,
  There's No Tortillas+ (O Solo Mio), *I Left My Car In San Francisco*+ (I
  Left My Heart in San Francisco) (the remaining six songs were
  included on the Ambiente Records *Parodies of Lalo Guerrero* album)

Break Records (1999)
Vamos a Bailar Otra Vez, with Lalo Guerrero (CDLAL02) (1999)
  Vamos a Bailar*, *La Cosa*+, *Tin Marín De Do Pingue** (instrumental), *El
  Carnalito** (Spanish), *Manzanita**, *Nunca Jamás**, *Barrio Viejo**
  (Spanish), *Tin Marín de Do Pingue**, *La Cosa** (instrumental),
  Marihuana Boogie*, *El Carnalito** (English), *Barrio Viejo** (English),
  Vamos a Bailar* (instrumental), *Nunca Jamás** (instrumental) (with
  the exception of *El Carnalito* and *Barrio Viejo,* all new recordings of
  songs originally released in the forties and fifties)

Compilation Albums
33-1/3 rpm LPs
Mexican House Party (Imperial Records, LP-9213) (released ca. 1962)
  *Pecadora, Frio en el Alma, La Mula Bronca, El Barzón, La
  Mancornadora, La Pachuquilla* (re-release of Imperial recordings of
  the late forties, the last two songs with the Trio Imperial)
Canciones de Manuel S. Acuña, Vol. 1 (Discos C.S.A.N. CS-61075 j-B)
  (ca. 1965)
Mentira and Nacozari (previously released on Colonial Records)
Texas-Mexican Border Music, Vol. 14 (Folklyric Records 9021)

El Pachuco y el Tarzán (with the Trio Imperial) and *Marijuana Boogie*
(Imperial recordings of the late forties)

Compact Discs

Jumpin' Like Mad: Cool Cats & Hip Chicks Non-Stop Dancin (Capitol
 Blues Collection CDP 7243 8 52051-2) (1996)
 Marihuana Boogie and *Chicas Patas Boogie* (Oh Babe), (Imperial
 recordings of 1949 and 1950)
Dos Grandes (Cepellin/Las Ardillitas) (Sony Discos SMK-83987) (1997—
 2000)
 *Clases de Ingles, Las Ardillitas en la Escuela, Los 10 Perros, Pánfilo
 en Texas, Agapito el Sapito* (all previously released on Capitol Pops
 EMI)

Special thanks to Jose "J.D." Delgado for his list of Vocalion and Real
Records, to Skip Heller for his gift of several RCA and Real Records,
and to Dad for answering my endless questions and providing all of us
with a musical legacy for the ages.

About the Authors

Lalo Guerrero

Lalo Guerrero, the child of Mexican immigrants, was born in Tucson, Arizona, in 1916. While he was a teenager, his mother taught him to play the guitar, and he played and sang with several groups while he was still in high school. One of these groups evolved into Las Carlistas, the quartet with which he began his recording career in 1938. During the next sixty years, he recorded more than 700 songs on several major labels. In the 1950s and 1960s, his music dominated the Latin American charts in both North and South America.

Guerrero is also a prolific composer. His first song, *Canción Mexicana*, was written when he was only 18, and it became such a standard in Mexico that it has been called the "unofficial anthem" of that country.

Truly bicultural, Guerrero writes in many styles including boleros, rancheras, salsa, mambos, cha-cha, swing, comic parodies, protest songs, and children's music. Many of his compositions are based on personal observations and his corridos have told of the struggles of Mexican Americans and of their heroes. Overall his music serves as a history of the Chicano experience.

Guerrero has received many honors, including the 1996 National Medal of Arts, a National Heritage Fellowship in 1991, and the Smithsonian's designation of National Folk Treasure in 1980. He has been called the "Father of Chicano Music."

Sherilyn Meece Mentes

Sherilyn Meece Mentes holds an M.S. in psychology from the University of New Mexico. She has taught remedial reading, film making, and general psychology in schools and colleges in New Mexico and California.

Mentes has produced award-winning travel and documentary films in Hungary, Poland, Greece, France, Scotland, Peru, the Netherlands,

Costa Rica, the United States, and the Republic of South Africa.

She researched, wrote, directed, and edited thirteen feature-length 16 mm films for the illustrated lecture field. She provided the film, script, and voice-over for seven one-hour video productions: *Bonny Scotland; Bonjour, France; Eternal Greece; Hawaii—Lovelier Than Ever; Costa Rica Unica; The Charm of Holland;* and *South Africa—A Personal View.* The videos on Scotland, France, and Holland have been featured on The Learning Channel and PBS.

Mentes presents approximately seventy-five to 100 lectures each year. She has appeared thirty-four times on the National Geographic Lecture Series in Washington, D.C.

While none of this may seem relevant to this book, Mentes' studies in psychology were motived by an interest in people—how individuals become what they are and why they behave as they do. Her fascination with different cultures and lifestyles led her into the travel film field. She became a teacher and a lecturer because she enjoys sharing what she has learned. All these traits combined led to the in-depth interviews over a period of two years that resulted in Lalo Guerrero's memoir.